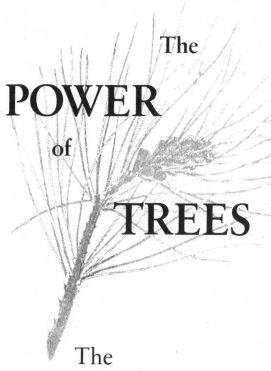

The

POWER

of

TREES

The
Reforesting of the Soul

MICHAEL PERLMAN

*To Jonathan
for the Jill of
the River
In peace
hope*

Michael

Spring Publications
Dallas

Published by Spring Publications, Inc., P.O. Box 222069, Dallas, Texas 75222. Text printed on acidfree paper in the United States of America. First printing 1994. Cover designed by Margot McLean, with production assistance from Slobodan Trajković. The cover image is a painting by Pamela Harris, Untitled (Green Aurora), oil on canvas, 1991, 72" x 60"

Distributed in the United States by the Continuum Publishing Group; in Canada by Maxwell Macmillan; in Europe, Eire, and the United Kingdom by Airlift Book Co.; in Australia by Astam Books Pty Ltd

Library of Congress Cataloging-in-Publication Data

Perlman, Michael, 1957–
    The power of trees : the reforesting of the soul / Michael Perlman.
        p.   cm.
    Includes bibliographical references (p.   ) and index.
    ISBN 0-88214-362-X (pbk.)
    1. Trees—Psychological aspects.   2. Nature—Psychological aspects.   I. Title.
BF353.5.N37P47   1994
155.9'1—dc20   94-4552
                                                        CIP

SHE WAS SIXTEEN. SHE HAD GLOSSY LEAVES AND BURSTING BUDS AND SHE WANTED TO STRUGGLE WITH LIFE BUT IT SEEMED TO ELUDE HER.

—Zora Neale Hurston, *Their Eyes Were Watching God*

WE REQUIRE AN INFUSION OF HEMLOCK SPRUCE OR ARBORVITAE IN OUR TEA.

—Henry David Thoreau, "Walking"

SOON WE WERE HEMMED IN BY TREES, WHICH IN PLACES ARCHED RIGHT OVER THE ROADWAY. . . .

—A sojourner in *Dracula's* Transylvania

THE FAMILY TREE IS IN THE COMPUTER [IN MOTHER'S FLOODED HOUSE]. MOM DIED A WEEK BEFORE THE FLOOD, AND I GOT TO FIND THAT COMPUTER.

—An Illinois man, during the 1993 Midwestern flood

I SEARCHED OUR YARD FOR MAGIC, GRAVITATED TO THE MIMOSA TREE WHICH MYSTERIOUSLY CLOSED ITS LEAVES WHEN I TOUCHED THEM. IT SEEMED A KIND OF FRIEND.

—Deborah Tall, *From Where We Stand*

Contents

Acknowledgments   vi

CHAPTER 1   Trees: History and Prehistory   1

PART I
Biographical Woodscapes

CHAPTER 2   Powerful Trees   19

CHAPTER 3   Trees and Human Biography   38

PART II
The Psychological Nature of Trees

CHAPTER 4   The Importance of Tree Spirits   81

CHAPTER 5   Trees of Pain and War   127

CHAPTER 6   Trees of Solidarity and Peace   152

CHAPTER 7   Walking in Aphrodite's Woods   190

Notes   222

Index   255

Credits   265

Acknowledgments

MANY PEOPLE CONTRIBUTED vital ideas while I worked on this book—ideas from which I still draw inspiration. I cannot mention everyone, of course; but those I am particularly grateful to include Michael Adams, Peter Bishop, Alan Bleakley, Charles Boer, Deanne and Robert Bosnak, Edward Casey, Stephan Chenault, Jane and Alan Clayton-Matthews, Mike Flynn, Ethne Gray, James Hillman, Robert Jay Lifton, Jennifer Manlowe, Herbert Mason, Howard McConeghey, Daniel Noel, Tom Quinn, Lucy Silva, Polly Smith, Charles Strozier, and Mary Watkins. All contributed something crucial to the spirit of my work. Especially I think of those who read part or all of the book in manuscript: Charles Boer, Mike Flynn, Ethne Gray, James Hillman, Robert Jay Lifton, Jennifer Manlowe, Polly Smith, and Charles Strozier. Without their help, I would not have fully grasped what most needed to be said.

My father and his wife, Donald and Cynthia Perlman; my mother and her husband, Harriet and Gene Hower; and my sister, Lisa, have given my work and me a lot of needed love and thoughtful criticism. I found that my father and Gene, who also carefully read various versions of the book, have considerable editorial talents.

I am deeply appreciative, too, of the incisive, respectful work of my editor at Spring, Mary Helen Sullivan, who oversaw the book's final, crucial pruning.

My warmest thanks go to all who helped provide a place for *The Power of Trees* to grow.

CHAPTER 1

Trees: History and Prehistory

AFTER HURRICANE ANDREW had devastated the Homestead area
of South Florida in late August, 1992, a newspaper article described something surprising:

> It was the trees that so many people spoke of.
>
> In the midst of the devastation, the privations and the pain,
> the people of Homestead last week sometimes stopped, mid-con-
> versation, and remarked on a pine tree that had grown up with
> them, an acacia that was a benchmark for their lives, a towering
> mangrove that was a testament to their own struggles, achieve-
> ments and now loss.
>
> They spoke of the scent of the leaves, the shape of a par-
> ticular trunk or crown, the shade from the burning South Florida
> sun and the stretches of green that had made Homestead special.[1]

The article's title evokes the absent trees: "Alien Terrain Replaces
What Was Once Home." Such images and feelings suggest that trees
can matter more to us, and in more ways, than we realize. So does
the movement of the story, which evolves in a specific way. First comes
a keen recognition of the importance of trees. Then come deeply
felt parallels between people's lives and those of the trees. And finally,
the trees themselves—their particular images and characteristics.

Trees are vital in many ways. Their ecological and aesthetic importance is often recognized, but this book explores something less
tangible—their psychological power. I do not believe we can fully
appreciate the ecological and aesthetic value of trees without
acknowledging that influence. My exploration moves in the direction of the Homestead story—from looking at situations in which
the importance of trees becomes plain, to exploring the way trees'

lives and human biographies speak to each other, and finally to focusing on the psychological presence of the trees themselves, their rich and resonant particulars. This movement ramifies in many ways through our private and public lives. It is the ongoing reforesting of the soul, the peopling of wooded imaginations.

We gain by beginning, in this era of global ecological concern, with stories of tree loss. Listen, for instance, to Pamela, a young woman working at a car rental agency, with whom I spoke when I visited the South Carolina "Lowcountry" in December, 1989, three months after Hurricane Hugo ravaged that area's woodlands. Hugo, she told me, "says to you, 'Look, you remember this tree that used to be there, and used to stand so tall, and you used to admire, it's not there any more.'" Pamela went on to talk about how preoccupation with "daily deeds" could lead to loss of connection with nature. In other words, the immediate loss occasioned by the hurricane opens to view another level of loss, that of alienation from natural forms.

Yet, the experiences of people in places like Homestead and the "Lowcountry" suggest that our estrangement from the nonhuman natural world may not be as total as we think. Otherwise, the loss of trees couldn't have turned Homestead into an alien place.

The psychological power of trees is not primarily something we attribute to them; it is never separate from their actual, *natural* life—or from decay, from openings to the underground, from death. Trees do tell us a lot about ourselves, of course; there are intricate relationships between tree and human worlds. To borrow one botanist's characterization of what takes place in gardens, there is a "negotiation" always going on between trees (together with other nonhuman natural forms) and ourselves—a dialogue. As in any serious relationship, there is give-and-take, and in this book I want to give a lot to trees—not just take from them. By looking at the various facets of this reciprocal relationship between trees and human persons, we discover that trees have specific psychological qualities.[2] The trees I have in mind are not all actual—they include trees of literature, of fantasy, of image. But actual and imaginative trees are always related—any encounter with an actual tree involves particular imaginations, and any encounter with an imaginative, fictive, or legendary tree discloses a presence of actual trees.

I write as a psychoanalytic psychologist especially attentive to the work of James Hillman, C. G. Jung, Robert Jay Lifton, and others who emphasize in diverse ways the importance of imagination in human life; and also as an active environmentalist with deep concern about issues of war, peace, and social justice. I draw from a variety of trends in recent psychological and ecological thought that come together to highlight the value of the nonhuman world—the *psychological* importance of physical things (stressed by writers in differing psychoanalytic schools) and the intrinsic value of nonhuman beings (stressed by differing schools of ecological thought). I hope what follows will contribute to a more psychological ecology, as well as a heightened, deepened, and broadened sense of what Herbert Schroeder calls "the psychological value of trees."[3]

As the aftermath of Andrew shows, valued analogies between the lives of trees and human persons are by no means confined to traditional tree lore. There are myriad forms of human–tree parallels. The analogy never implies a full and literal identity of humans and trees; always there is some awareness of the radical differences between us. But, conversely, that awareness of difference is itself never absolute; the multitudinous metaphoric analogies provided by root, branch, limb, leaf, shadow (and fallen tree or rotten log) touch us all, inform our lives and understandings. These analogies always involve a *simultaneous* sense of intimacy and difference between human and tree life. This coincidence of intimacy and difference, this joining of relatedness and estrangement, is from a psychological standpoint crucial to our understanding of the power of trees. Wherever trees and humans coexist, neither the parallels nor the differences between them can be consistently avoided or reconciled. That tension is basic to the world's tree stories—and relevant, as well, to many other kinds of relationships.

Such combinations of intimacy and estrangement and of likeness and difference ramify. Erotic vitality, for example, thrives on a joining of intimacy with difference, of "mutual recognition" that allows people "to enter into states in which distinctness and union are reconciled"—"the most intense experience of adult erotic life"; or on *"the alien in the context of the intimately familiar, and the prospect of the intimately familiar amid the alien."*[4] While the references are to sexual passion, something analogous holds for the course of other human relationships, including those with oneself. Our relationships, human and nonhuman, whatever their quality, inevitably involve combinations of similarity, sameness, and intimacy on the one hand; and of difference, distinction, and more radical alienation and estrangement on the other. In exploring what trees tell us about these combinations, we explore what they can mean for the nature of ecological relationship in its fullest sense—for Eros in its fullest sense.

To psychologically explore trees—or any ecological phenomenon—means to remain within the precincts of both likeness and difference. Neither can be overcome. We dance with paradox and sometimes suffer, sometimes celebrate, contradiction. We cannot return to a primary harmony with the natural world because we were never there in the first place. Estrangement is not only a human phenomenon; it predates us and forces itself upon us. For instance, Lewis, a Homestead native, insisted to me (when I visited that area in November of 1992) that "South Florida *should* get hurricanes," that they were not "foreign" to the area's ecosystems. Yet, his reaction to the stripping of the trees' foliage by Andrew's 165 m.p.h. winds revealed a contradiction: "My images of after the hurricane were very simple: hot, bright, *so* bright—and foreign. Because it didn't look anything like South Florida; South Florida has leaves everywhere." Homestead had become as strange for Lewis as for anyone. And a couple of days before we talked, there had been gusty thunderstorms in the area. Again, Lewis experienced "that—that eeriness. There was that dread. . . . I felt something comin' over me. . . ." Something foreign becomes, for Lewis, all-too-familiar—but no less eerie.

Our relationships with trees are both paradoxical and contradictory. Confronting this has been difficult for me—in part because we may manage to do away with much of the planet's familiar and unfamiliar flora and fauna, along with ourselves. I began this book with the conviction that a dangerous alienation from our natural, ultimately our *forest*, roots lay at the heart of the global ecological crisis. Though I thought I knew better, something in me had retained the hope that we could somehow return to an earlier unity with nonhuman nature. Perhaps a close exploration of the way trees present themselves in our imaginations could help us to do so. But my implicit image of "return to nature" has, in the course of my writing, been thoroughly confounded. Forests, after all, can be as eerie, as *foreign*, as the post-Andrew landscape. It is surely a meaningful coincidence that the words "forest" and "foreign" appear to have a common source—"the Latin *foris*, meaning 'outside.'"[5]

Yet there remains the kind of longing expressed in W. S. Merwin's poem "Witness":

> I want to tell what the forests
> were like
>
> I will have to speak
> in a forgotten language[6]

I think of the pin oak, Norway maple, and littleleaf linden outside my front window. I look at them, I love them. For they are always there. As are the ailanthus (or "Brooklyn tree"), a second and larger linden, sour cherry, Eastern hemlock, and Northern catalpa outside my bedroom window. We greet each other, but they're always first to say Hello, for their beings and their gestures embody ceaseless greetings to the world. I stand with them for forest preservation and restoration, in countryside and in city.

Yet I stand with estrangement as well. For, however discomfiting, estrangement threatens the world less than our self-destructive ways of evading it. Alienation itself may be psychologically as necessary as a sense of home—and, regardless, it touches us all. Robert Pogue Harrison, in his recent and deeply respectful study of forests in the Western imagination, underlines this point: we live "'at home' on the earth in the mode of estrangement," and forests can help us understand what that means.[7] Moreover, in spite (and because of) civilization's massive destruction of forests, there are ways in which we have in the course of our history grown *more* intimate with trees; the experience of estrangement from trees—including cutting them down and in other ways witnessing their deaths—paradoxically presents possibilities of a deepened relationship with them, and by implication with nonhuman nature in general. A deeper intimacy, and a deeper strangeness.

Paths in Trees

The Power of Trees follows two main paths: psychological interviews with a variety of people and explorations of trees in mythology, literature, poetry, and other collective imaginative forms.

Psychological life exists all around us, not only within us, and through interviews we can in a sense converse with this life—address it and be addressed by it. Daniel Noel says it well in his examination of the role of images of nature in the development of Jung's thought. Noel has retraced the steps of several of Jung's overseas journeys and noted the parallels between Jung's imagistic responses to those places and their particular ecologies. "The result," he says, "has been a sense of the dialogue of deep structures between psychological and terrestrial features in Jung's inner and outer travels." It is with an ear to such a conversation between "soul and earth," with each "striking, impressing, touching the depths of the other," that I spoke with people.[8]

Interview conversations (recorded with permission and then transcribed) allow us to hear some of the many divergent voices and images of the speakers' selves and to observe frequently occurring patterns and psychological themes. Those images and themes must always be understood within biographical contexts, and in most cases a significant part of my interviews focused on life-stories (the length of the interviews averaged about an hour and a half, and I was able to meet with twelve people two or three times). But they are also part of the larger world, its ecology, history, mythology, culture—that enduring conversation between soul and earth. Sometimes, slips of the tongue and other inadvertently expressed images and emotions can encompass simultaneously an individual's struggle and millennia of religious, historical, and social tensions.

Three months after Hugo devastated South Carolina, and again after Andrew slammed Florida, I visited the hardest-hit areas and spoke with residents. They had learned the hard way how difficult and conflicted the conversation between soul and earth can sometimes be. It will prove worthwhile to lend them our ears. I also interviewed a number of people in the New York City and Boston areas during the four years from 1988 to 1992, seeking to better understand connections between images associated with trees, patterns of human biographical life, and our sense of planetary ecological threat. I did not attempt any kind of systematic sampling, but rather sought to talk with ordinary people from a variety of backgrounds (about half having specific involvements with trees or ecology) and with widely differing views on what the human–nonhuman relationship is or ought to be. I recorded interviews with thirty-two people in all.

I also draw on a more formal psychological study I've worked on, which focused on the shifting relationship between planetary (particularly nuclear) threat and the American self during the waning days of the Cold War (1987–1990).[9] The study involved individual interviews (all in the New York City area) with Christian fundamentalists, economically deprived African Americans, peace activists, and civic leaders. As we proceeded we found that more and more people began to relate nuclear to other forms of ecological threat. Images of trees—especially threatened rainforests—started cropping up, and the fact that the study's main focus was broader only makes their appearance more telling.

Almost always, people willingly shared their time and their life-stories. Over time, many familiar themes emerged, but I was continually surprised by people's generosity. The transient but real intimacy of these encounters haunts me.

I've also learned much from meetings with sundry trees of literature, mythology, and poetry. Though I do make use of nature and environmental writings, the multitudinous ways in which trees are woven into the settings of works not focused mainly on trees or ecology are in some respects more informative still. The myth of "Aphrodite's Woods" (see chapter 7) is one illustration of this. For this reason the images to which I link people's life-stories are not necessarily from environmental literature in the usual sense. Looking at a more diverse range of works can help us expand our understandings of the ecological. But rather than trying anything like a comprehensive account of the world's tree tales, my approach will be to look closely at specific themes and their expressions in a limited number of works and traditions. For instance, that odd and weathered trees frequently capture our imaginations tells us something both about the trees and our biographical self-perceptions. Works by Toni Morrison on African-American experience and by Tim O'Brien on the Vietnam War turn out to have particular ecologies of trees, which are important partly because the authors' main concerns lie elsewhere. And traditional tales and myths—like those of the Kwakiutl Indians of the Pacific Northwest Coast and the Greek Goddess Aphrodite's vision of trees—prove to embody with imaginative precision the ecology and psychological power of their particular wooded habitats.

Important as well are the actual places I visited. In South Carolina, a national forest called the Francis Marion was virtually flattened by Hugo, and so I spent time talking with people who live and work and draw economic and spiritual sustenance from the forest. The Francis Marion is not a primary or pristine forest; it had been pastureland until the 1930s, and much of its acreage consists of trees planted for timber-harvesting, though there are also extensive areas set aside for recreational use. Local people may love and spend a great deal of time in the outdoors and the woods, while also working in the timber industry or in forestry. They do not always belong to what Will, whom we meet in the next chapter, at one point termed "your environmental groups." But they know firsthand what massive sudden forest destruction looks like, and how a storm can overwhelm any plan for managing a forest.

The South Florida area, while home to a number of nature preserves, is not dependent on local forests for its livelihood, although its subtropical climate makes it ideal for horticultural pursuits. While in the area, I visited the Fairchild Tropical Garden, one of the largest tropical botanical collections in the world. It was devastated by Hurricane Andrew, and the staff, aided by a large number of volunteers and botanists from around the world, worked feverishly in the storm's aftermath to save what they could. We can learn much by comparing and contrasting people's responses to the destruction of a timber-producing temperate forest and that of a carefully put-together tropical garden.

Back in New York City, I visited Bedford-Stuyvesant to learn about "The Tree Lady of Brooklyn." "Bed-Stuy," as it's called, is a poor and largely minority inner-city community, far in many ways from a large national forest or a tropical botanical garden. But in the midst of Bed-Stuy is the Magnolia Tree Earth Center, a thriving local environmental and cultural educational center. It was founded by the "Tree Lady," a resident, after she waged a successful campaign to save one tree, a *magnolia grandiflora*, native to the South, which had been transplanted to Brooklyn in the 1880s. It survived because it was sheltered from the winter winds by a row of brownstones, and preserving those city buildings was necessary in order to save the tree. Its evocative life mirrors a community's persistence in a less-than-hospitable climate.

The Francis Marion National Forest in coastal South Carolina, the Fairchild Tropical Garden in South Florida, and the Magnolia Tree Earth Center in Bedford-Stuyvesant, Brooklyn, are actual places and metaphors for a kind of path—a psychological exploration of the power of trees—that joins many different localities and touches on many social and cultural concerns within an ecological framework. I hope to confound, or at least call into question, a number of taken-for-granted categories associated with environmentalism and, in fact, much of industrial culture. These include our usual ways of dividing the rural from the urban, natural from artificial (or "built") environments, ecological from social-justice or peace-oriented concerns, human individuals and groups from each other, and trees from ourselves.

Biographical Woodscapes

In keeping with the direction of the Homestead story, the book moves from recognition of trees in this chapter through "Biographical Woodscapes" (section I) and then "The Psychological Nature of Trees" (section II). "Biographical Woodscapes" focuses on the particular ways in which trees reach into people's life-narratives. By biographical woodscapes, I mean the entire "family" of trees peopling one's imaginations and helping to shape one's human stories. Biographical woodscapes are more diverse, for example, than either a single "family tree" or a generalized image of a forest. They can include any tree, located in any place, fictive or actual—city street, television show, favorite novel, recurrent dream (or nightmare), haunting memory, tropical rainforest, empty lot, suburban yard, or steppe.

Through such imaginative diversity we can better appreciate how particular trees stand out in people's psychological lives. In the immediate aftermath of Hurricane Andrew, Homestead residents were "stopped mid-conversation" by reminiscences of trees. What gives such reminiscences their power? What makes for "Powerful Trees" (chapter 2)? They may be tall and imposing; more often they are the garden variety—unobtrusive, modest, vulnerable, even odd. Always what they evoke is something we hold dear—though they may be connected with powerful conflicts and take disturbing shapes. Some people talk quite readily about their "favorite trees" or make connections between trees and a sense of the sacred; others less so. In any event, trees have a way of making their importance, their power, felt in very different lives.

One way they do so is through our habit—deeply ingrained and near-universal—of drawing parallels between the "life-stories" of trees and our own biographies. In more generally considering "Trees and Human Biography" (chapter 3), I focus on the psychological qualities and forms of the human–tree analogy. What in trees gives that analogy its enduring quality? There are hints in the post-Andrew world: people thinking about a "pine tree that had grown up with them, an acacia that was a benchmark for their lives, a towering mangrove that was a testament to their own struggles, achievements and now loss." Such trees both reflect and shape our own multiple locations in life-and-death cycles, while their location in biographical woodscapes reflects the ecological nature of the soul, the meeting of the familiar and the alien within and around us.

The Psychological Presence of Trees

We are not only human; our lives are configured by nonhuman as well as human power. And trees, as people often say, can have their own personality or "character." To speak in this way is not anthropomorphic only, but an expression of the very real *psychological* presence of trees among us. Here is where "The Psychological Nature of Trees" comes in—"The Importance of Tree Spirits" (chapter 4).

The relationship between the human and tree worlds—and, more generally, between what I call the human and nonhuman in nature—is not only organic. Tree spirits, as I talk about them in chapter 4, are neither *immaterial* nor identical with the living matter of a tree; they are more inclusive (as well as elusive) psychological presences. As James Hillman claims, we can find "soul in manufactured things" as well as in trees.[10] In fact, tree spirits—the nonhuman psychological presences of trees—don't hesitate to utilize machines and technology. Trees can be psychologically present in the most unlikely forms and places. They can appear in the elvish and nymphic faces of the actual forest, but also in black-and-white photos of a World War II landscape (see chapter 5).

Though my emphasis is on contemporary forms of tree spirits, I take a close look at some older tree tales from the Kwakiutl tribe of the British Columbian coast, which the neighboring old-growth forests pervade (see chapter 4). The Kwakiutl do not fit easily into the usual picture of the Native American community in harmony with the forest. Kwakiutl culture was estranged from the deep forest well before the arrival of Europeans. Living by the water's edge, the Kwakiutl know the forest as the dangerous "other world." And yet they reveal surprisingly intimate and precise connections with trees and forest—intimacies with the Pacific Northwest coastal bioregion, and, perhaps, estrangement itself.

The spirited presence of trees is ambiguously shadowed; I do not gloss over their relationships with pain, death—and human inequities and evils (see chapters 4, 5). Yet there is considerable evidence—scientific, religious, literary, anecdotal—that trees can have a palpably restorative effect on human beings, in settings that range from pristine forest to communal park, from hospitals to prisons. This restorative power reawakens our evolutionary connections with trees, both in early forests and on the African savanna on which species *homo* raised itself up. A lot of people I've talked with will testify to the importance of "Trees of Solidarity and Peace" (chapter

6) and their psychological workings. So will many writers and poets, ranging from Carson McCullers and Aldo Leopold to Mari Evans and Langston Hughes. So will the Tree Lady of Brooklyn.

Finally we come to "Walking in Aphrodite's Woods" (chapter 7). Without knowing it, we have already been walking among them. They are present in the form of the fundamentally erotic closeness and estrangement between humans and trees. Whenever there is an intimate meeting of human worlds, worlds of trees, and the longing for beauty, we might say we're in Aphrodite's Woods, for we are in the realm of that Goddess, Goddess of lovers human and nonhuman.

It is strange how rarely the Goddess of luxuriant sensuality and love is linked with the love of nature, with ecological concerns, with the power of beauty. Her world of sensual and erotic display, of nightclub and bedroom, seems so distant from the backpack trail; we're not in the habit of juxtaposing thoughts of wild nights and the wildness Henry David Thoreau celebrates in his famous essay on "Walking."[11] We don't generally think of ecological concern as having erotic and sensual power (even though the image of the woods as a sexy place is hardly confined to Greek myth), and recent ecological thought has begun to appreciate the loss in that omission.[12] If, for instance, we are to talk about Greek mythological figures in relation to contemporary ecological concern, shouldn't we be talking instead about Artemis, Goddess of pristine wilderness and inviolate, virgin forest?[13] Maybe we *can* talk about her, and many other figures from many other places, but still see something important in the perspective of Aphrodite—see the relationship between trees, beauty, sex, aging, old-growth forests, death, and religion also from her point of view.

Entering "Aphrodite's Woods" is not the same as going back to a "timeless" or "primordial" forest existing prior to human interference with forest ecosystems—though these woods very precisely embody typical themes of just such a journey. The woods to which Aphrodite refers in the myth we'll explore are sacred, not to be "touch[ed] . . . with the axe." They grow in a setting where others have been "touched by mortals' axes," where forest destruction on a significant scale is already part of the ecological and cultural context. By the time this myth was recorded (approximately the seventh century B.C.E.), forests in Greece were felt to be at risk and many hillsides were denuded of trees and eroding.[14] One thinks of current images of Himalayan forests. The sacredness and beauty of such woods is not purely primeval, but stands out against the backdrop of a loss of trees to human hands. Here we encounter both the historical predicament and the prehistoric power of trees.

A Prehistoric Tree Animal

It remains worthwhile to return to truly prehistoric—pre-anthropoid—forests. For while we were never fully in unity with them, there are ways in which we have never fully left them either. Speaking from an evolutionary perspective, as I do in this book, requires considerable circumspection. Evolution, from a psychological standpoint, does *not* imply a linear movement from the "lower" and simpler past toward the "higher" future of realms of complexity and greater sophistication. Rather, there are constant and subtle movements back-and-forth between the early and the more recent, prehistory and history, high and low. There is more complexity (and more history) in prehistory than we may realize.

In this book I try to remain close to the perspective of a spirited little varmint from the forests of the Mesozoic era, whose descendants now inhabit forests of Southeast Asia—a type of tree shrew that appears to be an important mammalian ancestor. Approximately squirrel-sized, tree shrews related to this Mesozoic forebear "can and do move freely between ground and trees," as F. A. Jenkins says. They are not arboreal or terrestrial but both. Their versatility is related "to the fact that the forest offers, to a small mammal, an extremely uneven and disordered substrate for locomotion." Or, in language more like that of contemporary ecology, "the forest floor, the trees, and all the interconnecting secondary growth are not a smooth continuum but rather a ragged network of substrate possibilities. . . ." The forest topography favors "a highly flexible and versatile locomotor pattern" involving "flexed limb postures" and "irregular spacing of footfalls. . . ." Thus, analyzing bone and joint structures, Jenkins says: "Flexion and extension of the vertebral column, the mobility of the feet, and the flexed, abducted limbs may be interpreted as mechanisms to permit versatility in stance and locomotor pattern."[15] The tree animal's physical being evolved in the context of, and is sensitive to, various surfaces and textures of the forest, on all its levels. It is in that sense ancestor to Aphrodite's feeling for surface, texture, and form; and for the more general role aesthetic attentiveness to trees has played in human evolution, culture, and ecological concern.

This little creature is also a sophisticated image for evolution itself, for rather than ascending to ever higher realms, it is well-suited to movement from higher to lower levels as well. Its differentiation, in fact, depends upon close contact with lower surfaces, so that the frequent equation in evolutionary fantasy of "higher" with more "differentiated" states is subverted. Our ancestral tree varmint is intimate with verticality on all levels—more flexible than hierarchical.

A psychological ecology can learn something from following in the footsteps of this creature. It will "move freely between ground and trees," in various kinds of horizontal and vertical modes that remain close to floors of forests as well as their understories and canopies. It will stay within "the ragged network . . . of possibilities" by remaining "flexible and versatile" in its constantly evolving, always incomplete understandings of the psychological and ecological patternings within which we move. It will limn ecological dimensions of many local and planetary concerns (regarding the development of more humane and just societies and dilemmas of war and peace), without trying to encompass them in a holistic scheme. While the longing for wholeness is powerful, and holistic concepts valuable in ecological thinking, there is always the danger of excluding the ragged, uneven, "irregular" networks that more precisely figure the interconnections and juxtapositions of human and nonhuman worlds.

The spirit of our ancestral tree shrew is, in its Mesozoic way, a postmodern and iconoclastic one. It frees the ecological imagination to look in (what from a more conventional view seems) unlikely places for insights into the psychological power of trees. At the same time, we become freer to imagine and to address simultaneously the breadth and depth of our planet's predicaments, to recognize the complex forms of intercourse between areas of concern we have too often kept isolated. We become freer to recognize the animal spirit, the tree power, which can inhabit even computers, with their "tree" commands and directories and invaluable contributions to planet-wide ecological networks (branchings and leafings) such as those between American and Russian forest ecologists.[16] We become freer to move beyond dualisms of every sort, including that between the "organic" and the "mechanical." For such is the spirit of forests, as Robert Pogue Harrison observes: because "forests can easily confuse the psychology of human orientation," they form "a world of implications which renders our deepest structural categories superfluous or unreal."[17] Here is also a kind of initiation, a human *re*orientation—one in which we honor and call forth an innovative mammalian inheritance, the versatile spirit of a prehistoric tree animal.

PART I

Biographical Woodscapes

CHAPTER 2

Powerful Trees

TREES CAN EVOKE especially keen emotional responses from people. More often than not, those responses express a sense of solidarity or kinship between trees' lives and ours. But not necessarily. Powerful trees can take many shapes. Here I give some attention to trees that don't figure as powerful in the usual sense, that wouldn't work as emblems for the Tree of Life: the unwanted or destructive, the vulnerable or hurt, the old and weathered, and the soon-to-be-cut-down.

Wicked Trees

Animosity, anger, and estrangement can name our connections with trees, our experience of their power. In both South Carolina and Florida some people raged against specific types of trees after the Hurricanes Hugo and Andrew—the loblolly pine and an exotic type of ficus, respectively, which were perceived as having been responsible for a disproportionate amount of damage to the properties upon which they fell. These trees focused and concentrated people's suffering and frustrations with the lingering aftermaths of the storms.

Ed, a public relations director for a South Carolina state agency, spoke of lines of people, irritations, and even all-out brawls after the storm—in which people "like you and me" were involved. His frustration with the longterm effects of Hugo emerged in an angry observation: "Until you accept that [recovery will take years] you walk around in a damn state of wantin' to punch somebody out." Frustrating as well was the destruction of his work surroundings, which "we . . . [were] real proud of because of its uniqueness and its forest." Recovery of the forest will take more years than Ed, in his mid-forties, has left: "That's just been changed now for the rest of my lifetime." In spite of this loss, and because of it, Ed spoke against the loblolly pines, which he held responsible for much of the damage to homes and property. He told me people were saying things like "Any of those goddam pine trees left, I'm gonna cut 'em down, you know, solve the problem right now." Actually, Ed was saying that himself. His home had been demolished—by the storm tide, not falling trees. But "with this experience, a pine anywhere near *my* property is short-lived. I'm gonna get rid of it." In fact, Ed had already cleared "all the pines out" of his lot. Yet they were still a potent psychological presence, still animating Ed's anger.

Kevin, an urban forester in the Charleston area, observed that "there's a lot of animosity toward the [loblolly] pines." He claimed that people considerably exaggerated the extent of loblolly-related damage, saying that "whenever the opportunity arises [I] try to do a little bit of sermonizing on behalf of the pines." And, "I really feel like people are going to miss the pines a great deal as time goes by," because they are evergreens that provide color in winter and help block out traffic noise. Kevin was perplexed—in fact, downright irritated—by this bias against the loblolly. But even before Hugo, as it turned out, locals had "some negative feelings about pines"; since there are so many of them and they are tall, they are hit by lightning rather often, and this has led to "the misperception" that the loblolly is inherently attractive to lightning. Another source of animosity was revealed to me by Ted, a South Carolina biology teacher, who contrasted pines unfavorably with hardwoods, since "pine trees are strictly an industrial product." They are the chief timber-producing tree and so are haunted by memories of human industry, of alienation.

Ann, a Coral Gables resident involved in street-tree planning committees, was likewise taken aback by the virulence some people were feeling, in the aftermath of Andrew, toward the exotic type of ficus tree. At community meetings there were pitched battles between "pro and anti-ficus" contingents. One man who opposed replanting this type of ficus referred to it as a "wicked tree," while another, blaming one for the death of a smaller tree, called it the "culprit tree." This was strange to her; it was as if these individuals were "personalizing" the tree—as if the tree were sentient.

As in Ed's case, this reaction is in part an expression of psychic travail following a disaster. "Displacement" is one word that comes to mind: the trees symbolize and evoke the range of human responses to a "posttraumatic" situation. But a moment's reflection will bring to mind other images of "wicked" or otherwise baleful, potentially sentient trees. Consider what Treebeard, the treelike old forest shepherd or "Ent" in J.R.R. Tolkien's fantasy trilogy, *The Lord of the Rings*, tells us: some trees "have *bad* hearts. Nothing to do with their wood: I do not mean that"; they can be "sound as a bell, and bad right through."[1]

Elaine Scarry gives another, seemingly more mundane, but in truth much more fantastic, illustration of an offending tree that comes alive. A think-tank study entitled *Force Without War* recounts a deadly incident in the Korean DMZ in 1976, when "two American officers supervising the pruning of a tree . . . were attacked by North Korean soldiers and killed." This resulted in a series of counter-measures that climaxed when "a large force of American and South Korean soldiers entered the demilitarized zone and cut down the offending tree while armed helicopters circled overhead and B-52 bombers flew near the border."[2] The implicit "legal statute," says Scarry, is "any tree that protests being pruned by taking (or by permitting in its vicinity the taking of) human life will be subject to the penalty of death by more-radical-pruning." Such trees' sentience seems itself animated by death—and a desire for revenge. Even the absurdity of the military response to an "offending tree" suggests a kind of give-and-take between humans and trees not limited to the old, deep forests of (what we usually think of as) fantasy.

The psychological power of trees, as these examples show, is not to be equated with a love of trees or with a reverence for life. We'll encounter many more ambiguously powerful trees. I emphasize this in part because I am biased in favor of trees. For we need to let all sides have their say in order to fully appreciate what the psychological power of trees is about and why it is important.

Nature's Own People

David, a longtime resident of Homestead, offers a different, and more common, kind of response to the destruction of trees. Yet there is a psychological parallel between his reaction and the intense antipathy to trees that we've encountered—the evocative way in which trees take hold of his mind and animate his emotions.

At sixty-one, David has been married, raised his family, and lived in Homestead for forty years, but he was "born and raised" in London. He is also a veteran of wars. As a boy, he lived through World War II and the blitz of London; some of his friends were killed. After coming to the States, he joined the Air Force and served for twenty-four years—including "three times" in Vietnam. There he loaded bombs on aircraft and, while he did not himself see combat, "we got pretty close to it a couple of times" and "a lot of friends got killed." He retired from the Air Force in the 1970s, grew interested in landscape design, and became maintenance supervisor for the physical facilities of a Homestead community center. But then, during the fateful August night in 1992, he lived through Andrew and its aftermath—something that "to me . . . was worse than the blitz of London." He spent the night of the storm huddled in a closet with his wife and one son while Andrew "totaled out" his house. "I think I was more afraid than I've ever been in my life," and "I *didn't* think we were gonna make it, to be truthful." The next morning "we came out of the closet . . . and pushed all of the bedroom furniture out of the way. . . ." They "went out in the yard and just looked at the mess," and the London blitz came to David's mind: this "was really devastating. My trees and everything were just completely leafless— what trees I had left. I mean, I had trees disappear from my yard that we never have found."

Struggling to describe his response to the scene, David, who as a former military man characterized himself as "pretty callous" about death in war, became tearful after saying: "I had no feelings."

As he told his story, David moved back and forth between images of devastated houses and devastated trees. "It was pretty grim"; trying to save things from his house "was a waste of time." David plans to re-landscape his yard. But that won't help the "massive trees around the area that were just uprooted—and gone." They "were just—it was more like skeletons layin' there . . . because"—here David switches into the present tense as though to signal the vividness of the image in his mind—"there's no leaves left on 'em." But "you can go into my kitchen now, and there's still leaves imbedded in the wall" by the force of the wind.

One of the strangest things about Hurricane Andrew is that it brought people closer to nature—for instance, by not only stripping the trees' leaves but also driving them into the most hidden and interior recesses of wind-damaged homes.

Although David spoke rapidly, almost furtively, he very much wanted, and needed, to tell his story. And, he stressed, "people were what impressed me more than anything. People's attitudes changed so dramatically . . . they were just courteous. I mean, I've never seen people like that before. *Ever.*" Trees play a crucial role in David's description of human re-connection, as they do in his depiction of human devastation. He talked about how two men who had flown in to help with the restoration of the community center's grounds offered to do likewise in David's yard.

> And, uh, they pulled their blocks and tackles out and—I had three palm trees at each end of the pool at my house, and they stood 'em up for me. Started cryin'. I couldn't help it, it was just—it was pretty to see 'em come up, you know? Such a relief. I've never seen anything like that. Still feel it . . . those guys—helped put me on the track, those two guys . . . because a tree's comin' up, all the sudden we're goin' again.

So excited were the three men that one of David's helpers insisted on taking a picture of the first tree when "we had it three-quarters of the way up. . . ." That picture is etched in David's memory. But he recognized how important it was for his helpers as well: "They felt like they were doin' somethin'. Which they were." Like David, they were moved, in more than one way, by trees.

This *moving power* of the trees has important features. There is the physical activity involved in righting the trees, but this is preceded, and followed, by the *movement of emotion*, which brought David to tears again as he spoke. This in turn is preceded, and followed, by a *movement of images*, as David remembers the scene. The physical, emotional, and imaginative movement has interrelated vertical and horizontal aspects: "Because a tree's comin' up, all the sudden we're goin' again." David gets back "on the track," begins to feel able to get around. The organic image of the righted trees lends David a sense of vitality. But this organic quality does not exclude a movement of machines: the equipment used to right the trees, the camera used to take the picture, David's being "on the track." The "track" would seem to imply not only "train" but also metal linked by wooden ties. There is at least an echo of history here, in that humankind's movement into the machine age was made possible in large part by wood.

I do not know whether David was moved on some level by that historical echo. But the immediate and evocative forms of the trees, while not David's main concern as he looks back on the days after Andrew, plainly matter. As in the case of those persons who are moved to speak, and act, against "wicked trees," the tree itself is the animating power. Notice that this power bridges various qualities that usually appear in opposition: (1) estrangement from, and solidarity with, trees; (2) the psychological and physical; (3) the internal and external worlds; (4) the vertical and the horizontal; and (5) the organic and the mechanical. The trees are psychological presences that move the soul—sometimes to right them, sometimes to cut them down, always to somehow imagine them. So it is misleading to speak of "animism," or the projection of human qualities onto trees. To speak of "powerful trees" means addressing the ways in which trees animate the human.

Trees animate themselves. This was apparent in South Florida and South Carolina after hurricane winds stripped their leaves. Within two to six weeks, the surviving trees (together with other flora) sprouted new leaves and flowers. Somehow, this didn't seem quite natural. If they had lost their branches, they could look, as Ed put it, like "telephone poles" with "clumps of new growth." A minister in South Carolina told me: "We were so surprised . . . pear trees, apple trees, crab apple trees here in the village, were all in full bloom two weeks after the storm. I don't understand that. Nobody's explained it to me." Ted, the biology teacher, explained that trees "had to have green leaves in order to feed themselves . . . that was extremely interesting to me and the biologists that they did that when they were undergoing immediate, very severe stress. That was their response." For most people, the releafing of the trees was a potent source of hope. But there could be anxiety as well—expressed in religious or botanical images. The minister said that the "crazy Christians," or fundamentalists, thought the out-of-season releafing and flowering of the trees was "a sign of the end of the world. . . . And the nature people," or environmentalists, "said, 'isn't that strange?'"

After the hurricane winds make a place "foreign" (as Lewis put it) by obliterating familiar foliage, it is yet stranger when the trees "come back," as Ed said. In one way or another, the return of the leaves prompted a religious attention to plant life, whose very existence is, after all, somewhat strange.

I asked David about his reaction to the releafing of the trees. This prompted him to talk in religious terms. David—himself a member of an evangelical congregation—first responded with an image neither conventionally Christian nor conventionally ecological: "I think nature has a way of taking care of its own peop—own things."

"Nature's own people": here was something worth pausing over, one of those moments in a psychological interview when you hear a voice other than that intended by the speaker, observe the unexpected leafing of an image. Both to make sure I heard what I thought I heard and to prompt further expression of the image in order to probe David's relationship with it, I restated it: "Of its own people, so to speak." (Such restatement or reiteration is one form of what Jung called amplification, or concentrating on an image and examining it from different angles in order to better appreciate its psychological power and resonance, significance, and relationship to other pertinent matters. I employed this approach often in my interviews.)[3] Here David became a bit skittish. "Yeah, well, whatever. Anyway you want to put it." However you put it, he went on, "nature has a way of taking care of its own," and it's "the same way" with us. He felt a parallel between the regrowth of trees and nature on the one hand, and the human community on the other. In David's slip of the tongue, there is "the suggestion of an occult relation," in Ralph Waldo Emerson's phrase from his essay on *Nature*, between the human person "and the vegetable."[4] For Emerson, this is "the greatest delight which the fields and woods minister," as it evidently is for a part of David.

But then David emended himself: "The man upstairs take[s] care of us and takes care of [nature] too." There is a conflict of images here, one with a long history: "the man upstairs" versus "nature's own people." This is often cast in terms of the struggle between Christianity and paganism, or monotheism and polytheism, but such dichotomies, whether scripturally based or not, do little justice to the nitty-gritty contradictions and interplays of religious, mythological, and ecological imaginations that we find in different cultures.[5] Nevertheless (and partly for the same reason), the image of "the man upstairs" can be compared to a statement made by a Catholic priest seven years after Hurricane Gloria passed over Connecticut and tore a limb off a maple tree in the town of Milford. For in the place where the tree's cambium tissue and bark had begun to grow over the wound, one woman spied what "looked to her like the face of Jesus Christ."[6] The priest, in response, cautioned that Christ's visible signs should be found in other human beings, "not in trees. . . . To all of a sudden give miraculous power to a tree, I wouldn't see that as too positive."

There is again a link between David's response and the antagonists of "wicked" or "offending" trees: here, the trees' tendency toward sentience. David's characterization, expressing a sense of kinship or solidarity between human people and nature's people, finds many echoes. Ted said of the live oaks damaged by Hurricane Hugo that "they each have a personality" and that "it feels like a friend's been injured." A journalist, referring to the massive loss of trees in her native city of Charlotte, North Carolina (known, she said, as the "City of Trees"), had this response: "Next day, driving around town was like going to a friend's funeral." Steve, who works at Fairchild Tropical Garden, spoke for many when he said the loss of the garden and its trees was like "the death of someone close." This particular feeling for trees is not confined to storm-damaged areas of the United States. For instance, Mischa, a Russian writer, spoke similarly as he remembered confronting random forest destruction caused by the Soviet military near Vladivostok at the time of border conflicts with China in the late 1960s. "Even the death of a friend is instructive, after all. It teaches us something that we cannot learn in everyday life." And we hear from England, after the Gale of October 1987 (which felled millions of old trees), that "people treat trees as old friends."[7]

The sense of trees as personified beings remains very much alive, even though these kinds of characters live mostly in the interstices of our imagination and emerge most often in certain difficult times— times when the borders between our ordinary and our less ordinary, less familiar, selves and fantasies are likely to be more permeable. When the usual order of things and images is disrupted or reversed, occult relationships with "nature's own people" may be revealed.

"Respect"

Certain trees show their power through the respect they command. Some of these, of course, are monumental champions of the forest or historically significant trees in a human community. But some are quite modest—odd, misshapen, even dead. For instance, in a well-wooded area of New Hampshire stands a house called "Wolf Pine Ledge, [named] for the scraggly pine that grows there."[8] The surrounding taller trees remain in the background. "Wolf Pine" is powerful because scraggly.

Often, we seem unaware of the claims of these garden variety trees on our lives. But we may respect them more than we realize. Take Will, a forester and sawmill operator in South Carolina. I met with him twice, in December of 1989 and July of 1992. The first time we spoke, he introduced himself to me this way: "I was born and raised in western North Carolina. So I went," he said in a deadpan voice, "from a Hillbilly to a Swamp Rat." Two-and-a-half years later, Will said it a little differently: "I've come from a Hillbilly to a Swamp Rat." As I saw it, Will was a companionable guy, in his mid-forties, with decidedly conservative—timber industry-oriented—views on the debate over forest management. But Will, the rural Southerner, evidently considered that an urban Northerner might see him differently. I was not immune from similar concerns. In 1989, we met in the sawmill's main office, from which we could see and hear logs being fed through the huge, whining saws. Will gave me a brief tour of the mill. Even if I had not told him this was my first visit to a sawmill, I was sure Will would have known that I was in an unfamiliar environment from the ginger and, I felt, awkward manner in which I picked my way around the machinery.

"I'm an environmentalist," Will asserted early on, although he has spent his life as a forester—working for the U.S. Forest Service and in "the wood products industry." In the course of our conversations, he sought to counter certain stereotypical notions he thinks that many in environmental groups hold regarding foresters and loggers—images of "people who have the black beard, cross-and-dagger skull bones that rape and pillage the land." He was critical of the distinctions often drawn between loggers and environmentalists—including members of the most radical environmental group, and the one toward which Will expressed the most rancor, Earth First! They appeared willing to risk human lives to save trees, said Will, and they "would get along real well with Khomeini or somebody like that." But he also made a statement that may be in part self-referential—and whose relevance, in any event, goes well beyond Will's own story: "A logger and Earth First! probably share a whole lot more than what they ever even think they do." Take, said Will, "any of your [hard-core] loggers, you know, they all love a tree. . . . And they've all got trees around their house," which they would protect from somebody who wanted to cut them down, "'cause they're beautiful."

But Will was impatient with what he saw as idealized—and urban, Northern-based—ecological visions, with the notion that a forest once matured stays the same forever, Eden-like. "That's not nature." He surmised that most New Yorkers would view trees "as a thing of beauty" and "a sacred commodity," not to be disturbed. His "perception of a New Yorker versus somebody, you know, in the South—or even in your forest in upper New York state" was that *their* "perception of a tree would be totally different than what I would think somebody that lived in rural America's perception of a tree is." It could be, Will added, doubtless mindful of my Northern roots, that "this is maybe totally inaccurate. . . ." But he could not suppress a tinge of scorn when referring to "your urban foresters who are basically horticulturalists or whatever," who don't deal with the messy (and ugly) business of cutting trees.

When we met in 1992, I asked Will to talk more about "rural

America's perception of a tree." Will readily obliged, in the process telling me more about himself. In "rural America," he began, a tree may be planted around a house for "its aesthetics," but "any place else, it is something to be used." And if "a tree's in the way, you cut it down . . . it's just a tree." Whereas "An urban person would do everything in the world to save that one tree." But then Will found himself telling me about a tree he himself had saved.

Just a week ago, Will had been with his brother's family at their vacation home. One afternoon, looking for something to do and "to get away from the kids," his little brother had suggested they go cut down a "nasty-looking tree." But Will reminded him: "That's a dogwood, they're all gonna be gnarly"; and that in the spring when it bloomed it would be pretty. His brother replied, "Nobody's down here in the spring to see it bloom." But to Will, it would be pretty anyway, and who's to say if no one sees it. It's also part of the history of the area, associated with local arts festivals, and Will was surprised his brother didn't "put more importance on that bein' a dogwood."

The point Will wanted to make was "that would have been the last thing in the world a purely urban person would have thought about doing, was cuttin' down a tree because it was gnarly." But Will was also talking about the difference between him and his brother: "for me" the dogwood "was aesthetic. It wasn't hurtin' anything. . . . So I don't know that that wasn't a little bit different feelin'." In Will's case at least, Mr. Hillbilly and the imaginal urban person turn out to have some things in common—an appreciation of certain trees and their cultural value.

Will had already alluded to differences between himself and other members of his family. "My father, my brothers, and sisters are all engineers. I'm the black sheep in the family," he said with a laugh. It would seem that he was aware—and that, in one way or another, he was made aware—that he was going against the family grain in not becoming an engineer. When I asked him if that was in fact the case, Will denied it. He insisted that, though "I woulda been miserable" if he'd followed the family path (which at one point in college he considered doing), "my folks never told me that I needed to look at engineering. . . ." Yet Will immediately drew a parallel which would argue against his denial. His parents also "to my knowledge . . . never even asked whether or not you were goin' to go to college." For "that was just something you were going to do, but it was never said you *were*." Here Will unwittingly acknowledges that things unsaid can be very important. He *was* aware, if somewhat uneasily, of something that set him and other family members apart and drew him toward trees: "I don't know if I wasn't a more sensuous person than they are"—sensuous being "the wrong word," he said, perhaps implying that when young he picked up from his local environment the idea that being a sensuous male was wrong. Nonetheless, Will could appreciate the sensuousness of the old gnarly dogwood—a tree with which he might be said to share Hillbilly roots.

Jane, like Will, is in her mid-forties. But there the similarities would seem to end. Jane, a personable artist, educator, and dancer who lives in a liberal New York City neighborhood, often draws and paints trees, for "I feel so reassured" by their presence. She volunteered that "I have favorite trees" and spoke extensively of her religious feelings for certain ones.

One of her favorites drew from Jane the same kind of respect Will showed the dogwood. It is an old fruit tree, "probably an apple," though it doesn't live in her neighborhood. It may not be alive at all. She discovered it about a decade ago, "when I was discovering upstate [New York], having been pretty much in the city a lot." It is "a tree I see on the road" to the house in the Catskills that Jane and a friend bought. You turn a certain corner, and there, "jumping out at you," is the old tree. "And it kind of started wearing into my consciousness more and more and more." It shows its age. "I don't even think it's putting out leaves any more," Jane continued; "I mean, it's extremely fat and gnarled and . . . developed, developed by time and age. And," Jane wonders, "is it alive or is it dead, you know?" Alive or dead, it stands, "out by itself" on a road of memory, and it will continue to stand, because "it must be respected by . . . the people who own the land."

In talking about trees, Jane speaks a very different language from Will—one imbued with the eclectic spiritual sensibility of a contemporary, progressive, and cosmopolitan urban milieu, strongly influenced by feminist and certain New Age images. She has, for instance, at times "been aware of receiving power from the earth."

When she used to play tennis she would "do a lot of extra footwork in order to hit my feet on the ground, and it kind of got me into the rhythm, . . . and from the earth, came everything, came an energy, direct." Jane talked animatedly about this and about hitting "the hell out of" the ground when dancing, drawing a parallel to Native American rituals "of hitting the ground with your feet to get [its] energy." And this earth energy is parallel to Jane's sense of trees' vitality. "I think," she said, that the tree gets energy "the same way, from the ground." And "the ground seems so *hot* in a way, just full of good stuff." So the tree "has . . . an image of the ground being hot, like full of vitamins" or (since it's a tree, not a human being) "nourishment, nutrients. It makes the tree dance, it's so hot. . . . Deep, hot earth." And that heat is linked with trees; "sometimes when I'm looking at a tree . . . I just feel fire."

But as Jane talks about the old apple tree, certain features stand out that remind one of Will's old dogwood. The apple tree has an exquisitely defined physical presence, a gesturing "specificness"; "because it's so gnarled, as they say, . . . there seems to be a flesh quality to that, and a pain quality." This is because, more generally, "the accumulation of experiences in a way has accumulation of pain." Contemplating the tree, Jane observed wryly: "You know, after a while it's not size that we grow in, it's something else, obviously. . . . The tree has physical expression of that," of our psychological lives. But the specificity is the tree's own. She talked about it as the tree's "growth and development. Definition, articulation. Specificness of bark and bumps and all of that. Wrinkles and tumors," she said affectionately. It is as though the tree gives expression to and mirrors "every twist and turn" of experience, "is responding to the specificness of . . . its time and weather, and all the cars that pass by and . . . maybe its own destiny, too." The tree "says 'beauty,' it says 'power,' it says 'integrity.'"

Speaking of destiny, experience, "bumps and all of that," and pain: there are trees on Will's property, somewhat like that old gnarly dogwood, that have a similar character. They, however, were dealt a heavy blow by Hurricane Hugo, and a few remained on the verge of dying from the damage they had suffered when I spoke with Will in 1992. But he respected their woundedness: "My wife asked me, 'Will, the trees that are leanin', are you gonna go cut those out?' And

I said, 'No. Those trees lived through Hugo. Fifty years from now I want to be able to sit right here and say "That crooked tree right there lived through it."' You know—the trees that lived through it, to *me* are sacred. They stood up," Will added with a slight laugh, "a whole lot better'n a lot of us did." The gnarly dogwood and the survivors of Hurricane Hugo on Will's property are powerful in a similar way. Like Jane's favorite tree, they are odd, misshapen survivors.

In calling these trees survivors, I don't mean to leave out death, because death is part of their living power. Not only do they survive death (tumors, hurricanes), but death survives in them. Death is part of their "definition, articulation," as it is of our own. Sally and Dave might concur. Sally, a Brooklyn shopkeeper and environmental activist, grew up in England, where her home had a large garden with a great variety of trees. Many of them had been extensively pruned over the years, which in combination with their age had given them a "real" and "contorted kind of character"; their "angles always seemed like arms." One tree that stood out in Sally's mind was an apple tree known as Lady Sudely. It bore "an old-fashioned apple" which "wasn't . . . very distinguished"; it was "kind of . . . yellow" and not too tasty, but the tree was interesting to draw. Sally then remembered another apple tree, a "very old being who is smaller—like much of it is not alive" any more. Some of its smaller branches "had kind of fallen off"; it had been wounded in a storm and is no longer producing much fruit. Her father had tied some plastic on its top "to protect the inside," and this "was like some strange little *hat*. . . ." Sally thought about how the tree, "as it gets very old" and loses some of its branches, seemed somehow "wiser" than before. The interior presence of the dying tree grows.

Dave, a South Carolina wildlife biologist, spoke of a tree that had already died. Like many in the Lowcountry, he holds live oaks, with their tough, sinuously curved branches draped sensuously in Spanish moss, "in very high regard." But they needn't be living. "In fact, we had one live oak that had been dead for some time on our property [and we] just left it." I asked him why and he replied, "Well, [I] saw no reason to do anything other than that, for one reason. And, you know, birds perched in it, it provided some foraging for woodpeckers. . . . And I saw no reason to remove it. And that's the type of individual I am." Dave thus grants a place to a particular, highly regarded dead tree and also to an ecological image of death itself that becomes for him a form of self-definition.

There is a struggle in such definition. It isn't easy to combine life and death in yourself, though we all do—and all trees do as well. Odd, weathered, and scraggly trees seem to exemplify how it can be done, but they perplex and surprise us. When pondering the life and death of the old apple tree, Jane remembered "stories about" apple trees to the effect "that they die completely and then the roots [are still] alive and they send up another tree." So this tree "might not be putting out leaves and certainly not apples, but it might again."

That answer to the question of life and death was not wholly satisfactory, and the question came up again. After describing the apple tree, Jane showed me some pictures—several pen-and-ink sketches "of a similar tree." The tree, with "all these bumps . . . is just so developed," she exclaimed. Full, rounded protrusions, gnarled in a voluptuous way, mark the tree's old thick trunk and branches. It leans slightly to one side, which together with its detailed features evokes a sense of activity, of motion. Like the apple tree, it is "dancing." Like the apple tree, it had no leaves, as I noted aloud. "Yeah," replied Jane, "it's also in a dormant stage or dead or whatever." This might be a kind of "borderline condition . . . maybe it's something I'm trying to learn. About dead not being an absolute state." But Jane did not seem completely satisfied with her formulation, musing as she looked again at the tree: "A lot of combined, contradictory things there."

Jane felt the tree "inside myself as wholeness," but part of *this* kind of tree's wholeness is its lack of leaves. Of the latter, Jane said that "it's sad . . . you know, the kind of life that is a leaf is lost." There is in a leaf "such a different quality, in its moisture, and its greenness, and everything it brings together in the world in its greenness. And"—here the actuality of the tree reasserted itself—"but then again it's dead." But even if "it's permanently dead," Jane surmised that people would continue to preserve it, much like Dave with his dead live oak. For it would still be "a statement, it's still a physical thing that stands there, at least temporarily." Yes, affirmed Jane, "it's making a statement." Jane's reiteration was newly emphatic and had the aura of a small but important discovery. She had hit upon a more exact way of expressing her sense of the tree's combination of qualities.. "And it's dead. It's speaking."

Will had, somewhat unwittingly, defined himself (vis-à-vis his brother and other family members) in the course of telling me about the old gnarly dogwood. That self-definition went together with his respect for the tree. And death went along with it. For he next spoke again of the several trees on his land "that are for all practical purposes, dead. Or will be shortly. But I still trim around 'em, and mow around them, and maybe they'll live." While using fewer words than Jane, he is talking—as are Sally and Dave—about a similar, and unresolved, combination of death and life and persistence which gives certain trees their power. These sorts of trees have a particular character, one that can simultaneously define and reach past geographical, cultural, and biological locales. Such character commands respect on its own terms.

"A Quote Life-and-Death Decision"

It also happens that another kind of tree can command a certain respect, as my conversations with Will and Jane revealed. I mean trees being marked for felling.

I asked Will if he remembered the first time he felled a tree. No, he said, having cut so many in his life. But "I can remember, fresh out of forestry school, in my first job, . . . marking timber to be cut. *That* was hard. Because I was making a quote life-and-death decision." It did not involve marking mature trees in a primary forest, but the weaker trees in a pine plantation—trees considerably less "majestic" than others with whose felling Will has been involved. Yet, "it was still a decision of which ones do you let grow and which ones do you remove so the good ones can grow better. And it took me a long time . . . that first day, the decisions about life and death. I can remember that, and I aggravated the logger, because he was waiting for me to cut the trees."

I asked Will if this was a common experience among loggers, and he replied, "I would guess it would be." Then, reflectively, he added: "It's somethin' nobody says, it's probably almost an unspoken perception." This sounded similar to his family's habit of leaving certain things unsaid. When Will talks about "perceptions," as his remarks about environmentalists and New Yorkers suggest, there are likely to be intense and conflicted feelings, images, and ideas involved. The "unspoken perception" in turn involves a sense of the parallel between the deaths of trees and humans—and at least a tacit sense of the huge and complex relationship between death in general, killing, decisions regarding them, the value of life (one's own included), and how humans are linked to each other and to the planet's nonhuman denizens.

It turned out that Jane also has had, as she put it, a "little experience in paring down trees," on the vacation property in upstate New York that she shares with a friend. As "reassuring" as Jane finds trees, "we didn't like living in a forest. We needed more light and space" and wanted "to open up" their magnificent mountain view. In arguing for the value of forest management, Will spoke about a nearby old-growth swamp in a comparable way: "The understory of the swamp was nothing but a maze of small saplings strugglin' to survive in the shade. It wasn't at all the beauty of an open, lowland swamp. . . ." Will and Jane would probably recognize the commonality in their experiences of estrangement in the deep shadows of an old-growth forest. For both, however, the attempt to manage this wooded dark led to still more intimate contact with trees.

Jane and her friend contracted with "these really lovely loggers" to have some of the trees, "huge oaks," taken down. Jane's friend "stayed up at the house and I went down and walked among the trees and tagged" those they had decided had to come down. Like Will, Jane had to make physical contact with the trees she marked for cutting ("I was tagging trees that were so big that I couldn't get my arms around them"), and as for him, this was agonizing. "I felt awful about that," said Jane, "and I felt scared." What Jane felt so awful about was that "I personally" marked those trees that were to come down. She hesitated as she told me this, just as Will had hesitated to mark his first trees for death. Jane, like Will, was morally troubled. "I felt that it was *evil*."

The setting, of course, was quite different from that in which Will worked. The trees were far more vigorous than those for which Will made his life-and-death decision. This was an old-growth forest, not a timber plantation. Also, Jane, the urban Northerner, had been used to drawing trees and to celebrating them. And her reason for cutting the trees was, at least on one level, quite different from Will's. Jane herself might think it much crueler.

What Jane's and Will's experiences have in common, however, is that they are a kind of initiatory experience of *hands-on* forest management. Their stories can be seen as a re-enactment of one of humanity's primal scenes: going out into the woods in order to impose human designs upon the life of trees. Initiation experiences generally involve an anxiety-provoking juxtaposition of one's will and an awareness of forces beyond any human will. That's why anthropologists, following Victor Turner, speak of them as "liminal"— one is, in a sense, between worlds or unusually sensitive to more than one world at the same time. Death, moreover, lurks in the background, if not the foreground, of initiation narratives and is necessary to them. For Will and Jane, as they went into the woods in order to shape them according to human purposes, death was very much present.

But unlike Will, Jane found herself worrying overtly about an *arboreal* will beyond her plans. What if her actions called forth a response from the forest itself? she wondered. She was scared that "I would suffer the revenge." Suddenly, the trees took on a power of agency. "I felt," said Jane, "like somethin' would happen to me in the woods as I was . . . tagging them." It might look like an accident—"I'd fall off a log and break my head, or a snake would come and do me in. . . ." But it could also be that "just the tree wouldn't like it and . . . would do something to me." Exactly what form the tree's revenge might take was hard to describe. "I think," Jane surmised, "it would do it supernaturally somehow" or perhaps, she said after another pause, it would be "just a voice"—"That would scare me enough!" Then again, "whether it would be the tree itself I don't know, but, you know, it's some spirit that's attached to it or lives in it. Or is associated and protects it. . . . It's hard to distinguish."

Each image in this story is more unusual than its predecessor, though all of them have ready parallels with traditional lore—found wherever trees, forests, and human beings live together—of personified forest and tree powers. The story gives one the sense of the liminal process at work—the movement into a psychological space between this world and that one, the human world and the world of the forest. The sequence goes from a rationally explainable accident to the mythologically tinged image of snake vengeance and then to an image of something supernatural "the tree" might do. Jane's switch into the singular suggests that what was going on at that moment was an imaginative encounter between herself and the tree that personifies the forest—the forest's guardian, its exemplary figure of sentience and power, its Treebeard.

Jane and Will are especially sensitive to the lives of the trees they mark for death. Jane, in contrast to Will, has a conscious interest in the mythic imagination and in cross-cultural religious themes. But here what puts her in touch with one of the more ubiquitous of these themes—initiation into an awareness of death in the woods—is what connects her with loggers, and with that seemingly unmythological practice Will emphasizes—forest management. She and Will share, through their initiatory experiences of marking trees for cutting, a juxtaposition of acutely felt ecological concern with immediate awareness of the power of trees and of the human power to make (and reflect upon, and regret) decisions in favor of death. In that way, Jane's "little experience in paring down trees," like Will's "quote life-and-death decision," involves a disquietingly intimate form of estrangement from the forest, one in which the trees to be felled become the most powerful of all.

CHAPTER 3

Trees and Human Biography

Tree and Self

ALL NONHUMAN BEINGS, biologically alive or not, express and affect the soul in particular ways; but within the plant kingdom, none have so intimate and pervasive a link with the imagination and sensibility of human biography as do trees. This address of trees to human biography, to a sense of life's direction and character, is an important expression of their power.

The eighteenth-century writer Thomas Pownall says of North American forests that "the individual trees of those woods grow up, have their youth, their old age, and a period to their life, and die," like human beings. "You will see," he continues, "many a Sapling growing up, many an old Tree tottering to its fall, and many fallen and rotting away, while they are succeeded by others of their kind, just as the Race of Man [sic] is. By this Succession of Vegetation the Wilderness is kept cloathed with Woods just as the human Species keeps the Earth peopled by its continuing Succession of Generations."[1] Janie Crawford, the protagonist of Zora Neale Hurston's novel *Their Eyes Were Watching God*, imagines her life analogously, "like a great tree in leaf with the things suffered, things enjoyed, things done and undone. Dawn and doom was in the branches."[2] Trees speak with uncanny exactitude to our biographical lives—their sufferings, their joys, how certain things are done and left undone and *come* undone, and the leafings and branchings of our dawns and our dooms.

The persistence of the human–tree analogy, in spite of all anatomical or physiological knowledge of how different trees are from each other, let alone from human beings, points to the depth at which trees have a hold on our imaginations.

Over several decades of psychological practice and research, C.G. Jung carefully studied trees as they appear in individual fantasy, myth, and religion. His essay "The Philosophical Tree" considered the tree as an alchemical and psychological symbol—"the self depicted as a process of growth."[3] Moreover, he found that the appearance of trees in the imagination of his psychotherapy patients often seemed to quicken a growth of the personality. "Taken on average," said Jung, the tree as symbol elicits associations to "growth, life, unfolding of form in a physical and spiritual sense, development, growth from below upwards and from above downwards, the maternal aspect (protection, shade, shelter, nourishing fruits, source of life, solidity, permanence, firm-rootedness, but also being 'rooted to the spot'), old age, personality, and finally death and rebirth." Many of these themes emerge in the way Will and others talk about trees and their (that is, the trees' and their own) "life-stories."

Other psychological investigators enthusiastically note the capacity of trees, or tree symbols, to evoke soul, personality, biography. In projective tests (in which respondents are encouraged to fantasize and hence to "project" conscious and unconscious aspects of their personalities onto test items), drawings of trees are especially revealing. For instance, the Freudian-oriented psychologist E.F. Hammer, who authored a widely used survey in the late 1950s on *The Clinical Application of Projective Drawings*, writes that drawn trees in particular seem "to tap . . . enduring . . . intrapsychic feelings and self-attitudes"—deep, "basic layers" of personality.[4] Karen Bolander, a Jungian-oriented writer who in a 1977 volume focused more specifically on *Assessing Personality Through Tree Drawings*, says:

> In general, one might say that tree drawings are particularly rich as sources of insight regarding "life content"—whether we speak about actual biographical events or about the attitudes and feelings which are characteristic of the subject. One finds in the drawings indications of the person's relationship to mother and father; clues to hidden or repressed biographical material; a record of the more important romantic and sexual experiences of the subject; and indicators of traumatic incidents, which can usually be dated approximately by measuring their position in the tree in relation to the subject's age.

In the past decade, this last subject—trauma—has become a major focus in psychoanalytic writing. For example, a 1990 article on "Indications of Physical, Sexual, and Verbal Victimization in Projective Tree Drawings" examined the hypothesis that wounds on drawn trees—or drawings of dead trees—reflect prior abuse and victimization.[5] The authors quote Hammer on the value of tree drawings and find a link "between duration of physical abuse and multiple [wounds] on the tree." Severely traumatized patients they studied drew dead trees or "other extremist trees" such as stumps. (In exploring hurricane aftermaths, I follow a reverse procedure: looking at how actual wounded or dead trees project themselves into people's responses as part of a pattern of posttraumatic stress.)

All these authors describe the value of drawn trees in superlative terms. But they are not speaking about trees themselves, except insofar as they prompt projections of the human biographical psyche. Without denying the cogency of this psychological work on trees, I would like to take it a step further and propose that another kind of projection is going on as well—namely, that trees, as they are, project and reach into human biographical contexts. In other words, it's a "two-way street," as one friend told me when reflecting on some forestry work he had done: qualities of trees penetrate and fashion human biography. Trees, like all beings, are themselves shaping powers of imagination. Not only do they stand for the human; human selves are symbols of trees.

We find another clue to the nature of this "two-way street" in the way Jane describes her relationship with trees, drawn and actual, that especially fascinate her. "I really see trees," she said, "as a mirror of me." The mirror reflects her perspective on trees and her strong sense of a give-and-take connection between trees and herself. "I have a certain way of seeing them that I think is in my drawings and also when I'm confronting them live, where the individuality of the tree is pressing forward at me." Not only does Jane "confront" trees; they confront her. Trees like the old apple "spring out at me." Especially when sketching trees, she feels a kind of "equality" or symmetry between herself and the tree. She senses herself, in her relationship with a tree, to be standing upright, straight-on, each party facing the other, "being locked into this gaze with each other," almost like "belly to belly." The tree, like Jane herself, becomes a "dancer," and the dance becomes an erotic relationship. As in all erotic involvements, there is a transposition of self and other. That means Jane herself becomes in part the tree in the mirror, and this is how she and the tree could get "locked into this gaze with each other." The mirror becomes the medium of a complex dialogue in which each party has a view of the other; in the viewing, human self and arboreal other are transfigured and transposed, drawn closer together.

Under the gaze of the tree, something else happens as well—an intensified awareness of what it is that trees and the human body have in common: uprightness. Jane described this in terms of the "equality" of herself and the tree, the way in the mirror they would be standing straight-on, facing each other "belly to belly." A mirror image is usually one of standing; it embodies and displays human verticality. Standing before a standing tree stirs a movement of the vertical imagination, or what Gaston Bachelard calls a "vertical dynamism": it moves us into awareness of one of the bases of humanness and of treeness.[6]

I mean movement in a very concrete, physical—kinaesthetic—sense. The imagination of trees involves us in vertical motion, an involuntary perception of a force—upwelling, expansive, and downwardly stabilizing—that is shared by tree and self; a tacit feeling for the energy involved in standing upright; and awareness at some level of multiple significances of uprightness, implicit fantasies about growth and evolution—the biography of the human species and of each human individual. This engenders a feeling of kinship, well-expressed in a poem by Wendell Berry on his relationship with a dying elm tree: "Willing to live and die, we stand here, / timely and at home, neighborly as two men."[7]

Trees, of course, have been standing around since before *homo erectus*, and the recognition of that must have figured early on in the self-perceptions of *homo sapiens*. Our prehuman ancestors descended from the trees (and from the tropical forest onto the savanna), but in becoming upright they mimed arboreal growth, growing like trees. We grew away from trees and grew toward them at the same time. The cultural and psychological significance of this early experience of parallels between the bodies of trees and human bodies has received little attention in paleoanthropology.⁸ But our kinaesthetic imaginations respond to the human–tree parallel in equally significant ways today; we in our human uprightness can still sense trees within our standing.

Stand still for a few moments before a tree, and the imagination that moves you will be as primary as that of early *homo sapiens*. You'll probably sense how Jaime, a rainforest activist, standing before a huge tree in a tropical rainforest, could wonder, "What if I were also a tree?" and muse about what it would be like "standing up here beside all these giants." Jaime, a Filipino man in his mid-thirties, was describing to me the experiences which led to his activism. At first he hesitated to talk about this particular experience, both because of its apparently fantastic character and because the power of the tree stirred psychological conflicts about his own standing in the world. But once started, he warmed to describing to me his tree-self. "Probably," he said, "I would have huge roots so that I won't just tumble down whenever a big typhoon blow[s], and I would be supporting life, too"—birds, monkeys, and (yes, even) "reptiles." As a tree, "You have a sense of purpose," a sense "that you were doing something for which you were made by your Creator to do." He would be a nurturing and, in fact, quite sensual tree. "I'll have lots of branches and it's going to be very lush"; his leaves would retain moisture so that birds and insects could drink from them. Like Jane's tree-as-mirror, the tree becomes an erotic being; the green vibrancy of the leaves would be "attractive to the insects." There are various animal movements going on in this fantasy.

There could also be movement in another, typically human, direction. For being so tall, and being well over a hundred years old, you might also have, surmised Jaime rather hesitantly, "a sense of superiority [over] the younger trees." You could say, "'See, look at me, I'm already this old. Look at me, I'm already supporting all these kinds of animals. And you still have a long way to go. I am *proud*. I'm a proud tree. I can do all these things.'" This "proud tree" left Jaime feeling vitalized but also, for a moment, a little embarrassed.

There is doubtless a part of Jaime imbued with "a sense of superiority," as there is in just about all of us (though some, to be sure, boast only of modesty), and there is something in him ready to cut him down to size. The tree becomes a mirror of the human reach for pre-eminence. But Jaime is also describing the psychological effect upon him of standing by the great tree—*its* way of moving his imagination and influencing both his immediate self-perception and, at least tacitly, his biographical self-narrative. In this sense, Jaime's biography mirrors the power of the tree.

If we listen for a moment to a couple of echoing voices from other sides of the planet, we will better appreciate the larger force at work here. Mischa, the Russian writer, and Pamela, from South Carolina, were likewise moved by trees. Remembering his boyhood days climbing pine trees near his Moscow home, Mischa described his feelings about them: "Admiration . . . [because] they are lofty, they are proud of themselves, they're strong, they are noble." Like Jaime's tree, the image in Mischa's mind is of an older presence; he analogized the tree to "an old man who is careful about you, and who wants you . . . [to] be better, so to say." In "his" presence, you are called to "cultivate yourself somehow," to "transcend yourself" and become a more "worthy" human being. Pamela thought about transcendence of another sort in connection with her pained memories of downed trees that "you used to admire," that "used to stand so tall." She was also very much concerned about the struggle for racial equality, noting pointedly that as a black woman, she is well-acquainted with job discrimination. In imagining her hopes for the recovery of her home area from the hurricane, Pamela obliquely connected the renewal of the trees and the overcoming of racial barriers. She spoke of a time when "black and white" could come together, where "there is no type of segregation. As far as looks are concerned, I pray that it will be back. That I can see those trees standin' tall again. . . ." The metaphor of *standing* helps to set up a psychological flow between images of social growth—addressing, implicitly, Pamela's own future—and the admirable, inspiring trees. Jaime, Mischa, and Pamela express variations on the imagistic bond between forms of human "cultivation" and the admired life of trees.

Like human lives, trees gain power through a complex growth of interior space, of depth. Protection, nourishment, shelter, connection, and a sense of ecological affinity between human and non-human lives—all these, trees provide on many levels.

For instance, Jaime's more recent experiences among rainforest trees bring back childhood stories. When his father scolded him, Jaime would retreat into the emotional sanctuary of a guava tree in their yard. The tree is long dead, but it grew again, a lushly foliaged tree of stories, in Jaime's memory, after he recalled accidentally disturbing a wasps' nest while climbing in a fruit tree on his uncle's farm. Then, interjected Jaime with new animation, "I [just] thought of a guava tree when I was . . . about ten years old." In this case it is not a father's scolding but another stinging image that sends Jaime's memory up into that tree.

In the guava tree, Jaime explained, "I was building a little house." His residence in the tree house began when he was about seven. He would sometimes spend "maybe five hours or even more" in "my house on the top of the guava tree." And, he emphasized, "I was imagining that that was really my *house*." To get to it "I would climb up a 'stair.'" Once there, if alone, he would look around with a pair of plastic binoculars he had or "write on my small scrapbook." Often he played with friends he had invited over ("Come to my house"), scrambling through the branches "as if we were monkeys." This rather modern tree house featured a "telephone." Jaime and his friends set this instrument up "with these empty cans and a string attached" which ran across the street. They were, thought Jaime, "able to send some messages," and doubtless they did. He mused: "I felt comfortable during that time, you know? No wonder I have this affinity for trees! Now I remember why."

The guava tree was not nearly so tall as the rainforest trees, but had an affinity with them. It provided food: if Jaime was hungry, all he had to do was to pick a guava and eat it. It provided another potent substance as well—sap. "Sometimes," said Jaime, "I'd chew the guava leaf," because "the sap has some medicinal properties." These could be psychological, as suggested by what Jaime thought of next. "And then I would shout down to my friends that I am up a tree. 'Hey, you guys, I'm here!'" When I asked Jaime what this was like, his reply echoed the voice of the tall, "proud" rainforest tree: it "felt good . . . that I was on top of the tree, and they were just down there in the street."

At this point, Jaime became much quieter, pondering: "And what else did I do?" Sometimes he would do nothing but "stay put when some birds would come close to the tree and just observe them." To be able to just observe requires (in a child no less than the rest of us) a certain "serenity" or "presence of mind," as Jaime phrased it in talking about being in touch with rainforest trees, or, as he said in talking about the guava tree, simply feeling "comfortable." That presence has its own quiet power.

The guava tree's effects on Jaime presaged his rainforest activism; "I guess that's how I developed that empathy" for the trees. Jaime hadn't used that specific word before, but now, with considerable feeling, he emphasized it. "That's what people have to develop. They have to develop that empathy with trees." Empathy in this sense overlaps with his "affinity" for the trees. It means feeling with, alongside of, and into trees—a contemplative awareness of what it is like to be among trees and mindful of their presence, their vitalizing effects upon one. In talking about his affinity for rainforest trees, Jaime explained (using an arboreal metaphor unself-consciously): "You may say that you have the same roots. You have life—the tree has life. . . . You're both," he said, "manifestations of life itself"— "of creation, of God's love." And, he added, now implicitly recognizing (and reasserting) the distinction between himself and the "proud" tree, "That's why I have this certain respect for these trees."

Sally, the Brooklyn shopkeeper originally from England, recounted another experience of affinity with a tree. Her English home sported a large garden with many trees, a place of "what were really kind of deep spiritual experiences" she had as a teenager. One time, "I remember I was standing" near some fruit trees "and it was spring . . . and everything felt like it was really really growing, you know? And I remember very clearly having that feeling that I was like a tree. That I had that potential, . . . that it was possible for *my* roots to go down, straight down, through the lovely spongy fresh spring grass. And also, you know, for my branches to reach upwards." Having entered into the sensual image, Sally reflected on how it moved her and then mused about nature and spirit: "The feeling of it that was so important was the rooted and the stretching feeling, and the vertical feeling, the feeling . . . *which is the feeling of the tree*, that the trunk . . . often is a pillar, that it in a sense rises between the earth and heaven" [emphasis added]. And all of this was "part of

that particular feeling that I had at that time, that as an upright being, connected with the upright beings of the trees, that that was
the purpose"—"that trees and we have that potential to be the con-
ductors of that energy between the earth and the sky."

Like Jaime, Sally is a committed environmentalist who stresses
the importance of preserving the world's forests. But their "deep experiences" (Jaime's phrase) in relation to trees are spiritual because
they are bodily—an experience of the body of the tree in kinaesthetic
relationship with their own. Here is one of the most intensely intimate relationships between human and nonhuman nature, carried
by the old, enduring imagination of ourselves as having biographies
with tree-like qualities. It is, in fact, an involuntary experience of
the body's *ecological* soul.

Sally's description also reveals the complexity of the vertical
power of the tree, its *simultaneous* upward and downward thrust.
There is again the kinaesthetic dimension: in the encounter with
the tree, we feel our bodily selves to be drawn or stretched or expanded in both vertical directions. There is also the sense, not
necessarily conscious, of the simultaneous upward and downward
movement of the tree's own life-juices, of the roots drawing up
moisture and nutrients and of the food of the leaves circulating back
into the tree. The woodworker George Nakashima, in his book *The
Soul of the Tree*, describes the tree's physiological structure. The living
wood is concentrated in the tree's cambium layer, the outermost ring
of wood lying just underneath the bark. On the inside of this layer
(the xylem) the fluids are drawn up into the tree, while on the outside (the phloem) the sugars produced by the leaves flow downward
and grow into the tree's wood. (The new wood eventually passes
into the heartwood of the tree underneath the cambium layer, which
supports the tree's life while being itself largely dead.) Nakashima
observes that "the staggering total of fluids rising and falling in the
trees around the world constitutes a veritable Niagara."[9] Prior to
any familiarity with tree physiology, we sense this and are moved
by it.

If we examine our treelike sense of "affinity" and "empathy" more
closely, we find that it dovetails with two crucial aspects of human
biography—imagination and memory. The philosopher Edward S.

Casey notes that imagination and memory have in common a vertical orientation. Imagination moves upward from the actualities of life, "guides bodily being toward soul," toward expression in image, metaphor, story, reflective thinking, an expansive sense of possibility—toward "progressive *articulation*."[10] Memory moves downward into life's actualities, grounding us in the past, in continuity and history, in bodily being, and so "gives mass or substance" to biographical life or what Casey elsewhere calls "the dense earth of recalcitrant experience."[11] Imagination "breaks up and breaks out," while memory "consolidates." Importantly, both go on at the same time, holding together the variegated and conflicting tendencies within our psychological lives, "working as coeval partners" which continually create and re-create our sense of ourselves as biographical beings.

Casey does not refer to trees in his discussions of imagination and memory, but what he says about their "coeval" operation is curiously treelike. For instance, while imagination moves in *nonactual* realms and memory in the world of what does have or has had actual existence, there are "*images* which" they "share," which are a kind of common pathway, like a psychic cambium layer that joins or connects earth and sky. Images "help to account for the deeply rooted links between" imagination and memory and allow them "to find a common ground—a shared placescape. . . ." The connective power of image itself turns out to have a hidden link with the connective power of trees, which may have something to do with the ways in which imaginations around trees move inevitably (though not necessarily overtly) in the direction of memories (so that Jaime's entertaining of the possibility that he is also a tree animates his childhood memories, and Sally's experience of that same possibility, while already a memory, will lead her to still other levels of memory). In another discussion, Casey concentrates on the power of place itself to ground human being *between* extremes of "upmost and downmost, heaven and hell, peaks and vales, high-flying imagination and morbidly remorseful memory."[12] For "we need to take a stand somewhere in between—somewhere on earth, on the world's body. . . ." Again, the image is tacitly arboreal, suggesting a sensed correspondence between the interior life of trees and our own upright beings.

The felt connection between the tree, the treelike, and the human stance upon (and attachment to) the earth is articulated in many of the most deeply felt statements of people like Will, Jaime, and Sally, each of whom speaks in some way about a yearning for a wooded home. This connection, in fact, is one of the ways in which those on different sides in environmental debates turn out to have something important in common. For example, a man living on the Olympic Peninsula in Washington sided with local loggers in the conflict over the preservation of the old-growth forests in the area. He insists, echoing Will, that "I am not a preservationist but I am an environmentalist." He is particularly passionate in describing the rhythms of life on his family farm, on which he grows trees for harvesting. "Sometimes," he says, "it's neat to put your rain gear on, hop on a tractor, and go down to trim some trees." His words express a downward attachment to the place: "It's not necessarily a way of life, so much—it's a place of life. These are roots that most people never get to know." He stated this while walking "through a dark spruce grove."[13] Walking among those trees probably lent intensity and clarity to his thoughts. The arboreal attachment to place is present on several levels and in the foreground and background of the man's musings. Ironically, given the nature of the conflict over the old-growth forests of the Pacific Northwest, this man most definitely *is* a preservationist as well as an environmentalist: like his preservationist opponents, he wants to perpetuate a "place of life" that depends on trees, and on special roots.

What he says can be heard not only in connection with Casey's insights, but also with some words of an avowed forest preservationist and poet, W. S. Merwin. In his poem titled, revealingly, "Place," the narrator ponders the tree he would want to plant "on the last day of the world":

> I want the tree that stands
> in the earth for the first time
>
> with the sun already
> going down
>
> and the water
> touching its roots

in the earth full of the dead
and the clouds passing

one by one
over its leaves[14]

Merwin's poem, like the man's words quoted before, *takes a stand* upon a place against a backdrop of threat and loss, embodying the parallel between the stands of humans and of trees.

The "vertical" relationship between the soul of the human body and that of the tree turns out to have its own, quite complex, interior life. For it also grounds a *horizontal* dynamism which adds further vitality to the felt links between us and the trees. This dynamism is illustrated in David's movement from "a tree comin' up" to "gettin' back on the track"; his sense of *horizontal* possibility was energized (see chapter 2, p. 24). Both Jane and Jaime also sense a life-power flowing horizontally between themselves and the trees. In the forest, Jaime sometimes had an impulse to touch a trunk because he wanted to get its feel. "I want all my senses to experience the tree," and he "can certainly feel that it's also full of life." More, it "seems like life is flowing from the tree to me." And that's what "gives you a feeling of affinity with the tree when you touch it." This horizontal movement also is suggested by the images of "equality," the mutual gaze, the mirror, the two-way street. The one-on-one encounter with a tree often involves a distinct feeling of a dialogue, conversation, or mutual knowing between subjects. The "empathy" and "affinity" that Jaime describes, and which is reflected by Will's image of the crooked trees that "stood up" to Hugo, expresses this mutuality.

There is a related sense that an encounter between a human and a tree can be a meeting between two sentient souls. Bachelard quotes a passage from Rainier Maria Rilke describing a man's contemplations while resting in a tree's lower limb: "It was as if almost imperceptible vibrations came from the inside of the tree and passed over into his body. . . . He felt as though . . . his body had been in some way treated like a soul and prepared to receive an influence" of which he would normally remain unaware—"a subtle, yet pervasive message."[15] Sally related that her mother had one day had a powerful experience in their garden by an ancient mulberry tree that was one of the family's favorites, when "all of a sudden she got this really, really strong feeling that the mulberry tree was a person and that she could communicate with it as another being." A woman college student wrote about an encounter with a tree using similar terms. She, or at least her "cynical self," was surprised by the intensity with which she remembered a fig tree in the yard of her grandmother's house, a tree beneath which she used to play. Recently she had visited her grandmother and the tree, and as she stood before it, she experienced what she called a moment of "mutual communication." Donald Culross Peattie, in the foreword to his classic volume on *A Natural History of Trees of Eastern and Central North America*, talks about the value of "a speaking acquaintance" with trees: "When you have learned their names, they say them back to you, as you enounter them—and very much more, for they speak of your own past experience among them. . . ."[16] It is as though the tree becomes the locus of your life story and relates it back to you along with, and as part of, its own.[17]

In this way images of what makes human biographical life distinctly and *physically* human meet up with the imagination of a tree: the kinaesthetic senses of vertical thrust, of (horizontal) communication, and of soul or subjectivity. In a very real, if not *literal* way, trees do communicate something to us about the basis of our biographical lives and possibilities. But trees' way is one that intensifies our awareness of their nonhuman presence. It is as though they transform themselves into human persons—as though the numerous myths and legends about the transformation of humans into trees are the mirror image of what happens in our everyday lives: trees become embodied in human forms, in tools, materials, homes, images, what's in your hand, and in "the blood trees within us. . . ."[18] On the level of culture this is undeniable; on the level of biographical and bodily self-perception, it is usually only in less-guarded moments that we take seriously the shaping power of trees in our lives, their ceaselessly speaking images.

Because it is so intimately an affair of the body, an encounter with trees can also easily evoke one's important images regarding maleness and femaleness and can shape related images of sexual awareness and exploration. In Will's case such a meeting elicits what he self-mockingly refers to as "typical male chauvinist" images; for Jane, it suggests women's struggle *against* male domination.

Will "would guess" that his appreciation of nature came from the times he spent with his father and two brothers "in the woods workin'. You know, doin' whatever it is we were doin'. We were always the typical male chauvinist family," he said, wryly recounting how men's and women's roles got defined through the experience of being where the trees were. "The boys did the work outside, and [my] little sister did the inside work with my mom . . . we cleared land and moved rocks and put in fences and just enjoyed being outdoors." The continuing power of this male/female divide was evident when Will spoke of his protective feelings toward trees planted on his property. He warned his son against scraping them with the lawn mower. "You know, 'Don't you skin my trees.' . . . 'You can run over my wife's flower bed—those are perennials, they'll come back next year, but don't you skin that tree!'" Clearly, the womanly flowers do not measure up to the manly trees.

Unlike Will's sister, Jane grew up in an environment where gender equality was valued; her mother encouraged her to be physically "adventurous." Subsequently, she became deeply involved in feminism. She made explicit, sexual and religious, connections between her experience of the power of trees and her effort to reclaim "my heritage as a woman." Trees with "fire" in them are one element that helps shape her struggle toward that heritage. Where the roots of trees go is another, related one. In talking about the mirror of the tree, Jane observed that "the tree very definitely has . . . to have roots in the ground and leaves in the air." And, underground, what you find is space—"dark space instead of light space"—the "downstairs," "that whole world." It happened that about half a year ago, "I fell in love. And I *fell* into the other world. It was like the floor opened up and I fell in." Though her love went unrequited, the experience for Jane was "a wonderful falling into myself also." And "the person that I fell in love with was an Austrian woman." This involved "an extremely strong spiritual connection . . . and I felt in her . . . a way of finding the Goddess." She stressed also its "very strong sexual component"; this "was really necessary as part of the whole experience," and it has been crucial to Jane's self-affirmation as a woman and her growing interest in that part of Jewishness—the role of the Goddess in ancient Near Eastern and Semitic mythologies—that has, she said, for the most part had to remain "underground."[19]

The more general power felt in maleness and femaleness (in all its contradictions, its expansive and affirmative as well as stereotypical and constrictive forms) can also be imagined as a power of trees. The expansiveness is evident in Jane's religious and sexual explorations, as well as in the old "proud" trees Jaime and Mischa described (the ones that urge "you to be better, so to say"). Such imagining can have an idealized quality as well (in which case it can be simultaneously amplifying and narrowing). For instance, Ted described the live oak trees in the South Carolina Lowcountry as "the patriarchs," a word that evoked for him important leaders and "great presidents" like Teddy Roosevelt.

The role of male idealization is determinable in Ted's life. It seemed to me that he himself has tried hard to behave like a "patriarch" or strong leader, both through his role in his community and through many years of devotion to the environmental restoration of South Carolina. In addition to being a teacher, Ted is "a commissioned law enforcement officer"—which added to his responsibilities in the aftermath of Hurricane Hugo. At the time, he was feeling intensely both his desire to help his community and his inability to do so to the extent that living up to the image of a "patriarch" would require. (In reflecting on the plight of those who as of mid-December still did not have homes, Ted said, "That was really depressing. . . . Not bein' able to do everything that they needed done"; and "I wish I was a multimillionaire and could go in and fix everything for everybody.") Even before Hugo it had been a rough year for Ted. He had been confronted by unexpected difficulties at work, which had shaken his image of himself as being able to conform to his own exacting standards. More, his father (another personal connection to "patriarch") had died, a particularly difficult event because Ted and his father had been somewhat distant—as great men, and parents whose humanness is not fully accessible to their children, tend to be. Ted was left with a feeling of incompleteness in his relationship with his father, a thwarted connection, grief without resolution; at the same time, he was shouldered with a persistent and impossible-to-realize image of the ideal patriarch. I thought these emotional dilemmas too had something to do with the way he talked about the live oaks.

For Pamela, Jane, and Sally, the connective power and *perspective* of a tree were strongly linked with thoughts about the contribution women can make to society or to a planetary ecology. Some cogent women's writing, as in the case of Zora Neale Hurston, Toni Morrison, and Mari Evans (on whom see chapters 6 and 7), makes parallels between the form of the tree and women claiming their authority (and the power of an ecological sensibility reflective of women's bodily life).

But there is a risk of idealization here as well. For instance, when Jane associates the power of the tree to that of the Goddess and the underworld, she is referring to an oppressed and repressed aspect of life. But mythologies of the Goddess also carry death and the possibility of bloody mayhem. The underworld of Near Eastern Goddesses is shadowy and insubstantial—not a pretty place, but one of strangeness and pain. Those qualities are not only a result of neglecting women's heritage, any more than the strangeness of trees is only coterminous with human alienation. Sometimes, at least, making links between Goddess and tree involves an idealizing maneuver. Such a Goddess, strangely enough, thus has something in common with Ted's patriarchal trees. But there is also something in trees that supports the human tendency to idealize male and female forms.[20]

For Jaime, Jane, and Sally, trees also stir a more specifically sexual imagination. Strong and standing competitively higher than his boyhood friends, Jaime's tree self manifests a kind of phallic ecology. This potency took on a palpable sexual resonance, figuring Jaime's sense of himself as sexual being, "lush" and "attractive" to other forest life. He also described abandoning his boyhood tree for girls, and its subsequent death, evidently thinking that he may have taken some of its flow, its strength, its desire with him (leaving the tree sapped, as it were, of its dynamism, along with the earlier boyhood interests it evokes). One could say that Jaime sexualizes the tree. But at the same time the tree sexualizes him.

The upwardly, and downwardly, surging power of the tree is not phallic only. It also fires and shapes Jane's search for womanly self-affirmation. The dancing power of the tree links Jane to a womb-like place of "deep, hot earth"—not the only distinctly erotic metaphor Jane used. In her recent drawings she has stressed "getting into the space" between trees and has described those woodscapes in terms of trees with "all kinds of wild things hanging down from the top" and "bushy things" alongside them. This artistic compulsion, she said, was "my discovery this summer"—the same summer she discovered herself falling in love with another woman. Sally's account of her experience of being like a tree, when "it felt like everything was really growing," may also have erotic connotations. Her roots go down "through the lovely fresh spongy spring grass," an image which suggests, together with an awareness of the ecological, spiritual, and erotic depths of earth and trees, her sexual self-exploration. For Jane and Sally, the tree's moving power arouses the land.

Trees are generous; their forms readily vitalize male and female power of many kinds. But trees also confound simplifying gender categories. Jaime's guava tree has some of the maternal, sheltering quality that Jung points to, as well as a boyish strength. And Sally could not keep herself from thinking of one tree that she drew as manlike; it was one in a series in which a man was in fact transformed into a tree. And for Jane, too, a tree can house a male spirit (see next chapter). Trees do not have gender, nor is it fair to simply call them symbols for male and female, however defined. You could think of them as Carl Kerényi did with regard to the story of Daphne and Apollo (the former was transformed into the laurel tree to avoid the latter's advances)—as "naturally bisexual."[21] Trees *attract* the imagination of both sexes. If you are a man, chances are you think of trees in male terms, but you can and do think of them as having female qualities as well; if you are a woman, chances are you think of trees as womanly but can also see them as manly. Trees draw out your images of both genders. The metaphors get mixed; the mirror is a two-way street.

Trees and Human Life-Stories

A sense of how the human–tree parallel is kinaesthetically embodied helps us to better appreciate some of the ways in which it can reach into people's biographical self-narratives—their biographical woodscapes.

Jane is not the first to use the figure of the mirror to characterize the relationship between tree and human life. In a footnote in his essay on "The Philosophical Tree," Jung quotes a commentary on a series of emblems by a sixteenth-century Italian jurist, Andreas Alciatus. Alciatus described various human qualities—strength, vulnerability, good political sense, and so on—using drawn figures of various trees (in traditional mythological and social contexts). The reason for this, according to the commentary, is that "the tree is the image and mirror of our condition."[22] Alciatus himself could also be a tree. His biographical experience is reflected in one emblem of a transplanted fruit tree which he describes as a "stranger to our clime" that only now bears nourishing fruit; "it has a leaf very like a tongue, fruit very like a heart." At a colleague's urging, Alciatus transplanted himself, accepting a teaching position in France, where he flourished. The epigram recounts this: "Alciatus, learn from [the tree] how to spend your life. At a distance from your homeland you will be more prized. . . ."[23]

The transplanted tree as a mirror of the experience of emigration (and hence of feeling oneself a stranger, uprooted) and of the quest for a home crops up with great frequency. African-American experience is often and powerfully figured by it. Says Janie Crawford's grandmother (her "head and face" envisaged by Janie as "the standing roots of some old tree that had been torn away by storm. Foundation of ancient power that no longer mattered") in *Their Eyes Were Watching God*, "Us colored folks is branches without roots and that makes things come around in queer ways."[24] The photographer and novelist Gordon Parks writes in his autobiography of the stresses of his adolescent trek from his rural Oklahoma home, after his mother died, to live with his sister in St. Paul. He arrived "still snarled in the roots of racism," and he and his brother-in-law couldn't get along. He ended up in a boarding house. In his plight, "I started taking stock of myself. I was like an uprooted tree in a strange forest."[25] The forest was St. Paul; "I was . . . overwhelmed by the complexity of surviving in a big city." Trees shape Parks's ecology of travail and survival, estrangement and connection.

Parks's life eventually took root, flourished. Ivan, a homeless man in his early thirties who had recently moved from Baltimore to New York City (and one of the black participants in the study of the American Self), was not so sure of himself. A question about his experience of being African-American prompted anxious ruminations about his sense of dislocation and struggle, about whether he would eventually be able to claim "something that's mine," that is, to secure a grounded sense of self. Ivan had been married, with two children, and was recently divorced—and was not comfortable with that either. His next association, following immediately upon the discussion of African-American experience, had to do with that predicament—and with roots. "Look," he explained (to his attractive woman interviewer, and perhaps also to himself), "within the next two years I'm going to get married. I know that, and I've got to settle down, settle within myself and settle a firm foundation, just like a tree that you plant. You know if you plant it in shallow ground, it's not going to root. If you dig deep and plant the roots deep," it will. The tree that Ivan "plants" in the conversation says as much about his sense of uncertainty about whether he can find the deep ground of a home—"within myself" or within a family— as it does about his desire to do so. Since very early in his life, he has been unsettled in his depths. But Ivan's conflicted longing for roots has an ecological foundation. "I was born in the country. . . . That will always be a part of me, you know?"

In autobiographical reflections in his book *The Tree*, the novelist John Fowles talks about the differences between his and his father's views of nature—how he grew to favor wildness, while his father focused on the cultivation of his own garden. They had diametrically opposed attitudes to trees—Fowles's father's "little collection of crimped and cramped fruit trees" and "my America of endless natural ones in Devon," a rural area of England to which the family was forced to move during World War II.[26] Yet he later came to "see that the outward profound difference in our attitudes to nature—especially in the form of the tree—had a strange identity of purpose, a kind of joint root-system, an interlacing, a paradoxical pattern"; both, he now realized, sought "poetic" sanctuary in a world of trees that offers psychological nourishment and protection from the surrounding, frightening world.

Those roots Fowles talks about would seem to extend psychologically still farther—to actual America, among other places; to Ivan's story, with its themes of a quest for roots and the need for sanctuary among trees. The human biographical imagination everywhere is thoroughly interlaced with roots. (*Tree* roots are not always specified, though I believe an arboreal element is always implicit, given the singular parallelism between tree and human life. The specifically arboreal themes of verticality and uprightness appear in the frequent contrast between deep and shallow roots, which Ivan makes.) In general, one's roots are felt not to be fully recognized, and often there is concurrent with the imagination of roots a feeling of rootlessness, uprootedness, or some ambivalence about roots. Thus, Gordon Parks can feel the pain of uprootedness while at the same time being "snarled in the roots of racism," which immobilize him. Roots and rootlessness themselves have "a kind of joint root-system"; their fundamental psychic soil consists in the ongoing tension between the sense of ourselves as treelike and of our divergence from trees. The cultural phenomena associated with roots and rootlessness are in part expressions of (though hardly reducible to) this basic relationship between trees and the biographical imagination.

The ambiguousness of roots has much to do with feelings about home—a sense that home is that place to which we have a treelike attachment. When that connection is damaged or cut, roots are bared. Ivan's troubled thoughts about roots are illustrative. They compare to something that Dan, a forester who works outdoors in the Francis Marion, told me about *his* roots. In Dan's case, the damage to roots of home is a result of Hurricane Hugo. He would never consider moving elsewhere, he said, because "my family [has] lived in the South Carolina Lowcountry since before the Revolutionary War, so we have real deep roots here and have a very strong attachment to the land." The firmness of *those* roots contrasts with the roots of trees killed by the hurricane; his family "tree" remains embedded and at home while the actual trees have lost their roots (are "homeless"). Sally, on the other hand, was, like Ivan, homesick, at one point recently "pining to be back" in England. Immediately after recounting her adolescent experience of treeness, she said in a nostalgic tone: "There's such a strong connection between the land—in England—and the people"; it's "an intrinsic understanding" that people have, "even if they won't speak about it." The connection between this observation and her sense of *her* tree roots—and also her yearning for that English relation and thus her uprooted-ness—also remained unspoken.

Roots, in their psychological depths, reveal a treelike character and how that character shapes what we could call the biography of attachment. The attachments themselves can have psychological, cultural, social, religious, and ecological characteristics. In any case, roots' tenacity and vitality figure their enduring importance for human biography. The power of rooted connection is not, however, life-affirming in a simple and clear-cut sense; it can also connote inescapable entanglement in the past, its ambiguities and its wounds, as in Parks's and Fowles's stories. Even the experience of uprooted-ness, of the loss of grounding attachments (as in the cases of Ivan and Sally), can grow roots as deep as a tree's.

Dan was especially enthusiastic about the chance his work gives him to watch the total "life cycle" of trees. His specialty was supervising the replanting of logged-over areas in the Francis Marion, and he talked about his work the way a parent would talk about children:

> I call 'em my little babies out there. And [when] they get to prescribed burnin' around here and stuff, and they let a fire get out of [bounds] from time to time, and they burn up the stands of seedlins', I'll holler at 'em and tell 'em they're killing my babies out there. You feel that when you plan and work hard to get the site preparation done and the planting, you nurture little seedlins' along, you feel like you've invested a part of yourself in that.

Dan's was the most explicit statement of this theme—the human "parenting" of trees—that I came across in my conversations. One other man, Mark, a businessman in a town bordering the Francis

Marion, had taken a special liking to his community's revered live oak tree and germinated seeds from its acorns. These seeds grew into what he called "babies," to be planted by himself or others—a process that has not been, he said, without "miscarriages." And Mark shared what seemed an adult's fascination with a baby or young child in talking about these seedlings: "I think" that "people have an image that unless a tree is big and beautiful, then it's not worth having. . . . But I *love* the little trees . . . that you can plant and watch as they grow."

The "baby" tree often exemplifies and celebrates the birth and life-story of a human being, in part because its life will likely extend beyond the human life and so psychologically lengthen the latter. Many people have affectionate memories of trees planted in honor of their birth—a ritual practice in a variety of cultures that celebrates the *tree* of the human—and, implicitly, one's status as a human being in a larger ecological family.

The power of such a ritual appears in the account, in the *Odyssey*, of Odysseus's homecoming and reunion with his father, Laertes. Odysseus finds Laertes alone in the garden, wearing tattered clothes, planting a new tree, head bowed in grief.[27] That young tree tells us that something new is about to happen that will relieve Laertes' pain, that there was a young "tree" he did not, as he feared, tend in vain. The tree at hand is of course Odysseus—but Laertes doesn't believe it at first. Father and son each test each other; a remembrance of trees is the immediate precondition of the reunion. For when Laertes demands a sign that it is indeed Odysseus before him, his son first mentions a scar on his thigh from a boar wound. "And," continues Odysseus, "I can tell you the trees that you gave me, here in this garden, when I was little—when I followed you around asking you about every tree." Laertes had responded to his boy's exacting curiosity: "And you named each of the trees and told me about them. And you gave me thirteen pear trees, ten apple trees, and forty fig trees." The trees were given to Odysseus, essential seed and fruit of his father's work, his soul—and Odysseus's as well. The naming was deliberate, ritualistic—sixty-three trees in all. The archaic sense of the human as a form of planted tree is as crucial to Odysseus's identity as the wound in his thigh. Wound and tree, appearing together, figure the years of painful separation of father and son, but also the fruit of their prior and anticipated memories, and their familial self-definitions.

Odysseus is not directly named in the story as himself a tree. Rather, the relationship between his soul, his father, and the trees is an indirect one, but a kind of mutual mirroring nevertheless goes on. We often encounter such indirectly mirrored parallelism between the life-stories of human and tree. For instance, Kevin, the South Carolina urban forester, remembered two silver maples that he and his siblings planted when they were children, "and as we grew up, they grew up." The implication, unstated, is that the silver maples are part of the family. A friend of mine described the growth of an elm tree planted in honor of his twelfth birthday using the same phrase: he watched as it "grew up." Jane's images of the mirror and of "equality" aptly characterize these memories—as they do those of Ellen, a New York shopkeeper, who remembered herself as a girl planting a pine tree, about a foot tall, by the side of her parents' house. "It was *my* tree," said Ellen, and "I used to go out and see if it was getting as tall as I was."

In a poem titled "Native Trees," W. S. Merwin subtly probes the inescapable parallelism between a human sense of self and the growth of the tree. [28] It is a portrait of family alienation—alienation from one another, from trees, from origins. On one level, the problem is exactly the lack of a sense of kinship between self and tree: "Neither my father nor my mother knew / the names of the trees / where I was born," and despite his persistent questions do not really even remember if there were trees where *they* were children. Now, reflects the narrator, they lived "where there were no questions / no voices and no shade"—none of the ambiguities and depth one finds among trees. The psychological situation of this family is on this level precisely counterposed to that of Odysseus and his father, who *name* each other as they name again in memory the trees where Odysseus was born.

Yet the problem in "Native Trees" is posed in such a way that the human–tree affinity asserts itself even as it is mourned by the narrator: the sense of a forgotten human actuality and the consciousness of native family trees as that actuality's locus grow together in the poem; the place of birth is among unnoticed and forgotten trees—as if to suggest that the human identity becomes truly human only when placed with trees and in familiarity with their native identities. The parents' fingers touch only "surfaces of furniture"—the surface furniture of themselves, not the deeper trees from which, presumably, the furniture is wrought. Merwin evokes images of humans being "born" from trees—and found among them (or about people who grow on the land like trees).

The narrator's questioning, like the mythic images, persists:

> Were there trees
> where they were children
> where I had not been
> I asked
> were there trees in those places
>
> where my mother and father were born
> and in that time did
> my father and my mother see them
> and when they said yes it meant
> they did not remember
> What were they I asked what were they
> but both my father and mother
> said they never knew

The ambiguous parallelism of tree and self is expressed here in the poet's use of "they" in the last half of the stanza to refer, in alternation, to the parents and to the trees—suggesting not only that the parents don't know their trees, but also that the parents *are* the trees who don't know their own roots or who they are or their native origins or their own true names. Even in their ignorance, forgetfulness, and self-estrangement, the parents are "Native Trees."

In Annie Dillard's novel *The Living*, we find further outgrowths of the life–death parallel between humans and trees. These appear in the life of Rooney Fishburn, a pioneer from Illinois who settled on Puget Sound in the 1850s. In Illinois, Rooney had a very different relationship with trees than his connection with the old growth in the Pacific Northwest. Back where he grew up, he "loved a grove of old pines" near his parents' house and "used to travel out of his way" to stand in their special light and shade.[29] But here the huge trees "seemed a condensation and embodiment of the rain and the crushingly heavy rank growth a man fought with all his muscles every day of his life, and hated with all his sore heart. . . . his task was to crack the dome of shade and help the sunlight down." As Dillard's image sensitively suggests, Rooney and his compatriots saw themselves as light- and life-bringers to their edge of the world; clearing the forest, if not specifically God's work, was surely creating a new world.

In this setting, *felling* trees instead of planting them could thus parallel human birth. In fact, Rooney's first daughter was born the day he and a Lummi Indian completed cutting down two trees:

> Both . . . came groaning down at once. They cracked a score of other trees, smashed the earth, and the earth rebounded. . . . Splinters, bark, and sunlit dust spun where the trees had stood. When it was all over he stood still in the stunning, expanding silence to listen towards [his] cabin, and he heard, distant and high and frail, what he was listening for: a baby's cry.

This is not where the story ends, however; even those who cut trees down can grow, live, and die like trees. Rooney's eldest surviving son, Clare, thrives in the Puget Sound area, becoming among other things an expert at felling trees. When working in the woods as a young boy with his father, Clare "loved to keep company with the motionless, live tree trunks." Later, as a teenager, "he planted apple trees when everybody planted apple trees" and enthusiastically tried grafting plums and pears onto them; at that time he also took to drawing—expressing in his own way what psychologists of the next century would rediscover with their tests: "He tried to draw the Douglas firs, the way their trunks grew straight and close as rushes, and their black branches high above swooped like skirts." Clare himself is exceptionally tall, and his wife at one point wonders to herself: "When had she seen [the] fir forest without his towering beside her like one of the trees?"

Clare also imagines dying like a tree. His life is maliciously threatened by another man, tall like Clare; at one point they encounter each "other's dark form rising above" a crowd at a town celebration, "the way a grand fir breaks from a ridgetop line of Douglas firs and sticks its mussed crown in the sky." Clare worries: "If a man believes he will fall a certain tree," he probably will; and "if a man believes that your death fits his plans," then it does. And Clare, even in his own yard, could feel "immense . . . and stripped, like a barked tree" in his vulnerability.

It happens, as well, that the final arc of Rooney's life is no less like that of a tree's because his relationship to trees has taken an adversarial turn and he is stooped "from . . . tree work" by the age of forty-one. He is digging a well on his property and strikes a pocket of deadly gas with his shovel: "Rooney fell over on his spade. He lay in the hole. He had gone down like a tree, head last."

Old Trees

Old trees are pre-eminent in biographical woodscapes. Their aesthetic specificities show their age and ours; old trees are the odd ghosts of the future, of where we will go. They foreshadow the final communion in human biography between ourselves and what is non-human. The future we see in old trees reverberates back through our images of biographical life—including the weathering and death of old images of self.

Let us listen to what Sally says about the old trees in the garden of her childhood home and enter into their biographical, familial interiors. The apple tree she used to draw, for instance, "had aged with my father. And that was the case with the mulberry tree [the one which had appeared as a "person" to Sally's mother]. I was really struck by that with the mulberry tree, because in its younger days it was such an effusive tree," but now its three main limbs have to be held together by a wire and one of its limbs has to be propped up. "It's quite possible," she said, that the mulberry tree "was three-hundred-years old, you know?" Sally's image of the tree's "younger days" is not literal or actual in nature, but it seems to be the way the tree tells its life-story to her. Because its life-story spans several human generations, it is able to exemplify them, lay bare their essentials. She then drew the parallel between her father "when he was old and leaning on a stick, [and] the tree—of which part of it was leaning on a prop . . . it was leaning more strongly on its support just like my father was. . . . I got a real sense of affinity between my father and the tree as they all grew older."

The trees of the garden also revealed a hidden affinity with patterns of trouble in Sally's family. Her father had died a few years before we talked, and Sally had more recently been having numerous dreams about the garden which she recognized as in part attempts to come to terms with her father's death and life. Sally is very much aware of religious connotations of gardens—"it's also the Garden of Eden and all these other things, right?" There is a very personal level of meaning in that Sally constantly played in the garden when a child, and "in my innocence it was my kingdom" along with its trees and other flora and fauna.

In a recent dream, Sally and her father were walking in the garden, "in a real state of closeness, which we had never really had when he was alive." Sally and her dead father walked arm-in-arm toward the garden gate, and "there was a line of little new apple trees" along the way; she especially noticed "one with red apples and one with yellow apples, right?" These were mythological trees, Sally said—though also "sort of like Golden Delicious and Red Delicious apples. . . ." They were, she added, "a gift for my father," but there seemed an undertone of sarcastic anger in that gift—Golden Delicious and Red Delicious apples, perfect in their artificiality, are hardly like the apples her father "allowed himself"—"the ones with the bugs in them. . . ."

Dream trees, like actual trees, can have beguiling contortions and complexities. Though Sally related the red to essential physical life and the yellow to gold, "the Elixir of the Spirit," these trees also assert a different awareness. We will remember that yellow was also the color of the not-very-distinguished apples of the Lady Sudely that Sally had mentioned. That in turn suggests a *yellowing* and *aging* of the innocence in which Sally had formerly played. [30] Yellow can be a lemon-bitter color, and something of this emotional coloration came through when Sally talked more about her father's extreme and rigid insistence on thrift. This "was a very big issue in our whole lives, all the way through, in the whole family, all our lives"; the family lived "permeated by the idea that, as he had felt, we were not really good enough to have the best." They had to use everything "up to the last drop," said Sally with a bitter inflection. Bitterness can consume, and Sally's father's attitude "*ate* into my mother . . . she felt very injured by it." Sally was also talking about herself.

And she was talking about the trees, for "when I come to think of it, I don't think that the degree of care" given by her father to the garden's trees in his later years "was as respectful as it could've been, whereas they kept on giving." He had his way of "nurturing" them, but as Sally thought about it now this seemed to have more to do with his own concern for order and pattern than for the trees themselves. She thought he didn't give the mulberry tree very much help. "I think," she continued, that her father "probably could have examined the tree more carefully" as to whether the tree's supports should have been adjusted. "He would prop things up," she said, with again a hint of bitter sarcasm, "when they were about falling on the ground, you know?"

Without directly saying so, Sally saw in her father's treatment of the trees a mirror of family difficulties—and she tacitly identified with the trees. The garden grows into a dense forest of psychological affinities, ambivalent and complex, between the trees and the human family. The "little new apple trees" in the dreamed garden sum up this familial-ecological pattern, the emotional nuances that together bear their fruit as Sally struggles to find a way toward a new affinity with her father through mourning his death—and the difficult contortions of his life.

Will's biographical woodscapes also reveal troublesome patterns of dying and mourning. His parents were active, alive, and well into their eighties when we first spoke. But the following January, as Will subsequently told me, his father had suddenly died, right in the middle of "puttin' in fence posts" on his property, when "he passed a blood clot." Will thought this was the best way for an active man like his father to die "if you're gonna go": "He would've hated to [have] gone slow."

The key word here is "slow": Will himself would hate to go that way. But he would not mind dying among trees. "I'd much rather a bear eat me than a hospital room," he said; "I'd much rather go the way my dad did. . . . just healthy and alert and playin'—and then the next day, gone." Though he wanted to emphasize that this was a good way to die, Will's tone was one of perplexity. It seemed to me he had a lot of suppressed grief. This death was one of those things that (like Hurricane Hugo) could not be managed in the usual way, or properly anticipated. But Will, like the rest of us, could not help anticipating his own death. In this, thinking about death in "the woods" did help. It could be in the "rollin' hills" of North Carolina, his childhood home, for "you go from adulthood back to childhood, you know?" And the forests there are "much prettier"—diverse and (not uncoincidentally) untouched by Hugo. Perhaps a woodland swamp would also be suitable, but, in any case, "I'd like to do it in the woods."

And in those woods, Will would not be alone. Listen closely to the yearning of those places, and you'll hear echoes of Will's self-defining characters—Hillbilly and Swamp Rat: "I've told my family, 'If I ever get Alzheimer's, or that old, . . . take me to the mountains or out in a swamp, and open the door, and tell me to walk that way.'"

Another "interesting story" takes on added appeal in connection with this image of *the woods of death*. It is about the "life-story of a tree" grown for harvesting in the Francis Marion. "When I first moved to South Carolina," Will began, "I came to work for an older consulting forester . . . in his sixties." Will marked for cutting a stand of timber that had reached a mature "rotation age." By "rotation age" Will meant the cycle that begins with timber cutting, proceeds through preparation for replanting and the replanting itself, and continues with managing the stand until, forty or more years later, the trees are cut and the cycle begins anew. "In a given area [of the Francis Marion], you could see in just a few miles, every life-stage of a tree. Or of a forest. You could see places that were freshly cut, that looked nasty." Will continued, now in the present tense, journeying for a moment in memory to the forest as it was before Hurricane Hugo. "And then you can drive a mile down the road, [to] where the seedlins' have taken over, the young pine saplins' are up, it's gotten green again, they've done a controlled burning and a site-prep to prepare it for this point, it's again regenerating to that beauty. Drive a few miles down the road and you'll see trees that are fifteen to twenty years old. So," said Will with considerable feeling (and a shift into the past tense that marked the end of his trek through the forest-that-was), "you were able to watch the entire life-story of a tree in just a very few miles."

This was not the only time Will drew parallels, tacitly or explicitly, between generations of trees (their "life-stories") and of human lives, both in terms of the time it takes to reach "maturity" and the physical processes of growth and decay. This parallelism is for Will a way he contemplates and seeks to grasp his own life cycle. Though all crops have life cycles or "rotation ages" that in turn are linked to a variety of psychological, cultural, and ecological (and, ultimately, cosmic, religious, or mythological) cycles, the process of growing trees—or more generally the *story* of trees—is often felt to come closest by far to the human life cycle. At a conference on logging in the Pacific Northwest in early April 1993, a logger told attending President Bill Clinton: "I cut trees for a living, just like my father and my grandfather did before me. I like to think that some of the trees that started life when my grandfather was cutting are old growth today. Mr. President, you are going to be old growth some day, too."[31] Will's story illuminates the role of a mythic image, a life–death cycle, in the tradition of American forestry—and in recent disagreements about what forestry's role should be.[32]

It is, moreover, in a sense a primary story of Will's life as a forester, or an origin myth—and also an imaginative anticipation of his own *last* story. "I came in," Will went on, "to help" the older forester "with his actual woods work that he was no longer capable of doin'. The . . . land that I marked was also a piece of land that he marked [for a] first cut when he first moved to South Carolina"; it "was the first piece of timber that he cut and regenerated. So he had seen one timber stand go its complete cycle. And that was a goal to him." And he said, "I have fulfilled a desire"—that "he had . . . seen, and managed, a forest through its complete rotation. He harvested a mature forest, he regenerated it—natural regeneration—and he'd come back and started again. And . . . he died just a few years after that." His purpose, his story as a forester, had been fulfilled, so that death could become part of an ongoing "rotation" of forest ecology.

Yet, in the timber "rotation," trees are not left to die on their own. As we talked about another side of "the entire life-story of a tree," Will's attempt to keep a certain kind of death out of the picture emerged. "You can manage things," said Will in contrasting (what he saw as) urban environmentalism and rural common sense. "A *managed* forest is beautiful. An *unmanaged* forest can tend to overtake itself." For instance, there are "your environmental groups that" did not recognize that the massive, uncontrolled forest fires in Yellowstone National Park in the summer of 1988 might have been less severe "had that been a managed forest. . . ."[33] Will asserted that had the Yellowstone fire "been a controlled burn," of the sort practiced in the Francis Marion prior to Hugo, "it wouldn't have damaged anything," would even have encouraged the growth of browse for animals like deer and of seed-plants for songbirds.

At this juncture Will's point of reference subtly shifted—from the scene after the fire in Yellowstone to a generic "mature" or, as he subsequently clarified, "climax forest." "There are," he continued, "no songbirds in a mature forest," and in such a forest "the diversity of animal life in general" is much less. "There's nothing there for an animal to eat. You have to have the diversity of the young versus the old in order to maintain your wildlife." Whereas "when you get to a pure climax forest, all you have is one product."[34] The way Will talked about climax forests also has a powerful psychological resonance, touching upon questions regarding "the young versus the old," places "almost void of animal life" (how Will initially characterized the Great Smoky Mountains National Forest), and the densely tangled connections between life and death.

It turns out that Will's defense of the old dogwood tree goes against the grain of most of his images of old trees. His images moved him at this point from the climax forest to an unmanaged old-growth swamp (see p. 35). It had been bought and preserved by an environmental organization, and "I've been through it several times." Death now speaks starkly in Will's own words and images:

> To me, it was a dying forest. The virgin trees that are there were in very poor health. They were dyin', the tops broke out of 'em, just through the age and previous storms. The understory of the swamp was nothing but a maze of small saplings strugglin' to survive in the shade. It wasn't at all the beauty of an open, lowland swamp, where you have the . . . smaller trees growing healthy and

vigorous. That's the difference between a climax forest [that] is an old-folks' home, and a growing, mature forest that is a nursery. You know, a pre-school nursery. You know, an old-folks' home can be sad. A nursery school, that is a place of joy and excitement. You can look at all of the little people and what they're going to be and what they're going to develop into. You know, that's the two parallels that I personally make between a climax and a growing forest.

A forest of dying trees tells a story Will doesn't like.

But Will was sensitive to the tale. In a climax forest, he reiterated with emphasis, "the trees . . . are dying. Sick. Diseased." If only he could take me to see the swamp (in its pre-Hugo incarnation), with its "*huge*, old dyin' trees, and saplings so thick you couldn't walk through 'em in the ground. And then turn around and take you to a managed hardwood swamp." Both in Yellowstone and in the Francis Marion after Hugo, he continued, there will be a "massive die-off of deer, which is a waste. The poor animal is starving to death, he's in misery, he's dying a slow death. That's basically the same thing I see in a climax forest. A slow death to the tree."

Though we spoke about this in 1989, prior to Will's father's death, here is also that "slow death" that Will's father would have hated. Part of the usefulness of Will's profession for him personally is that it helps to hold at bay the specter of dying as trees do in climax forests or as people do in old-age homes. But holding such death at a distance by killing trees can nonetheless be difficult—in part because of that ever-present parallel between humans and trees. While talking about the value and beauty of youthful trees, Will abruptly, and uneasily, felt compelled to clarify something: "By no means am I advocating euthanasia for old folks. You know, that is wrong, I mean, you ought to be able to grow to your potential"; but "on the tree, it helps the beauty to keep it growing vigorously." The human–tree parallel had come so compellingly into Will's mind that he had to point out that people differ from trees. Still, the forest of dying trees stirs questions about how he will grow old and die, in what way and how far the sadness will grow, and whether it or he will have any value in the end.

In his forestry career, Will has sought management and control. But in his obliquely expressed grief over the loss of his father, that image of management also dies a certain death. Will resists the tale of the old-growth forest, but in the end turns himself over to the trees.

Woodscapes of Darwin

Certain themes in the relationship between trees and human biography can be found in Charles Darwin's evolutionary tree of life. Darwin introduces us to this tree in his chapter on "Natural Selection" in *On the Origin of Species*—though, as his unpublished notebooks make clear, he himself had been familiar with it for over twenty years as he worked on the image of the tree, drew it, reflected on it, revised, refined, and complexified his theory of evolution.[35] The psychologist Howard E. Gruber examined the evolution of Darwin's own thinking in the latter's notebooks. Gruber observes: "Darwin's picture of nature as an irregularly branching tree attributed to nature some of the characteristics that I saw in his thinking."[36] And the tree, *with its irregularities*, shaped those same characteristics. Gruber further suggests that Darwin's other famous evolutionary image, that of the "Tangled Bank," was defined in part by his experiences of nature—of the tropical rainforest—during his five-year voyage on the *H.M.S. Beagle* (1831–1836). There is in Darwin, as he articulates his theory of natural selection through the survival of the fittest, a formative power of trees.

Darwin sought to account for natural diversity within a unifying evolutionary schema. He also aimed to formulate and express within that scheme the diverse details of his own thought processes— and, Gruber says, "the fundamental duality that at any time some must live and others die."[37] Thus Darwin was led to what he called in the *Origin of Species* "the principle that the greatest amount of life can be supported by great diversification of structure. . . ."[38] It was entirely natural that the image of a tree, with its diversity of structure, would impress itself on Darwin as a supporting image of life and the principle of evolution—a life-support image that includes death.

Shortly after introducing his principle of diversification, Darwin presents an abstract diagram of two evolutionary trees and expounds their logic.[39] The sensuous tree stands at the conclusion of the chapter:

> The affinities of all the beings of the same class have sometimes been represented by a great tree. I believe this simile largely speaks the truth. The green and budding twigs may represent existing species; and those produced during former years may represent the long succession of extinct species. At each period of growth all the growing twigs have tried to branch out on all sides, and to overtop and kill the surrounding twigs and branches, in the same manner as species and groups of species have at all times overmastered other species in the great battle for life. The limbs divided into great branches, and these into lesser and lesser branches, were themselves once, when the tree was young, budding twigs, and this connection of the former and present buds may well represent the classification of all extinct and living species in groups subordinate to groups. . . . From the first growth of the tree, many a limb and branch has decayed and dropped off; and these fallen branches of various sizes may represent those whole orders, families, and genera which have now no living representatives, and which are known to us only in a fossil state. . . . As buds give rise by growth to fresh buds, and these, if vigorous, branch out and overtop on all sides many a feebler branch, so by generation I believe it has been with the great Tree of Life, which fills with its dead and broken branches the crust of the earth, and covers the surface with its ever-branching and beautiful ramifications.[40]

"Natural Selection" becomes a revered tree. Religious and aesthetic feeling burst like its buds as the image carries Darwin along, transmuting itself from simile into metaphor. At the same time, Darwin's tree evokes other trees of religion and mythology: Trees of Knowledge and of Death. It is really a combination of trees, a kind of imaginal forest within one tree, which seems to stir Darwin's excitement over "ever-branching and beautiful ramifications." Natural selection is not the only evolutionary movement going on here; there is also an evolving *return*—to the image of a tree.

"Darwin," says Gruber, "looked at nature with deep emotion." He delighted not only in unifying logic but in "irregularity and entanglement" and "wildness"; his tree is an erotic image.[41] The sense of eros impelled and shaped Darwin's arduous theory-building that his notebooks portray. The tree played a crucial role in the evolution of Darwin's theory, its sometimes "irregular branches"—those that survived and those that were discarded.

But we haven't yet followed up on a hint of a further source of Darwin's arboreal imagination: his biographical experiences with trees. Is there, within those experiences, evidence of a still more specific influence on Darwin's arboreal reasoning? Darwin's account of his voyage on the *Beagle* suggests that there may well be.

That record contains engaging descriptions of natural and human phenomena, but trees per se remain generally in the background. Yet an intense emotional response to trees and forests does come through on occasion. "Epithet after epithet," says Darwin at one point, "was found too weak to convey to those who have not visited the intertropical regions, the sensation of delight which the mind experiences"; and Darwin cannot resist describing the forest as "one great wild, untidy, luxuriant hothouse, made by Nature for herself. . . ."[42] And in his concluding retrospect, Darwin says: "Among the scenes which are deeply impressed on my mind, none exceed in sublimity the primeval forests undefaced by the hand of man; whether those of Brazil, where the powers of Life are predominant, or those of Tierra Del Fuego, where Death and Decay prevail. Both are temples filled with the varied production of the God of Nature. . . ."

Writing about his visit to New South Wales in southeastern Australia, Darwin pictures a sparser, more severe realm of trees. It is this minimalism that would seem to more specifically shape Darwin's Tree of Life, paralleling the above-noted connection between his description of tropical rainforest scenery and the image of the Tangled Bank. In New South Wales, Darwin found, "the trees nearly all belong to one family"; their "foliage is scanty, and of a peculiar pale green tint . . . hence the woods appear light and shadowless. . . ." Still, they never lose their leaves. Thus, people "lose perhaps one of the most glorious, though to our eyes common, spectacles in the world—the first bursting into full foliage of the leafless tree. They may, however, say that we pay dearly for this by having the land covered with mere naked skeletons for so many months. This is too true; but our senses thus acquire a keen relish for the exquisite green of the spring. . . ." The great tree of the *Origin of Species*, with its "green and budding twigs," is no naked skeleton of winter, but seems very much a Tree of Spring, of renewal. This detail, and the collective experience it embodies, remains implicit— but powerfully so—in Darwin's description of the Tree of Life. The connection to Darwin's biographical woodscapes is only revealed by contrast, in his recollection of the English countryside as he visits New South Wales.

Yet even the Tree of Life embodies Death as well, in the form of its dying branches that drop off and the dead (disorderly) brokenness which "fills . . . the crust of the earth." Though Darwin means to contrast the evergreen forest of New South Wales with the deciduous forests of the North, he goes on to mention a detail which links them. "The bark of some of the Eucalypti," he says, "falls annually, or hangs dead in long shreds which swing about with the wind, and give to the woods a desolate and untidy appearance." The untidiness here would seem to parallel as well as contrast with the untidiness of "Nature's hothouse"—and, still more particularly, those "dead and broken branches" that fall from the Tree of Life. In arboreal landscapes, life and death can be equally untidy. Part of nature's irregularity involves its disturbing juxtaposition of life and death, exuberant growth and depressive loss. There is, after all, something ominous about bark that comes off its tree and "hangs dead" and "swing[s] about with the wind." And Darwin's Tree of Life grows into its own—and life's—executioner.

Intimacy, Estrangement, and Evolutionary Trees

In stressing the widely and deeply felt intimacy between trees and human biography, it may seem that we lose sight of the obvious and radical differences between the life-stories of trees and human beings. But that sense of intimacy always coincides with the sense of difference; something in us can never lose sight of the differences, even if we are not always reflectively or consciously aware of them.

Robert Pogue Harrison observes that "we dwell not in nature but in the relation to nature" and, as noted earlier, that this "relation remains one of estrangement from, as well as domestic familiarity with, the earth."[43] The psychological power of trees appears in our relation to them and in the juxtaposition of radical difference with an equally radical intimacy. (Which means also that the "nature" to which Harrison refers is itself always *in relation*, as deep-ecological thought emphasizes, and that estrangement is a natural part of relationship.)[44] The power grows when we look at this juxtaposition up close—at how it appears in images—and then, finally, in relation to human biography in a larger context—that of our (human and nonhuman) evolutionary tree(s).

It is commonplace, a sort of ritual, to assert the basic difference between human and nonhuman nature and to try and define it. In broad terms, that difference has to do with humans' uniquely complex and irreducible culture-creating capacities. But the awareness of difference itself, and the question of how we come to grips with that awareness, is perhaps still more basic in human experience, whether one focuses on differences between human individuals and groups, or what Harrison identifies as the problem of (human) estrangement from (nonhuman) nature.[45] The way trees and human biographies come together illustrates ways in which difference and intimacy can themselves come together, remain distinct and in tension, and therefore enhance each other.[46] One philosopher ends up illustrating this when he begins a discussion of ecological arguments for the intrinsic value of plant life by observing that "the distinction between plant, animal and human life has very deep roots."[47] The irony in that last image is worth a pause. It is an image of tenacious difference, but also one suggesting our special intimacy with trees. It suggests that we (trees, humans, others in nature) may be intimate precisely through our differences.

In a world wracked by massive violence in the name of (ethnic, national, religious, racial, or other) difference, it may be of particular value to look more closely at the imagination of difference in relation to trees. Perhaps we can glimpse possibilities of different—more paradoxical and more humane—ways of coming to grips with what divides us: a deeper appreciation of difference that could connect us.

The psychological nature of the link between trees and the human story appears in the following images. The first is from Heather, who recounted a trip to one of the world's great tropical botanical gardens near Oxford, England, where she observed a ficus tree whose roots were being trimmed by a gardener because they were overcrowding some other plants. Interested in her response to the implicit theme of managing nature, I asked Heather if she could imagine the gardener's bodily experience of cutting the root. Quickly, she replied that "it wouldn't be like cutting off a finger." In stressing the difference, Heather also expressed her body's kinaesthetic empathy with the root, simultaneously imagined how cutting it might well be "like cutting off a finger." An image of *cutting* paradoxically *connects* Heather's bodily sense of herself and the tree, puts her empathetically *in touch* with the tree. Radical difference and radical intimacy are again not cancelled out but given added power by the fact of their juxtaposition.

This image turns out to be psychologically quite similar to one that Jane shared. In the Catskills, Jane has observed trees "that hold onto rocks like a big hand" with roots. Again there is the spontaneous kinaesthetic empathy. Jane wondered whether such tree roots "are getting any nourishment"—or whether, perhaps, they're being hurt. For "you see rocks that look like they're going right through trees. Actually it's a tree growing around a rock. But," Jane added, "the tree looks like flesh. And the rock is just cutting right through it, it looks like. But actually it's not that at all." Like Heather, Jane juxtaposes a parallel and a difference between root and hand, and her imagination moves between them. There is a kind of flesh-and-bone kinship that gains power precisely by persisting in the face of the knowledge of difference.

Another image, now from Vladivostok in Russia, when Mischa first came upon the area of forest devastated by the Soviet military during earlier border conflicts with China: "I remember . . . the land itself . . . twisted in . . . a brutal and horrible manner—uh, I just feel the way, I guess [the] father or mother feels, or the child feels, when he sees [respectively] his child or his parent wounded, being cut by a knife or something." Mischa, in his early forties and a father of two, must himself know such feelings from the vantagepoint of both child and parent. And such emotions revolve around connection and kinship, as another of Mischa's images suggested: "I felt that, well, somebody from my own stock, from my own kind, has been tortured and killed." In that devastated forest, Mischa discovered both an ultimate estrangement from, and ultimate intimacy with, a family of trees.

With an inhuman but hand-like tenacity, the human-tree parallel continues to grip our imaginations, growing around the hard, sharp logic of our modes of estrangement from nonhuman nature. Some individuals, among them Jane and especially Jaime, can be moved to wonder openly if our kinship with trees implies an arboreal sentience—if trees can feel like we do or "psych out" things, as Jaime puts it. Their wonder remains clearly provisional, but it does remain. On the other hand, someone like Will with his knowledge of forestry and his firm commitment to a pragmatic rationalism (his emphasis on the *use* of trees) would dismiss such speculations as an artifact of urban romantic environmentalism, if not superstition. But Will was subject to similar imaginations, most notably around the theme of "euthanasia" and his respect for trees that "stood up" to Hugo better than most people.

In stating this, Will is being no less provisional, no less serious, and no less metaphorical than his urban Northern compatriots. That combination of seriousness and metaphor is basic to the bond between trees and human biographies and is engendered by the radical differences and intimacies between them. The power of trees in the human biographical imagination comes from, to use and somewhat alter Jane's phrase, "the incredible relationships between rocks and trees," between a sense of hard, unyielding difference and the psychological flow that links trees and humans as it shapes both our living and dying.

How is it that things have evolved this way? Why does our estrangement grow so rock-hard, so knife-edged? Such questions return us to evolution. Remember that Will and Jane shared a desire for human "management" of the forest—for open space, for "more light." We can imagine that desire as an evolutionary recapitulation: the movement of our prehuman ancestors from the deep forests to the more open savannas. In their contrasting ways, Jane and Will gave expression to and reiterated that movement. So too Annie Dillard's character, Rooney Fishburn, who went from his attachment to a grove of Midwestern trees to his war against the old-growth giants of the Pacific Northwest.[48]

Environmental preference studies show that humans prefer particular arrangements of trees—"groves . . . widely scattered, . . . open at eye level, with overhead canopy and a uniformly textured ground cover." It may be "that this environment is attractive because it resembles African savannas on which the human species evolved," for "in that sense it may represent our most primal image of 'home.'"[49] The more deeply-shadowed primary forests could have become associated with predatory threats to early human survival, and so we may, in the course of natural selection, have "evolved an inborn preference" for "places where [one] could see without being seen."[50] That would suggest that, however much we love forest trees, something in the makeup of each of us is estranged from them. Not our whole beings, but something in us.

We can fruitfully imagine that "the psychological value of trees is greatest when they resemble settings that had special significance in our evolutionary past." This would also provide a perspective on the polyvalent complexity of their psychological *power* and the parallel evolution of our intimacy with, and our estrangement from, the homes of trees. A native New Zealander told me that for the people there—both the Europeans and the indigenous Maoris— the deep forests are, as he put it emphatically, "home." He noted with disappointment that many visitors don't seem to see it that way, but rather are disquieted or depressed by the forest's density. But to something in us, the deep forest *is* home. Says one tropical biologist: "Less than two million years ago our australopithecine ancestors probably spent considerable time living in treetops. Before that, our ancestors probably spent 60 million continuous years living in an arboreal environment. Tropical treetops were the womb and nursery of humankind. This arboreal phase, critical to our evolution, has left an indelible stamp on both our body design and the workings of the human mind."[51] Before we were human, we were intimate with trees. And, going back still further—to our Mesozoic tree shrew—we can add the entire texture of the forest.

In chapter 1, I noted that *versatility of stance* was this tree-animal's specialty. In that is a possibility of psychological complexity—in this case, the shifting forms and combinations of intimacy and estrangement that come to the fore in our encounters with trees. Both, as suggested earlier (pp. 41–43), are embodied in the image of *homo erectus* itself. What this means is that our relationships with trees can become more densely forested, paradoxical, as we evolve in prehistoric and historical settings. This is how Jane's desire for open space—a kind of estrangement from the forest—brought her into closer physical *and* psychological contact with trees, into contact with what she was impelled to describe as nonhuman, a tree spirit. And tree spirits people Will's uneasy image of the old swamp, with its sentient "saplins' strugglin' to survive."

PART II

The Psychological
Nature of Trees

CHAPTER 4

The Importance of Tree Spirits

Strange Trees

TREE SPIRITS BRING to mind times, places, and worldviews far from our daily lives. We're not in the habit of thinking of tree spirits as here, under our noses, or of ourselves as in their midst; instead we associate them with ghosts of a distant past, "tribal" consciousness, or psychological "projections." Depending on our inclinations, we dismiss their existence altogether or perhaps strive to re-cultivate relations with them (metaphorically and otherwise) as part of an attempt to (re-)harmonize our relationship with nonhuman nature.

But our ambiguous evolutionary relationship with trees suggests something quite different—that the felt presence of tree spirits evolves in connection with our *estrangement* from the forest. Some of the most vividly sentient trees we've encountered so far are those in the dense forest of unease, the ones the human desire for "open space" marks for cutting. Perhaps this is why tree spirits often intimate death as well as life-symbiosis. But there is another possible ramification of our evolutionary image—that tree spirits, as *psychological presences*, not only thrive in the perduring nexus of intimacy and estrangement but also are at least partially capable of adapting to the machinery of the present and future. As flexible as our Mesozoic tree-animal forebear, they can appear at unexpected moments and in unexpected guises—like "the family tree . . . in the computer" which the Illinois man sought to rescue from the 1993 Midwestern flood (see epigraph). Imagine it this way: tree spirits, taking advantage of contemporary communications technology, filling books and airwaves and electronic mails. The shapes of trees from anywhere in the world, pervading our living rooms, movies, and dreams, quickening our longing for beauty and our ecological concern. Trees communicating with us and with each other, as they do in old tree lore, now with new means. Their access (at least, their *potential* access) to our imaginations is unprecedented, in spite and because of our location in a time of global ecological loss and forest destruction and in a place of estrangement.

Through looking at specific characteristics of tree spirits as they appear in contemporary imaginations as well as in older traditions (such as the Kwakiutl of the Pacific Northwest coast), we realize that our own experiences are as genuine as those of any earlier time. The point of this chapter is that, when it comes to tree spirits, we're as archaic as any people.

Treebeard Returns

In summarizing what can be learned about climate change from the study of tree rings, a *New York Times* science writer makes a pun: as "the lords of the rings, trees have the advantage of being found around the globe. . . ."[1] She means J. R. R. Tolkien's *The Lord of the Rings* and, of course, the Ents—tree-shepherds of the forest. Treebeard, chief-Ent, is back in the news.

Treebeard first appears in the second volume of Tolkien's trilogy, *The Two Towers*, when the hobbit protagonists, Merry and Pippin, come upon him standing on a high shelf from which they seek to view the peculiarly treeish forest in which they are traveling. At first he looks like an "old stump of a tree with only two bent branches left: it looked almost like the figure of some gnarled old man. . . ."[2] Tolkien's portrayal lovingly appreciates the aesthetic qualities of trees, while a humorous undertone celebrates the distinct character of personified trees and their provisional nature. Also their "gnarliness" and oddness. Treebeard tells his (hobbit) guests that "you can lie on the bed. I am going to stand in the rain. Good night!"

Treebeard himself has a "strange voice." He is a

> Man-like, almost Troll-like, figure, at least fourteen feet high, very sturdy, with a tall head, and hardly any neck. Whether it was clad in stuff like green and gray bark, or whether that was its hide,

was difficult to say. At any rate the arms . . . were not wrinkled, but covered with a smooth brown skin. . . . The lower part of the long face was covered with a sweeping grey beard, bushy, almost twiggy at the roots, thin and mossy at the ends. . . . [The eyes were] slow and solemn, but very penetrating. They were brown, shot with a green light. . . .

"One felt [said Pippin] as if there was an enormous well behind them, filled up with ages of memory and long, slow, steady thinking; but their surface was sparkling with the present: like sun shimmering on the outer leaves of a vast tree, or on the ripples of a very deep lake. . . . it felt as if something that grew in the ground—asleep, you might say, or just feeling itself as something between root-tip and leaf-tip, between deep earth and sky— had suddenly waked up, and was considering you with the same slow care . . . given to its own inside affairs for endless years."

Above all, Treebeard cares for trees and for those who feel as he does. Treebeard says, "I do not sit down" because "I am not very, hm, bendable," which may be reflected in what turns out to be his rather inflexible insistence on the value of letting all things go wild. It is also a quality which, as we know, is not always to a tree's advantage. Yet there is something to be said for Treebeard's tenacious hold. When he carries his new friends down from the shelf on which they found each other, his "rootlike toes grasped the rocks."

There is a deep interior affinity between Ents and trees; some of the former, says Treebeard, are "growing sleepy, growing tree-ish," while some of the latter "are quite wide awake, and a few are, well, ah, well getting *Entish*." For "trees and Ents . . . walk down the ages together"; like trees, Ents are "better at getting inside other things" than human beings are, but like human beings, they are "changeable"; the combination makes them "steadier" than we, able to "keep their minds on things longer." That capability for *long-term* imagining, together with the Entish capacity to *get inside* others, is worthy of our own extended contemplation.

Ents' affinity with trees, though, never changes. Even their variety is treelike. Some are like "beech-trees or oaks"; others "recalled the chestnut: brown-skinned Ents with large splayfingered hands, and short thick legs. Some recalled the ash: tall straight gray Ents with many-fingered hands and long legs; some the fir (the tallest Ents), and others the birch, the rowan, and the linden." It seems that they most love the trees to which they are closely related. Quick-beam, a young Ent, is rowan-like, and "whenever he saw a rowan-tree he halted a while with his arms stretched out, and sang, and swayed as he sang." Nothing wounds Ents more than the death of their companion trees; at one point Treebeard, his eyes flashing like "green fire" (when Aldo Leopold was young, he shot a wolf, only to "watch a fierce green fire dying in her eyes"), says of wanton tree-felling caused by an evil wizard: "Many of those trees were my friends, creatures I had known from nut and acorn. . . ."[3]

Tolkien's Ents suggest how our own spirits may be guided by those of trees. For if you are an Ent, a treelike creature, you are *shepherding* that which is part of you, your ancestry. And the lords of the rings are the spirits of the trees, shepherding in their memories many histories. In the case of dendrochronology, the "ringing" trees shepherd the history of Earth's climate—and, in their scientific adaptation, help shepherd, help shape, our longterm ecological concern.

A Leaf, an Old Folks' Home, and a Tornado's Legacy

It is a loss and an absence of trees that will send Treebeard and his Ents into action, make their presence known. There are, in fact, many ways in which tree spirits adapt to a loss of trees. One is illustrated by Ellen's (the New York shopkeeper's) response to a report on the effects of Hurricane Hugo on the island of St. Croix, whose trees the storm had defoliated. She thought of a story by O. Henry called "The Last Leaf," which she had read long ago, and vaguely remembered it concerned "a child or an adult, and they were very very sick." She was more certain that "outside their bedroom was a tree. And I guess it was fall and winter was coming. The leaves started to fall, and the person that was sick was semi-giving up. And they said, 'When the last leaf goes, I go.'" So "somebody in the house . . . went out . . . and painted a leaf on the window, or painted a leaf somewhere, so that the person wouldn't go when all the leaves went."

The images from Hurricane Hugo, which Ellen had seen only on television, evoked a season of human death. But O. Henry's story has its own power in this respect. This became clear to me when another woman mentioned, during a talk on tree photography, that "The Last Leaf" was *her* favorite tree story. She remembered that the tree in the story was an oak.

But both memories are mistaken. There is no tree in "The Last Leaf," only "an old, old ivy vine, gnarled and decayed at the roots," its leaves almost gone and their absence highlighting its skeletal structure.[4] In the story, a "Mr. Pneumonia," a "red-fisted, short-breathed old duffer," attacks an old woman and then the painter who paints the ivy leaf on her window. The old woman lives; the painter dies, having inadvertently memorialized the leaf of *his* soul. The narrator mockingly concludes that this was the "masterpiece" the painter, an old drunk, had ever been ready to paint but had never gotten around to starting.

These mistaken tree memories, however, aren't only mistakes. For any tree remembered is present in one's imagination. In this case, the image of "leaf" contains the presence of "tree"; we could say that a tree spirit inhabits the "leaf" of our schematic imaginations. So it is natural that Ellen and the photographer should read O. Henry's story as being about a tree. Their memories show the spirit or soul of a tree, the effects of its resident and shaping power. This can be said of other members of the plant kingdom as well: trees inhabit them. That is, the psychological power of trees is such that they are often present in other vegetable images, both specific and generic. That's why, for instance, I would say there is a presence of trees in imaginings of *deeply rooted* proclivities, habits, or things. So in that way "The Last Leaf" does embody the storymaking power of a tree; one could say that a tree spirit resides in the title itself, rather than being projected into it by a mistake of memory. Tree spirits are present in the way "leaf" is imagined—as they are in lines from Shakespeare's *Sonnet 73*, which the photographer recalled:

> That time of year thou mayst in me behold
> When yellow leaves, or none, or few, do hang
> Upon those boughs which shake against the cold,
> Bare, ruined choirs where late the sweet birds sang. . . .

Absent trees, or tree spirits, also reside in Will's characterization of a climax forest: the Old Folks' Home. The nonhuman nature of these folks emerged when I asked Will (in 1992) about his personal experiences visiting nursing homes. His reply was surprising: "Never have." No member of his family has ever been placed in one. His impressions of actual nursing homes come solely from television—"the atrocities that you see now on *60 Minutes*. . . ." More strikingly, Will did not now remember drawing the comparison between old folks' homes and climax forests—even when I quoted him his own words. So from where did these old folks come? And to where did they return when they left Will's memory?

Providing a clue, a poem of Wendell Berry's evokes "the ghost of the old forest/that was here when we came."[5] It could be that those old folks who appeared so vividly before Will in our first conversation were ghosts of a forest, of the Francis Marion, whose dead and broken trees Will was, in his way, mourning. By the time we talked again, those old tree ghosts had gone deeper into the ground. Will himself had somewhat rebounded emotionally and was not eager to return to the pain he had felt and that still lingered in his depths. He had some reason not to remember all that had been spoken in our first conversation. He did bring up once more the Yellowstone fires in 1988, saying that they "just . . . broke my heart"—likely a way of talking about what the destruction of the Francis Marion did to him as well. But in talking about the climax forests in the Great Smokies and Pacific Northwest, Will focused more on their sensual beauty, whereas in 1989 he had emphasized trees with "the tops broken out of 'em" that were diseased and dying slowly.

It wasn't until we talked in 1992 that I realized that Will's description of the latter could be recognized as an indirect way of speaking of trees that had been killed, or were in the process of dying, as a result of Hurricane Hugo. It was their souls and spirits that peopled the Old Folks' Home into which the Francis Marion had been transformed. Ghosts lived in Will's remembering and forgetting.

Another way that trees can be present in their loss is depicted by Gwendolyn Brooks, an Afro-American poet, in "Tornado at Talladega." She describes how, after that tornado does "some landscaping,"

Certain trees
stick across the road.
They are unimportant now.
They cannot sass anymore.
Not a one of these, the bewildered,
can announce anymore "How fine I am!"
Here, roots, ire, origins exposed,
across this twig-strewn, leaf-strewn road they lie,
mute, ashamed, and through.[6]

Brooks's poetic indirection effectively underscores her affirmation of the struggle to expose the "roots" and "origins" of racial injustice. (Her images are reminiscent of Langston Hughes's poem "Warning," which tells us to "beware the day" that "Negroes, / sweet and docile," revolt, as when the "wind / In the cotton fields . . . uproots trees."[7] The psychological power of trees is not the main subject of either poet, but lends itself with ironic effect to both.) Most revealing is Brooks's image of the *ire* of the trees—"ire" specifying hatred and animosity as well as anger; this is the clearest indication both of the poet's social concerns and of the active presence of trees. The image is both an original way of probing an American predicament and thoroughly in keeping with the larger tradition of tree lore—of awareness of those whose ire, in various senses of the word, can be aroused. We'll have more to say about images of "roots" and "origins" also. The poem's tornado exposes the underside of rootedness and gives voice to Trees of Ire.

The Souls of Tree Spirits

"The trees appear personified."[8] With this succinct observation, Franz Boas characterizes the trees of Kwakiutl mythology; but it applies to tree presences everywhere. To speak of trees as persons needn't imply literal animism; rather, in James Hillman's terms, it means giving a place to the psyche's propensity to personify as a way of defining what or whom is felt as valuable, powerful—"as a necessary mode of understanding the world and of being in it."[9]

Trees, of course, are not alone in the personified world. Everything can speak—human artifacts and industrial pollution, as well as ants, carrots, rivers, mountains, clouds, stars. W. S. Merwin, no champion of unchecked industrial growth, can allow in a poem the voice of streetcars "singing to themselves *I am iron,*" just as Pamela can verbalize what Hugo tells us about trees and "daily deeds"; and Lewis (the Homestead resident) can have words with Andrew: "You could have wiped out everything, but maybe you coulda left me [one particular] tree."[10] To say that things appear personified is not to say they appear in idealized form. The personifying of things expresses the sometimes intimate and sometimes distant conversation between soul and earth, the human and nonhuman, the organic and constructed worlds.

Michael Pollan, describing how a gardener can learn from pruning trees, well illustrates a simultaneous movement toward a deepened personifying of difference and of intimacy between human and tree—a move from a *humanized* tree to an *ensouled* one. The experienced gardener can develop a "sympathy" with trees that allows him or her "to cut the tree's limbs back hard": the seasoned "sense of where a plant's 'being' resides . . . is very different, I think, from the novice gardener's."[11] The latter is disturbed by the idea of pruning a tree "probably because he looks at a plant more or less anthropomorphically"; but with practice "he'll develop a more complicated and less anthropomorphic understanding of how, and where, a tree lives. He'll probably come to think of the tree as having something akin to a soul that is distinct from its parts, and for which the limbs sometimes (at transplanting, for instance) represent a burden it may be glad to be rid of." It is located, perhaps, at "the fulcrum of the tree's roots and visible parts, . . . maybe just below ground level. . . ." Pollan here acknowledges that the *image* of soul is a particularly congenial, perhaps inevitable, way of describing the experience of tending trees. The soul has its own (*in*human) feelings—it may be "glad" to be rid of unwanted appendages; it is a personified presence. And it is "below ground level," not apparent to anthropomorphizing eyes; it hangs out in an underworld, where the dead are.

There is a parallel to this gardener–tree involvement in the development of relationships between human beings. As Jessica Benjamin puts it: "The distinction between my fantasy of you and you as a real person is the very essence of connection."12 The gardener, likewise, learns to distinguish his or her *human* fantasy of the tree from the tree's own actuality. But that actuality *remains an image.* It becomes the essential connection between human and tree. One comes to feel what Jaime and others refer to as "empathy" or "affinity" for the tree as a being with subjective presence—not a human, but an arboreal subjectivity. The distinction I would emphasize is not between "fantasy" and "reality" but rather between what Samuel Taylor Coleridge referred to as "fancy" and "imagination," or what the old alchemical philosophers called the "true" and "false" imaginations.13 In this case, fancy or false imagination precedes the alchemy of close, extended, concrete contact between gardener and tree. False and true imaginations, in that sense, must be separated from one another in order to make room for a deeper imaginative intimacy—a concrete contact which is a real imagination involving a relationship of souls, a truly deep ecology.

To extend the alchemical parallel, the human–tree interaction joins the concrete and pragmatic to the power of metaphor. Through our specifically human involvements with trees, their nonhuman impressions become more deeply ingrained in us. (This holds, for instance, in the "initiations" of Will and Jane—as they acted upon the trees in marking them for cutting, the trees acted upon them, leaving enduring impressions.) This interaction is not a linear progression or one-way development from humanized to personified tree. The humanized tree has its place (and its corollary in the "arborized" human). Any alchemy involves a constant reiteration of intimacies, likenesses, differences, and separations. The truth is that true and false imaginations are to an extent always entangled and certainly are always potentials in relationships, human and other. That's why we find stories in which trees think they're human, as well as humans that think they're trees.

In order to relate in a fuller human way to tree spirits, we must bear in mind another distinction. What Pollan says regarding the gardener's relationship with an actual tree must be extended to all our relationships with trees as psychological presences: trees that appear in folklore, myth, religion, literature, poetry, dream, reverie—trees that are fictive but, like actual trees, very real images. It means, for instance, a cultivated attention to the specificities and needs of

tree images in Sally's dream of her father and the two apple trees
(see chapter 3, pp. 64–65); in Annie Dillard's novel *The Living* (see
above, pp. 61–63 and below, pp. 103–05); and in our explorations
(below and in chapter 7) of Kwakiutl tree lore and the myth of
"Aphrodite's Woods" itself. It means to look carefully at the shifting patterns of paradox, tension, and contradiction that emerge as
people talk about their responses to trees both actual and fictive—
responses which can be considered as the abodes of tree spirits. We
must keep in mind, for instance, the tension in David between
"nature's own people" and "the man upstairs"; the true imagination in Ellen's false tree memory of O. Henry's "The Last Leaf"; and
the similar contradictions in the way Will and Jane talk about their
experiences marking trees. Each image gets a fair and respectful hearing, because even when they fight each other, they are talking, telling us about each other. Each has its own value, its own character(s),
its own place in nature. Or in what could be called the Ecological
Pandaemonium, the cacophonous Forest of Image.[14] If we can allow
our imaginations and concepts a versatile tree-varmint stance, we
can go anywhere in this forest and let the interconnections be as
ragged as they actually are.

I've been reluctant to use the term "anthropomorphism," or the at-
tribution of human forms to nonhuman nature by a human subject. I'd prefer, in fact, to eschew it altogether, because we don't get
very far with it. Although it seems "rational," "scientific," it is actually an obfuscation, a hindrance to a more imaginative and ecologically attuned rationality. We do sometimes find, even discover,
ourselves in nature, and there can be a humanizing element in "empathy" with trees. We experience nature making *us* human, humanizing us, and nature's capacity to take in human qualities. The concept of anthropomorphism is inadequate both to our experience and
to the ecology of the nonhuman, for it tacitly confines the sphere
of power and agency to the human subject. That's not really what
we experience. In various ways, the nonhuman realm also actively
responds to human activity and takes us into itself; we need more
precise ways of talking about our human location(s) in nonhuman
nature. So in talking about "the human in nature," I don't mean what

we project onto nature but our location, mediated always by psychological combinations of likeness and difference, *in* nature.

Similarly, we might say that we are, or bear within us, *intimations of trees*, for nonhuman nature *locates itself within the human.* A nonhuman treeish nature can place itself in a human story, and a human story place itself in trees. In myth and folklore, this is often portrayed as a (human) person being transformed into a tree—and in that way becoming a tree spirit.

From this angle, we can reconsider the Greek myth of Apollo and Daphne, the nymph whom Apollo pursued and who begged one of her parents (Earth or the river god Peneius) to save her from his advances. Thus, she was turned into the laurel tree, and Apollo henceforth wore her branches as a crown or wreath. As Ovid and earlier mythographers portray the myth, Daphne is very much like Diana or Artemis, the Goddess of the Wild, of virgin, pristine forest—perhaps her double. In Ovid's retelling of the story, Daphne begs her father to help her keep her virginity, her free-roaming woodland spirit; her freedom, appropriately if paradoxically, lies in her becoming a tree. The myth depicts, in fact, the freedom of imagination, of soul or psyche, to dwell *within* trees. The myth of Daphne and the laurel is one of *return* of soul to its archaic tree-nature, in the context of a flight from a particular sexual involvement (with Apollo, God of a certain kind of "high" cultural *progress*) and all it may signify.

The sequence of the myth, the transformation of human into tree (or return of tree spirit to tree), can be imagined as something that happens once and for all. We can also think of it as something that happens over and over in our lives. In that case, the myth leads us to consider what goes on when we imagine ourselves in treelike terms. The mirroring which Jane so vividly describes is, in addition to being an instance of human–tree parallelism, a reflection of the treeness in us; in the "mirror" of trees, we see the true trees of ourselves. Or at least ponder, as Jaime did: "What if I were also a tree?" Or, while listening to wind-rustled poplar leaves, wonder fleetingly (as did a graduate student): "What if it were *my* leaves rustling?" Annie Dillard describes a parallel experience. Out one day after a snowfall, she spies a coot and wants to get a good look, hiding behind a cedar trunk. As the bird scurries about, seemingly unafraid, Dillard becomes aware by contrast of her own embodiment of stillness, "thinking that after all I really was, actually and at bottom, a tree, a dead tree perhaps, even a wobbly one, but a treeish creature nonetheless. . . ."15

We can come into sustained and energizing communion with trees at certain times, but more often there are brief moments in which treeness emerges, as in figurings of speech—"finding roots," "branching out," and, more obliquely, "taking a stand." Treeness might take an unromantic shape—our periods of "woodenness" or "fruitlessness" or feeling rotten inside, loglike. It can take the form of affectionate kidding—my father regarding me and saying, "The apple never falls far from the tree." All such trees that we momentarily become take their place in some woodscape. They are rooted to a spot but, at the same time, display a protean mobility.16 They may be enactments of an evolutionary desire to return to trees.

Daphne's transformation into a tree can also reflect historical and cultural pain, a pattern of seeking solace in woods, in the interior presence of trees. A return of soul to the trees, inspired by fear and flight, may be an important theme underlying the recent return and strengthening of concern for the actual trees of the world and their dwindling forests—the tropical rainforest, old-growth forests of the Pacific Northwest, the Russian taiga. The fear is of the final disappearance of "untouched" nature and woods; we are discovering in that fear the power of trees and a possibility of protection, a treelike endurance.

The myth also *does* happen once and for all. Seen this way, it entails an irrevocable loss of mobility. When desire moves into trees, there is new life, but also new death. Daphne *dies* into her tree; it is her living coffin. But because she dies, the tree spirit of Artemis lives. Apollo, Artemis's brother, shares her longing for the pristine, as Peter Bishop observes. While Apollo is separated forever from Daphne, he gets closer to her in the form of his own sister. He "finally gazes in awe and reverence at the purest expression of untamed Nature—the tree itself."17

Remember Ted, who thought of the live oaks (and, in part, of himself) in a rather idealized way as "patriarchs." Ted went on to tell how painful the storm's aftermath had actually been for him. When he saw that his compulsive need to try and fix everything for everybody in his community—that is, to be the ideal leader—had kept him from spending any meaningful time with his family for three months, he burst into tears. Perhaps Ted on some level recognized, and mourned, his father's pattern of emotional estrangement and its expression in his own life. After that, the Live Oak People revealed themselves in a non-patriarchal way, for Ted was less distant from them than from his father. When we finished talking, we walked outside together, underneath one live oak that had suffered only moderate damage. Looking at its broken-off and regrowing branches, Ted remarked: "They each have a personality" and "It feels like a friend's been injured." He gave me directions to get back on the highway to Charleston, saying that I would pass one live oak that survived the storm. Of that "old fella," Ted said, "he took a beating in the storm but held up." That tree, specific in its woundedness, features, and nearby location (in contrast to the distant, idealized "patriarchs"), would tell me I was headed the right way.

Ted's movement from distant patriarchal trees to that nearby beaten-up "old fella" is a movement into intimacy with the tree's own soul or spirit. It mirrors the way Ted let his guard down in confiding how difficult things really were for him, which allowed a deeper expression of his feeling for the "personalities" of the trees. The relationship becomes more deeply human, yet less anthropomorphic. As with the gardener, the actuality of the tree is more present; there is more difference between the tree and the human quality, more sense of what the tree has weathered and more feeling for it; and precisely because of the psychological differentiation, the relationship is closer.

Here we come to a distinction similar to that between the anthropomorphic and the personified, except that it is more specifically a question of spirit—a religious and theological matter. That is, the movement in Ted's narrative also discloses an important distinction between different ways of imagining tree spirits. Some ways of imagining them are more soulful, more particular, closer-to-home, than others.

In the last chapter I noted how the tree kinaesthetically embodies memory and imagination—the upward and downward motions of psychological life. The upward movement of trees is, in Peter Bishop's phrase, a "spiritually satisfying" one.[18] Trees are prominently associated with the spiritual: striving for the light, for enlightenment (e.g., the Buddha under the Bo-tree fending off the enticements of desire), for higher power and for contact with upper-worldly divinities, for abstract refinements and ramifications of thought, for unifying and integrating principles. Much tree *symbolism*, in scientific (including evolutionary, conceptual, classificatory, and analytical "decision" trees) as well as religious thought (e.g., the cosmic tree of many traditions, the Kabbalistic tree of the Sephiroth), has a "spiritually satisfying" character in one or more of these senses; it emphasizes less the particularity of a given tree and more a universal, abstract, even technical arboreal form. One could say that spiritualizing and generalizing images of trees grow beyond other images of them.

Bishop is skeptical of this kind of growth. He notes that "trees have been captured by the archetype of spirit," by "interpretive concepts . . . [that] have come to obscure the complex phenomenology and ecology of the tree itself," as well as our appreciation of "a plurality of possible imaginative arboreal moves. . . . So often we cannot see the trees for the concepts."[19] But since "the archetype of spirit" also has its abode in trees, we can't leave it out. If we are like trees walking (in the image of the blind man given sight by Jesus; see Mark 8:24), then like trees we may reach for ways of holding soul and spirit together—in images of "nature's own people."

That won't be easy. Remember how "the man upstairs" interceded when David spoke of nature's people. But it's too easy, as suggested earlier, to think in terms of the opposition of Christianity and paganism, or monotheism and polytheism.[20] It is more interesting to look at religious conflicts associated with trees on the trees' own terms. That means considering how the soul–spirit tension in trees manifests in contemporary individuals' lives and in different religious traditions.

David's and Ted's fantasies both show a certain tension and distinctness between abstract, "patriarchal" images and the soulful specificity of "nature's own people." So also the contrast between Will's "old folk" and "old, gnarly dogwood," on the one hand, and the "beautiful" trees of the idealized, "managed" forest on the other. But such tension was particularly strong in Jane's description of an overtly religious experience in a wild apple orchard one fall afternoon.

Jane's images linking trees and the search for women's spiritual roots are in part similar, we saw in the last chapter (p. 53), to Ted's idealized patriarchal oaks. This similarity emerged in connection with her experience in the apple orchard: "I was just overwhelmed with the glory of" the trees and apples. "And I just saw it as on fire, and it was a holy fire. It was a holy fire. . . . I felt I had seen God in an apple tree," that it was "like a vision. And I feel very blessed." It was not, however, a God beyond the tree or nature—"because I don't think there's anything 'beyond.'" This assertion expresses Jane's feminist sense of the spirit as immanent and may echo an ancient worship of Near Eastern Goddesses. Certainly it reflects the "immanentist" trend in contemporary women's thought on matters of the spirit.[21] But as a preface to her account of her experience, there appeared another character that Jane didn't like: "an image of a cartoon God climbing around in the tree." This bothered her because it seemed "to take away from" the experience of the fire. Jane was irritated when I drew attention to him; she didn't like "this interruption from the god in the tree." It was like "when you were about to be in touch with what you really felt, and suddenly, somebody made a joke." Also, noting his maleness, Jane "really resented the gender peeping in."

But the two Gods were not as far apart as they seemed. For "the god in the tree" reminded Jane of cartoons telling the story of Hanukkah in a Jewish children's magazine for which she had been art editor. Jane was surprised to recognize the connection between the holy fire and the cartoon God of Hanukkah, slapstick humor, and children: "the miracle of the lights," as she said—the *tree* of the menorah, with its eight candles representing the days during which, according to the story, the besieged Jews in the temple in Jerusalem held off the Romans. Jane then saw the connection through "the fire. Because the miracle of the lights is the miracle of the fire." In this way a fire surging upward from the underworld through trees, which Jane associates with women's religious and sexual experience, is related to a rather awkward male character who mimes in his postures the contorted branches of a tree. The idealized fire of the tree spirit gets tempered and ensouled. There remains a vulnerable, raw foolishness in the tree.

The tension between ensouled and more distant, rarefied tree spirits is not confined to Western religious terrain. Consider the importance of trees in the Japanese religious imagination. In early Japanese (Shinto and pre-Shinto) religion, particular trees and forests were felt to be abodes of the *kami* or inspiring power of the sacred. The *kami*, as Joseph Kitagawa notes, was sensed as a general, pervasive quality of world but also, if perhaps secondarily, as a "plurality of . . . separate beings and objects," or what could be called "spirits." *Kami*, in the plural, inhabited all of the natural world, as "symbols . . . not understood symbolically." That is, things were "not . . . representations of *kami* but . . . *kami*." This is not exactly the same as literal belief (though it could become or move in and out of that) but involves aesthetic feeling and a sense of "direct participation," of sacred and (at least tacit) personified presence *in* the material being(s).[22] Trees could speak. The forest, or "the place where trees grow thick [*Himorogi*]," was one of the primary origins of Shinto shrines, for in it "the spirits of the Kami lived and [the early Japanese] felt a kind of divine atmosphere. . . ."[23] Thus "people began to worship a certain area which was surrounded by thick trees and enshrined Kami there"; the "Himorogi" shrine grew out of forest-feeling. Eventually, the *Himorogi* came to mean a single sacred tree "where the spirit of the Kami was believed to be present."

Thus, powerful trees took hold in the cultural forms and sacred architecture of early Japan. But the arboreal forms and associated religious concepts tended, over time, to become more abstract and "symbolic" of spiritual states, evolving or growing away from themselves. (We see again that the evolutionary imagination itself, in spiritual and religious as well as scientific formulations, can be simultaneously an expression of treelikeness and a departure from it.) Thus one writer can say: "In primitive times people believed that through . . . trees [enclosed in shrine precincts] the spirit of the kami could be understood; but today the tree is only an expression of the divine consciousness."[24] The problematic nature of notions of the "primitive" and of stages of religious development is not unrelated to the spiritualizing of the tree. As well as being *spiritualized*, trees in Japan could became *nationalized*; the *sakaki* tree thus came to embody and vitalize the Japanese nation—its "natural" essence. This tree was used in rituals preceding World War II.

Such developments contrast sharply with vivid images of tree spirits and their relations with human beings. One Japanese folktale, for instance, tells about the lovely woman spirit of a willow tree that a young man saved from the axe. Tree spirit and youth fell in love and married, but at first the man did not know his wife was arboreal. Then, however, the tree had to be cut down. The young wife told her husband that she was the spirit of the tree and would have to die with it. The treelike beauty of such a person shows through in a Noh play about a sad old woman, Komachi, who remembers when "crowned with nodding tresses, halcyon locks, / I walked like a young willow delicately wafted / By the winds of Spring. . . ."[25] Such images, which here combine elements of Shinto sensibility with Buddhist and Zen Buddhist understandings, show a quite different way that tree spirits can evolve and develop, one that stays close to the particular aesthetic power of trees.

The lore of tree spirits, persisting in Japan alongside their more abstract evolutions, revealed they can be odd as well as beautiful. There are also, for instance, the *tengu*, who are the *kami* of certain mountain trees, usually "pines and cryptomerias," and who "are part bird and part man in appearance, winged with long beaks or noses. Sometimes tengu are red in colour and they often wear cloaks and small black hats. . . . Sometimes they are depicted as wearing cloaks of feathers and sometimes of leaves."[26] A shifting interplay of human and nonhuman, and animal and tree, takes place in spirits like these. Foliage becomes the wings of trees. What stands out is their imagistic "specificness," to use Jane's word.

Such tree spirits are often considered low men on the totem pole of religious evolution. That is as it should be: they are not *higher* beings in the sense of abstract religious, political, or scientific arboreal metaphors; they are not forms of light. They maintain a variety of colors, shapes, propensities, moods, and relationships with humans and animals. In terms of James Hillman's distinction between spirit and soul, they remain in the vales of trees and their play of shadows rather than their upward-thrusting peaks.[27] They are spirits with both soul and body. That physicality (whether or not their trees are actual or fictive) is crucial. In his essay on the nature of spirit, C. G. Jung questions "the actually very remarkable opposition of spirit and nature" in much conventional religious thought.[28] To which the trees in the wind must sigh in relief.

Such opposition is of little importance here, and tree spirits will always manage (as with David, Ted, Will, Jane, monotheism) to subvert it. Remember the Buddha, too, who as he meditates under the Bo-tree is seen, according to legend, as not only The Enlightened One but a tree spirit. This implies an evolution *into* tree spirit, its specific realization.

But we should bear in mind something else Jung says about spirit: it "still has the spookish meaning of the soul of one departed." Tree spirits are inherently soulful and never as unambiguous as trees that are purely light or holy fire, in part because they stir the spookish and the departed. And those who may be about to depart. The *soul* of trees and tree spirits consists in their plurality of reference, metaphoric reach, ambiguousness, and presence at the nexus of life and death. Tree spirits manifest in the vivacity and complexity of image-patterns associated with and evoked by trees. These lines from Gerard Manley Hopkins's lament for the felled "Binsey Poplars" are about the souls of tree spirits:

> My aspens dear, whose airy cages quelled,
> Quelled or quenched in leaves the leaping sun, . . .
> > Not spared, not one
> > That dandled a sandalled
> > Shadow that swam or sank
> On meadow and river and wind-wandering weed-winding bank.[29]

Let us pause for a moment and consider where we are. We have discovered a basic tension between different ways trees enter the imagination—a tension between an ambiguously soulful particularity and a tendency toward spiritual idealizing and generalizing. This tension appears within different spiritual frameworks—Christianity, Judaism, Japanese religion, and the person of the Buddha (the tension within Christianity being between "nature's own people" and the God upstairs, or an image of Christ manifested through a particular maple and, say, the abstract cross or human community).

The same difference ramifies in the images of the individuals we've heard from, as in the cases of Jane and Ted. For Jane, trees can spark a conflict between the need to affirm women's heritage through an idealized Goddess-image or a holy fire and a more pained, awkward, and gender-inclusive vulnerability that mimes trees' twistings. In Ted's case, the focus moves from an idealized and distant "patriarchal" live oak to a weather-beaten "old fella" close by. That conflict is involved here is evident from the tension between Ted's wish to fix everything for everybody and his own pain; it was his unburdening of the latter that led us to the more vulnerable tree. In fact, after giving me directions, Ted had me follow him home, where he showed me a live oak that had lost its crown. Pointing to it, he again burst into tears and then checked himself: "I'm just an old softie." Getting into the trees with Jane and Ted, we go from rather abstract and idealized figures—Goddess and patriarchs—to a cartoonish, silly God and an old softie. [30]

Trees of Fear

Some trees have a less welcoming nature than others. The following image from the old Anglo-Saxon epic poem *Beowulf* illustrates this arboreal sense. It describes the monstrous Grendel's lair, where

> the groves of trees
> Growing out over the lake are all covered
> With frozen spray, and wind down snakelike
> Roots that reach as far as the water
> And help keep it dark. [31]

The trees are necessary actors in a darkness. Their role is to "*help keep it dark,*" to intimate possibilities of night, gloom, and menace, without participating in any actual assault. But they can be very alive. Janie Crawford's grandmother, in Hurston's *Their Eyes Were Watching God*, recounts her escape with her baby from a slave plantation in Florida, when for some days they were forced to hide in "de swamp by de river. Ah knowed de place was full uh moccasins and other bitin' snakes," but there was no choice. [32] "De noise uh de owls skeered

me; de limbs of dem cypress trees took to crawlin' and movin' around
after dark, and two or three times Ah heered panthers prowlin'
round." We all know of "tree shadows that haunt the woodlands of
childhood, holding fear in their branches."[33] But Trees of Fear are
not confined to those woods.

Ellen, the shopkeeper, remarked that trees at night "look a little scary. . . . They're silhouetted against the sky, you know, and
they're sort of black looking, you know? They're not warm and
friendly looking . . . like in the daytime . . . they take on shapes,
like when you're a little kid and you're sleeping and you see the boogie
man in your room." Ellen spoke of a place where "there could be
things in trees"—"the jungle." She's never been there and has no desire
to go. Especially, "I'd be very afraid to be left at night in the jungle,
with the trees. . . . I would just imagine things all the time."

Ellen did not like imagining these "things" and had no problem
saying so. Jaime, the activist who loves the tropical forest above all,
also, as it turned out, imagined fearful beings in trees. For him,
however, this was a problem, given his very different feelings about
the forest. We are still in a terrain of tension between spiritual realities
of trees. But here it more directly involves the *ecological* imagination.

When Jaime was a child, he remembered, "some old folks would
tell stories about . . . horrifying people who live in trees or something"—"nonhuman beings." Their favorite dwelling-places are "in
the forest or . . . in big trees," and no doubt they "have a counterpart around here." In another way, they are specific to Philippine
tree lore. These nonhuman tree beings appear as "giants that smoke
cigars"—"very old people, big eyes, long faces." There are also elves
that live in "new trees," but it was the cigar-smoking older "horrifying people" that Jaime remembered most vividly. All of this, Jaime
said dismissively, was "superstition, passed on by old people" and
mostly confined to "the provinces." He didn't think it affected him,
though he was scared to travel alone at night. "But other than that,
they didn't scare me. They didn't scare me at all."

Why does Jaime insist he wasn't scared of the horrifying tree
people? It is easy enough to say they live only in provinces of superstition. But it turned out that something else was troubling Jaime—
the disjunction between his rainforest-activist image of trees as benevolent and life-supporting, on the one hand, and traditional Filipino

tree lore on the other. As we can gather from Jaime's remarks, this lore is thickly forested with tree demons who are hardly benevolent. Rural Filipinos, says Maximo Ramos, a folklorist, "keep away from trees at night and prefer to stay indoors. . . . They let no large trees grow in their yards. When a Filipino buys a residential lot, the first thing he generally does is to cut down the trees on it."[34] Or, should he be afraid to do so, he takes other measures to keep demons away. Jaime struggles with a conflict of landscapes, ecological and demonological.

"When I was a child," Jaime was not so sanguine about tree demons—and, it became clear, a particular tree. "Even my friends would tell me, 'Don't go very near that old tree because there's a fairy or something. An evil fairy who lives there.'" The tree, maybe fifty feet tall, had "a huge trunk," with "branches that spread out" and arched down toward the ground, "thick, very lush. . . ." Trees most likely to house demons or elves in the Philippines tend to have the physiognomy Jaime remembers.[35] Generally, when picking fruits from trees or cutting them down, some rural Filipinos retain a custom of first asking permission of any elves that may inhabit the trees. Ramos gives an illustrative petition:

> Your excuse, please:
> Be not angry, friends,
> For the priest asked us to fell something.

You can guess what happens next in Jaime's story. "Did you go there anyway?" I asked without needing to. Jaime's reply: "Just the same, we went there to pick the nuts." He laughed, recalling the fear and excitement. He and his friends would take only "a few pieces and then scram." The setting was just right: "strange. . . . kind of dark," probably just before a thunderstorm. They didn't stay long; "as soon as we had our loot," laughed Jaime, "we ran away so fast! You know? Laughing." The build-up to the caper lasted much longer. Mindful of the danger of disturbing the evil tree spirits, beforehand "we had to murmur something" or "chant something like: 'Please give us just a few of these.'" The petition had to be very gingerly and tactfully phrased, as in the illustration Ramos gives. And having gotten into the tree, they couldn't assume they'd escape with impunity. "I think my friends were saying, 'Please let me go down the tree.' 'Excuse me, we'll be passing this way.'"

Jaime recognized that this was "a ritual of some sort." It is no less an initiation ritual than Jane's and Will's timber-marking experiences. Jaime is admitted into the world of the Night Forest. He allowed that there was "not a chance" he'd ever visit the old tree at night. And, in general, "I don't think that's the best time to go to a tree." None of this, added Jaime, has to do with "the tree itself, but these spirits living in the trees" or "making the trees their abode."

But, as Jaime also said, the demons find certain tree features homey, so I asked him to describe the old tree. He replied: "It's not scary at all. It's not. No. Far from it." In fact, "as I see it now, it's very supportive." That is, he now imagined it in ecological terms, as he had the rainforest trees—as sustaining life. Snakes, maybe, but not demons. This does mean you have to "take away the imaginations about evil spirits. . . ." Jaime's ecological vision—now joined to the part of himself that sees these "imaginations" as only imaginary, as superstition—requires this extirpation, or at least attempts it. In this case, however, there turns out to be an unexpected connection between ecological consciousness and "the man upstairs" in David. "Nature's people" can pose problems for both.

For Jaime, the ecological metaphor of *supportiveness* is, moreover, a form of psychological forest management, curiously akin to that which Will employed. Even though Jaime wants to preserve the very thing Will is so dubious about—virgin forest—the two men have something in common in the way they are disquieted by certain trees. This commonality suggests an occult relationship between traditional images of forest management and ecological images that emphasize the life-supporting character of the forest—a similarity that consists partly in the difference between the idealized and the particular tree.

To return again to that old tree. I asked what it would look like if Jaime allowed the old imaginations back in. Listen closely. "It's very weird," Jaime says, quietly. "It *is* spooky, yes." It is spooky "because it's an *old* tree. And even the bark . . . has irregular shapes" or "some lumps." And remember those branches "arching down. . . ." The tree is "*huge. It's old,*" says Jaime, in the same emphatic tone that Will uses to evoke the "*huge,* old" dying trees in the climax forest. But this tree is all too alive. Fortunately, says Jaime, "It's more of the story behind the tree that's making it scary. But otherwise, as I've said, it's a very nice tree."

Often (as in Grimms' fairytales and in Jaime's case) it is the young who must undergo an initiation amidst trees of fear. The feared trees are initiatory demons, revealing to us our estrangement from them, and from the more familiar world we had inhabited up till this point. These demons, as in the case of Ellen and Jaime, stir the characters of our childhoods, perhaps so that we may re-enter the Kingdom of the Estranged as children—experience estrangement in a newly immediate way.

However, as illustrated by the cases of Jane, Will, and Janie Crawford's grandmother in "de swamp by de river" risking death for freedom, not only the young undergo such initiations at the hands of woods. And no matter how young or old one is, the initiation brings intimacy together with estrangement.

There is such intimacy in a story in Annie Dillard's novel *The Living*. In my last chapter (pp. 62–63), we met a tall treeish man—Clare Fishburn, whose life was threatened by another. The demon tree's name is Beal Obenchain. From his childhood on, Obenchain suffered episodes of "empty, extinguishing grief . . . for no reason"; it was "an airless demon that blew him into bits and hammered and scattered the bits."[36] One time, immobilized by the demon, "he had stood on the beach, a hollow boy still as a log . . . while it pounded him like a piling into the sand." It was when the grief lifted (especially just afterward) that Obenchain could be violent, in this case killing a calf; through sacrificing another life he escaped with his own, "gloriously. . . ." Obenchain could be called manic-depressive; and he might be said, more particularly, to personify the violent side of the American frontier spirit.

But here it is more the inhuman than the human in his nature that concerns us, the *demon* that renders Obenchain peculiarly treelike: a "hollow boy," "a log," "a piling," and later, when confronting Clare Fishburn, "a grand fir." That his is a treelike hollowness is brought home by the fact that the adult Obenchain, secretive and "mysterious and disreputable," a thief and murderer, lives in the forest just outside of town in the stump of a huge cedar tree—"hollow at the butt, and two or three feet thick in the walls—a ready house." Over a period of a year, Obenchain crafted his quarters; he is aptly pictured at one point emptying "a cedar bucket on his house's dead roots" and, at another, "mash[ing] over the forest trail": "He was like the Skagits' [a local Indian tribe's] fearsome, noisy spirit which lived in swamps, wore moss on its head, and walked knocking down trees or making fire seem to flicker up their trunks."

That Obenchain is also an *initiatory* demon becomes clear as his threat to kill Clare goes to work on the latter's mind. For Clare is initiated, and re-initiated, into a deepening awareness of death that begins right after Obenchain comes to tell him that, on a day of his (Obenchain's) choosing, he will kill him. Clare "found he could not recollect why he had been so all-fired busy, all these years, congratulating himself, like everyone else"; he had known as a boy that death was all around him, "but it had slipped his mind." Clare had become involved with the life and ceremony of his town, at the cost of an earlier spontaneity, a plainer vitality. Obenchain, who is also a grim spirit of Clare's own neglected forested imagination, is thus not entirely wrong when he thinks contemptuously of Clare that "he was a foolish man of common clay, who derived his sentimental convictions from others . . . and talked about 'pleasure' as though everyone agreed that pleasure was the first-rate thing." Now, feeling himself "already exited" from life, Clare begins to ruminate philosophically, while the raw beauty of the Pacific Northwest presses in upon him with much greater immediacy. He sees "the whirling scheme of things" under the aspect of transience and recalls that, when he had studied English history, he had wondered how "leaders waxed overwrought about nothing—about events that did not come to pass, or that did, and settled in, like tree trunks that fell and made a ruckus for a moment but were soon webbed over by moss." His imagination has left the affairs of the town, gone into the old-growth forest, the forest of death.

After three months, his wife perceives the change in another way; "No longer the pleased, blithely unconscious boy he was during their early marriage, and no longer the piddling, unconscious, institutional man she feared he was becoming, he had wakened and hardened. . . . He was losing, curiously, his self, and seemingly finding the world a wider place without it." He becomes more estranged from one part of the world, more intimate with another.

The story of Clare and Obenchain can be compared and contrasted with an appearance of treeish spooks recounted by Gordon Parks in the prologue to his autobiography. Parks, as we've noted, speaks about his experiences in a big city and with racism in arboreal terms: from Kansas he arrives as a youth in St. Paul "snarled in the roots of racism" and as "an uprooted tree in a strange forest." The last phrase already suggests not only Parks's treeness, but less-than-friendly tree demons. His emigration to the North figures as an African-American variation of Dorothy's trek in *The Wizard of Oz*, which begins with a wrenching separation from home and quickly takes one into the forbidding forest. For Parks, the "strange forest" has to do with the intrusion of racial estrangement into his most intimate struggles with himself.

The strange forest appears in Parks's account of episodic nightmares. He had been having chest pains accompanied by bad dreams after traveling abroad in the 1980s and set about trying to find their source. So "I began searching out the disquieting foliage of dreams past."[37] Nothing clear emerges—but note that trees are there. Then Parks receives an invitation to Birmingham for a photography project, which causes an upsurge of memories ("Birmingham, Alabama! A city blacks once called Bombingham"). Parks had visited the area in the 1950s, as a reporter for *Life* magazine, when "racial tension was so thick in the air I seemed to smell it. This was the Deep South, the hostile territory. . . ." Before leaving for Birmingham then, Parks thought about "the shootings and lynchings," about African Americans "butchered and hung from trees" by the light of flaming crosses.[38]

What we note so far is not any explicit presence of tree demons, but the presence of trees in a terrain of racial terror. Then Parks has a nightmare before leaving once more for Birmingham. It begins in a nondescript location in the Deep South, in "a heavily wooded area where the air was overpoweringly sweet with the scent of magnolia." There is again the *foliage* of dreams, and there are trees whose scent, sweet as it is, reveals a very different "smell." That is, Parks's old terror—and rage—is evoked. "Then, one by one, large white houses began bursting up through the earth, their facades frowning, smiling, sneering, even laughing. Suddenly there was a wilderness full of them, and I felt trapped, unable to escape their presence or their glares." The nightmare, continuing, seems to initiate Parks into a deepened awareness of the role of racial pain in his life. The dream is not only a recapitulation of the past; as it progresses, hostile whites appear with "chalk-white faces," which suggests the initiatory mask of death. Faces painted deathly white are no rarity in traditional initiation rituals in various parts of the world, if not as common as the journey among trees of fear.

The tree demons in Parks's dream are the white houses bursting up from the ground and eyeing him. They are part of the strangeness of the forest, even in a form as radically altered as it is by the particularities of African-American experience. It wouldn't be in keeping with the "disquieting foliage" of the situation to fit Parks's dream into an initiation schema and leave it at that; but the initiatory themes highlight the presence and persistence, in an unlikely setting and an unlikely manner, of *personified* tree powers. The "strange forest" of St. Paul and the "wilderness" of the pre-civil rights-era Deep South are not the wilderness as we usually think of it. But nor are they unrelated to the more usual type of tree demon.

Dangerous Tenacity

Treelike presence, never without its shadows, is not always a good thing, as illustrated by the demonic roots and trees in Gordon Parks's nightmares. Human suffering, racial and ethnic prejudice, injustice and the inequalities of hierarchies, collective enmity, evil—and, ironically, patterns of ecological destructiveness—have a peculiarly treelike tenacity, deeply rooted, just as we imagine, expressing a distinct combination of inhumanity and the human. We can distinguish, if never absolutely, actual trees from the effects of trees and tree spirits on our actions; tree spirits in human hands can be ruinous to forest ecosystems. This is only infrequently, or obliquely, associated with the overt shadows of Trees of Fear. In this neck of the woods lurk other, less obvious shadows of trees.

Listen again to Darwin's description of the evolutionary Tree of Life (quoted in the last chapter): its budding twigs, as they branch out, try "to overtop and kill" those around them, just as some species have "overmastered other species in the great battle for life." Notice that one of Darwin's metaphors for extinction is war but another is the growth of a tree. Another image, this one from a *New York Times* editorial of Memorial Day, 1992, "The Rings of Memory": a grove of trees was planted in Central Park to commemorate some American veterans killed in World War I. The editorial figures national war memory as a tree: "Each year adds a grainy ring to the wood inside the trunks. It encloses what grew before and in turn is incased by a future that in nature always comes. What we know and feel about bravery and belief is also wrapped, present around the past and by the future, in the rings of our remembrance."[39] This illustrates how national continuity through memory can be shaped by the figures (spirits) of trees. This shaping has value, but wartime remembrances are notoriously exclusive; victims on the "other side" are mostly forgotten, left in the shadows. That forgetfulness is then also formed by trees.

There are, in fact, whole armies of trees. A famous example is the witches' prophecy in Shakespeare's *Macbeth*: "Macbeth shall never vanquish'd be, until / Great Birnam wood to high Dunsinane Hill / Shall come against him" (IV.i.:92–94).[40] Elias Canetti, in his study of *Crowds and Power*, lyrically describes how the northern temperate forest has shaped and inspired German military feeling. In that forest,

> each individual tree is always taller than a man and goes on grow-
> ing until it becomes a giant. Its steadfastness has much in com-
> mon with the same virtue in a warrior. In a single tree the bark
> resembles a coat of mail; in a whole forest, where there are many
> trees of the same kind growing together, it suggests rather the
> uniforms of an army. For the German, without his being clearly
> aware of it, army and forest transfused each other in every possi-
> ble way. What to others might seem the forest's dreariness and
> barrenness kept for the German the life and glow of the forest.
> He was never afraid in it; he felt protected, one amongst many
> others. He took the rigidity and straightness of trees for his own
> law.[41]

In this *transfusion* of army and forest are roots of authoritarianism and militarism. Nazi ideology followed this pattern, fusing genocidal impulses with "a pious quest for the natural and authentic."[42] Nazi propaganda could explicitly model the cultivation of national chauvinism in children upon the stoutness of an oak tree, but still more demonic—because beautiful—was "the last sight which greeted those who were to be exterminated, before they confronted the expression which crowned the gate to Auschwitz, 'Arbeit macht frei'[:] . . . a large tree, striking in its luxuriance."[43] When Sethe, the protagonist of Toni Morrison's novel *Beloved*, ponders the well-treed plantation where she had been enslaved, we can hear echoes: perhaps in hell "fire and brimstone" were "hidden in lacy groves."[44]

Nazism is perhaps the starkest illustration of where such transfusions of human and nonhuman can lead. But it is hardly a problem of German history only; it involves, among other things, a power of trees—one way their verticality can shape individual and cultural imaginings, and their foliage collective patterns of self-deception. In at least one nuclear-war contingency plan prepared in Britain in the early 1980s, a human–tree parallel functions as a way of keeping the actuality of nuclear horror, and hence of humane moral feelings, in the shadows. "In a way," the document asserts, "a nation is like a forest and the aim of war planning is to secure the survival of the great trees. . . . If all the great trees and much of the brushwood are felled a forest may not regenerate for centuries. If a sufficient number of great trees is left . . . if felling is to some extent selective and controlled, recovery is swift."[45] This expresses the culture(s) of dissociative technological thinking that Robert Jay Lifton and Eric Markusen have identified in the "genocidal mentality."[46] But in this case, dissociation, scientific technicism, nationalism, and *organic* forest are all interfused. *Macbeth*, which also concerns woods of self-deception, is a strangely fitting commentary on this "forest."

The connection between trees and the military imagination needn't always lead to an embrace of literal militarism and national chauvinism. Yet the presence of trees, their spirits, can be involved with and invoked by reactionary nationalistic and political movements and lend vitality to authoritarianism and mass violence.

More generally, a power of trees inheres in the ingrained character of an unequal status quo, the drive to maintain that pattern, the deep-rooted images that structure and infuse it with beauty and desire (no less real because they serve to shade out unsavory social actualities), and that stabilize it. Here we confront the contribution of tree spirits to more mundane cultural self-deception and moral evasion. Will and Jane both say something about where the lushest and most beautiful trees were (or had been) located: a "habitated forest" outside of Charleston that contained "the *old* homes," where those Charleston residents who could afford it moved during "the heavy mosquito season"; and a Long Island "town [that] has resort mansions built at the turn of the century. And those houses," said Jane, "have wonderful, big, leafy deciduous trees on them." In neither case can the trees be isolated from the social and historical ecology of their time of planting, or their roots from the human sweat upon which those wealthy homeowners depended.

And the pattern still holds. Joan M. Welch, a geographer, studied the Boston neighborhoods of North Dorchester and Roxbury, which on their peripheries remain white and middle class but whose cores consist of poorer nonwhite neighborhoods. She found that "the structure and health of the urban forest" in these areas "is determined as much politically" as by "the physical parameters of tree survival"; that discriminatory housing and economic policies underlie ongoing neglect of trees in the nonwhite neighborhoods.[47] More broadly, the sharpening social and economic divisions in the United States during the past couple of decades have involved (as Lewis Lapham, writing after the 1992 Los Angeles riots, observed) the abandonment of urban areas in favor of well-treed and sedate suburbs, or the "feudal countryside," by those with economic means.[48] The presence of trees in the formation and bifurcation of American social terrain, past and present, is not inconsequential. Keith Thomas notes parallel transfusions between social and arboreal developments in seventeenth-century England where "poets saw in trees a parallel to the social hierarchy among humans" and where "the analogy between great families and great trees, giving shade and protection to lesser beings, was well-established. . . ."[49] They also give the more fortunate shade and protection *from* the less fortunate—more precisely, from sustained awareness of social inequities.[50]

This insulation can also be a form of protection, as Lapham notes, from the bewildering but stimulating *freedom* and multiplicity of the city. The hierarchies infused by tree spirits affect many social and political dilemmas. Here is another manifestation of "vertical, spiritually satisfying growth. . . ."[51] The hierarchical spiritualizations of trees, of which their military images form a part, might benefit, as we all might, if they were disentangled from an *unconscious embeddedness in social forms*, or the tendency of social-ideological "mythologies," in Roland Barthes's sense, to "*naturalize*" those forms and render "history into nature."[52] A humane ecological ethic requires such a disentangling—a movement from unreflected notions of *essential* nature and social order to a recognition of the inevitable, and ambiguous, *presence* of tree-nature in human society.

A similar ambiguity, to which the anthropologist Liisa Malkki directs us, abides in "the metaphorical concept of having roots."[53] Mostly our roots seem vital, life-affirming; but, as the testimonies of Gwendolyn Brooks and Gordon Parks attest, there are some lifeforms whose roots affirm destructiveness. Much nationalist, as well as scholarly, discourse associates concepts of rootedness with "deeply territorializing concepts of identity" and "taken-for-granted ways of thinking about identity and territory." Being rooted in a place, in the taken-for-granted sense and particularly in its nationalist variety, implies a world "composed of sovereign, spatially discontinuous units" since "one country cannot at the same time be another country. The world of nations is thus conceived as a discrete spatial partitioning of territory; it is territorialized in the segmentary fashion of the multicolored school atlas." One's roots thus imagined are at the same time *literalized* and *abstracted*: they can be in one place only, with the bounds of the place set by national and cultural principles which are at best tenuously related to place-specific ecological concerns (however much that relation is ideologically stressed, as in the case of the association between forest and national military). And the roots in question are particular to what she calls "Arborescent Culture"; "the naturalizing of the links between people and place is routinely conceived" by means of roots which "very often . . . are specifically arborescent in form." Again, we note ramifications of arboreal *spiritualizing* as well, when Malkki notes that these kinds of concepts "are not simply territorializing, but deeply metaphysical."

And they tend to exclude, and to naturalize and essentialize that exclusion. The idea is "that each nation is a grand genealogical tree, rooted in the soil that nourishes it. By implication, it is impossible to be a part of more than one tree." That arborescent exclusivity and purity is present in nationalistic (ethnic, religious) quests for "roots" and "land" that take on murderous, even genocidal forms.

It is also impossible to be part of more than one such root system. Hence Parks's and Brooks's difficulties with roots of racism—and the struggle to move beyond "roots" that reflect an imposed inferior social or economic status. (Thus, an African-American pastor remarks that, in order to find his religious calling and his talents, he had to move "over and above and beyond where your original roots might have been"—in his case, growing up poor in Harlem.)[54] In this way, whole groups can be rendered immobile, attached to trees in ideologized soil. This, of course, does no justice to the ecology of forests; and it is not the way our ancestral tree-animal knows roots.[55]

We can give the hierarchical tree model or spirit a name: Old Man Tree. The tenacity of human divisiveness and inequality we have been witnessing—shaped indeed by trees—is a contradictory ecology. It corresponds to what Jungian psychoanalysts have called the mythological image of the *senex* (Latin for "old man"), the Old King, the Old Oak, the tyrant who shades out all who would compete with him for power; who, rooted to the spot, must keep all in their place. Old Man Tree ramifies throughout culture (and not only Western culture), but has too rarely been seen for the tree spirit that he is. Thus his effects remain unconscious, in deep shadow, and in oversimple habits of thinking in terms of tree models that have unsavory political corollaries—and, paradoxically, in our ecological destructiveness.

Treebeard, the chief Ent, has something of this spirit in him, which emerges when he tells how the Ents and "Entwives" got separated from each other long ago. In their youth, all were together, "but our hearts did not go on growing in the same way: the Ents gave their love to things they met in the world, and the Entwives gave their thought to other things"; while "Ents loved the great trees, and the wild woods, . . . the Entwives gave their minds to the lesser trees," to the deliberate arrangements and order of field and garden, whose inhabitants the Entwives could "grow according to their wishes, and bear leaf and fruit to their liking. . . ."[56] Treebeard, something of an arboreal chauvinist, can lapse into rather arbitrary dichotomies between the wild and spontaneous on the one hand, and the willed and cultivated on the other—between *forest* and *garden*. (Perhaps there is something of Treebeard's spirit in Will's negative comparison of his wife's "perennials" to his trees.) Later on, he lets the defanged evil wizard out of the tower where he has agreed to keep him because "above all I hate the caging of live things, and I will not keep even such creatures as these caged beyond great need." The wizard proves to be still capable of maliciousness, much to the disadvantage of some great trees.

Yet that is not all there is to Treebeard, and Old Man Tree is not as singular as he himself is thought to be. Think again of the various forests of old trees in lives like Will's, Jane's, Jaime's, and Sally's; of the precise and odd twists and turns of old wood in which tree spirits also dwell. Once again, we witness a tension between odd and particular commonalities of trees and their disparate, spiritualized abstraction. If the tenacity of our political and social evils is as imbued by treelike presences as I suggest, it may be of value not to eschew tree metaphors and arboreal evolutions but to imagine trees more, and more carefully, discerning the ramifications of their images without necessarily following them literally; to hold steadily in mind our need to distinguish authoritativeness from authoritarianism; and to grasp in a sustained way how the longing for beauty and the upright life can sometimes have, and sometimes shade, ugly consequences.

The importance of tree spirits consists partly in the way their presence reveals how troublesome is our human tenacity, transfused as it is with their nonhuman nature. The foliage of danger and hate can be seductive—luxuriant, proliferating.

Witnessing Trees

Other ways trees may witness human goings-on suggest possibilities of salutary historical self-reflection. Nick, a social activist of Catholic upbringing, remembered visiting the Garden of Gethsemane, where one can "absolutely document" Christ's passion because the place has been unaltered. Especially, the nature of the place draws Nick: "olive trees," which can "live to be several thousands of years" old. So "that there were living witnesses, so to speak, . . . those trees which were alive then and are alive now." Nick had been discussing in an interview religious sources of his activist work; at this juncture his imagination, beginning with the olive trees at Gethsemane, takes a different turn: "I do have a strong feeling about things like that, like trees . . . which have lived a certain kind of nonhuman experience, but an experience nonetheless. I can see how . . . Druids felt that way about a particular tree, or people who are very connected to nature would have a very strong feeling about a particular mountain. . . ."

Nick, like so many, is unable to avoid the sentient imagination of the trees and gives voice to the confluence of (human–arboreal) intimacy and difference that we've been exploring. (Notice how his Christian imagination leads him not away from but deeper into trees and back to "Druids." In terms of our evolutionary framework, this means not a "reversion" to a pagan image but an ongoing ecological differentiation within his Christian-based ethics.) But in this case, Nick specifies that the "living witnesses, so to speak," live a "kind of nonhuman experience"; he is not making a human–tree parallel but struggling to articulate what is distinctly nonhuman in the "experience" of a tree over time. The tree expresses a nonhuman way of seeing human history.

Trees as witnesses of human and world history, including monumental and celebratory or commemorative trees, turn out to be a particularly important manifestation of tree spirits. As Mischa put it (implicitly stressing the *active* power of the tree), trees "gather" memories over time. Historical memory becomes a form of *tree memory*. Roland Bechmann, in his volume on *Trees and Man*, says concerning old communal trees that "tradition often recalled . . . all the events throughout the centuries [that had] occurred around it and that it had 'witnessed.'" For "the 'memory' of the tree is real and concrete; the tree registers in its flesh, in its concentric layers, all the events that affect its environment."[57] These are Treebeard's "ages of memory."

More than a book could be filled with stories about witnessing trees; the deeply felt connection between trees and history is in fact one of the more powerful motivators in efforts to preserve trees and forests. A few more illustrations will be enough to make the point. W. S. Merwin—himself deeply involved in efforts to preserve the remnants of Hawaiian lowland rainforest—says in one poem about a cosmic tree that was chopped down: "It remembered everything."[58] Through various trees, Jane remembers women's heritage; and Sally, that of England. Says Wendell Berry of his dying "neighborly" elm tree: "In us the land enacts its history." Trees as *enactments of history*—that is hardly a usual way of thinking about them; yet it is an image imbedded in day-to-day experience of trees, which becomes apparent especially in strong experiences that mark *our* memories like trees—or the tree spirits in our memories. Aldo Leopold, in the second of his *Sand Country* essays, talks about a hundred-year-old oak that was killed by lightning, which he subsequently harvested for firewood. "We let the dead veteran season for a year in the sun it could no longer use, and then on a crisp winter's day we laid a newly filed saw to its bastioned base. Fragrant little chips of history spewed from the saw cut, and accumulated on the snow before each kneeling sawyer. We sensed that these two piles of sawdust were something more than wood: that they were the integrated transect of a century. . . ."[59] As the saw bites deeper, Leopold then details, year by year, the environmental history "written in concentric annual rings of good oak."[60]

It is a difficult history that trees often witness. Consider the following poem by a Kurd writing about Saddam Hussein's violence against his people during the seventies and eighties, entitled "The Roots":

> The birds which are killed in the skies
> Though the stars, the clouds, the wind
> And the sun do not see them
> The horizon plays deaf,
> The mountains and waters forget them:
>
> Yet some tree
> Must witness the criminals

And write their names
In its roots.[61]

What distinguishes this *witnessing tree* from the unobservant or forgetful stars, clouds, wind, horizon, sun, and waters? This forgetful cosmos likely reflects the historical Kurdish experience—that is, as a people forgotten and sacrificed to the geopolitics of fossil-fuel power. For what reason, then, the poet's faith in a remembering tree? Though he is hardly concerned with actual trees, it is the presence of a witnessing tree that lends power to the human depths of suffering and anger he is focused on, just as for Nick the witness of trees lends intensity and particularity to his religious and ecological feeling. In both cases, trees give immediacy and endurance to historical memory, and a life-affirming form of tenacity.

After Hurricanes Hugo and Andrew, what was often most disturbing about the loss of old trees was a concurrent sense of loss of historical witness and memory. Ted, for instance, noted that many live oaks, two and three hundred years old, were present through the development of "our entire country" and some even before that. I asked him what historical images he had in mind, and he first referred to the Francis Marion National Forest:

> Francis Marion himself [a Revolutionary War general] . . . was around, however many hundreds of years ago that was, under some of these same oak trees . . . during the Civil War, these same trees were right here. When Lincoln was president, or Jefferson, all of the great presidents . . . George Washington, over at Hinton Plantations—a state park seven or eight miles from here—had lunch under one of the big oak trees there. You know, those are the sorts of things I think about. . . . The rum-runners during the days of Prohibition. I think about the Indians along the coast. . . .

Ted concluded his post-Hugo reverie with an inadvertent pun: "You've seen the movie *Gone With the Wind*? . . . a lot of it was filmed right down the road here, and a lot of those trees are gone."

Kwakiutl Tree Stories

With the present power of trees in mind, we can better understand the importance of tree spirits in an older tradition, that of the Kwakiutl of coastal British Columbia. The Kwakiutl imagination is rich with stories in which the souls and spirits of the old-growth forest move about; they press skyward and also down and back into history and myth and the land animal and ocean worlds. They extend into the community in the shape of the "totem" poles—actually crest or heraldic poles figuring the animal ancestors of particular families or groups—we associate with the region. There is (thanks to the anthropologist Franz Boas and others after him) a wealth of anthropological information on the Kwakiutl, which allows for many illustrations of how the patterns we've encountered can hang together in a tradition set in the neighborhood of big trees—and their underground, often subtle ramifications.

The trees of Kwakiutl tradition (as in the Amerindian world in general) are understood to be people of a particular kind. "You know," an old man says, "about all the Myth people—all the different quadrupeds, and all the different birds, and also all the different crabs: they were all like men, and also the trees and all the plants."[62] They are not human in the conventional sense; they are "myth people," somewhat like the "horrifying people" Jaime talked about, like the "person" of the mulberry tree Sally's mother encountered, like the tree on Jane's property that "wouldn't like it" if it were cut down, like the "old folks" of Will's post-Hugo imagination—like "nature's own people." This way of imagining origins seems the reverse of the common theme that *human* people originated from trees, although the Kwakiutl tell stories to that effect as well. The idea is that *people* of all kinds come before the humans that we know.

Still, the Kwakiutl were never shy about asserting the importance of the human in nature. Their society (as was the case to different degrees with all the tribes of the Pacific Northwest region), traditionally divided into ranks of noble, commoner, and slave, fits into no ideal image of an egalitarian, primary society. The power of trees could become political, as in a chief's proclamation: "I am the only great tree, I the chief! I am the only great tree, I the chief! You here are right under me, tribes! You are my younger brothers under me, tribes!"[63] Whereas "in many . . . American Indian cultures, the world is considered to be innately harmonious and man merely becomes syntonic with its orderliness," for the Kwakiutl the cosmos "is innately discordant, conflictive, and self-destructive"; it takes work and the continual suppression and modification of personal desires (particularly hunger) for humans to cooperate with each other and with the spirit-world.[64] Still, the Kwakiutl preoccupation with hierarchies, with potlatch (gift-giving) ceremonies, and with wealth has frequently been overstated and interpreted in an excessively literal way, missing how (as the anthropologist Stanley Walens notes) "the process of metaphorization is the fundamental process of their cognitive mode. . . ."

The old-growth forests, as the chief tree suggests, play a fundamental role in the "metaphorization" of the Kwakiutl world. Such forests, after all, are rife with wealth and feed on self-destruction. In the habitat of the Kwakiutl, the forests are profuse with giant red and yellow cedar, yew trees, fir, hemlock; there are stands of oak, maple, alder, and other species. The animal life on land and sea is prolific; the Kwakiutl didn't have to worry about scarcity of food but obsessed constantly about the devouring power of hunger—in the human world and beyond. A forest whose layered life grows and rots as intensely as do those of the Pacific Northwest coast must have very great hunger.

The dense undergrowth itself consists of more than one world. The Kwakiutl cosmos, consisting of sky, human (and large animal) world, small-animal world, and sea, involves the forest's lower layers. Walens, noting that "the ground of the human level is the sky of the world of small animals [like] . . . insects, worms, reptiles, and amphibians," suggests how this cosmos is shaped by the forest world: "The growth rate of plant matter . . . is so rapid that new plants grow upon the remains of fallen trees far faster than those trees can rot away. The result is an accumulation of vegetal matter that is in some places more than twelve feet deep and so tangled and dense that its upper surface supports the weight of people. It is in this level that the small animals live."

The trees, and the cedar tree in particular, have a power in the

Kwakiutl world that they never lose—not even when trees are barked or cut, their forms transmuted into human artifacts. Even wood-chips from tree-felling keep their *nawalak* or "supernatural power." Traditional Kwakiutl tree-barking and felling rituals paid the most careful respect to the soul of the tree.[65] This deference is motivated by pragmatic concerns—including a concern for the welfare of the soul, and its ire. When a tree must be harmed for human purposes, it is particularly powerful. You have to sense and relate to the sacred-ness of a being before it will allow you to capture safely its soul.[66]

"The people of olden times" told why it is important to leave some bark on the trunk when stripping a young cedar tree. For "if they should peel off all the cedar-bark, . . . the young cedar would die, and then another cedar-tree near by would curse the bark-peeler, so that he would also die."[67] This act, exposing the tree's interior, exposes the bark-peeler to ire. That the ire of trees is present even when the right precautions are taken is clear from the prayer of a woman to a tree she has found for barking: "Look at me, friend!" This language already suggests that the woman senses in the tree a power of sight; her prayer puts into words a kind of "mutual gaze," as Jane said about her mirroring tree. The *mirroring relationship* is expressed by the woman's next statement: "I come to ask for your dress, for you have come to take pity on us. . . ." That is, the woman and the tree have come together; not only has she approached the tree but it has approached *her*. There is also a cosmological implica-tion: the prayer seems to restate the prior world-engendering rela-tionship between "us" and the cedars. The tree is world-engendering partly because, in the prayer's words,

> there is nothing for which you can not be used, because it is your way that there is nothing for which we can not use you, for you are really willing to give us your dress. I come to beg you for this, long-life maker, for I am going to make a basket for lily roots out of you. I pray you, friend, not to feel angry with me on account of what I am going to do to you; and I beg you, friend, to tell our friends about what I ask of you.

We can hear an echo of Will in this prayer—his emphasis on the *use* of trees (even in the making of "your sweater," he told me).

The souls of trees approach human beings so the latter can put them to use. But this perspective is not, however, anthropocentric; the trees are active agents, and the fact that they can be put to use reveals their independent power—their soul and spirit. The nonhuman source of human creative capacity stands out.

We can see Will's utilitarian and human-centered stance from a Kwakiutl perspective: whenever he talks about the use of trees, he is also talking about their soul. His hesitation when first marking trees for cutting can be seen in the same mirror as the Kwakiutl woman's prayer. Both (human) people are seen; being seen, as it often does, here suggests conscience and guilt. The woman's actions are witnessed by "our friends," the trees; perhaps Will's concern about "euthanasia" is not only his own, but the result of an inward ire, and witness, of trees.

Protection against the ire of trees can only come from the trees themselves. This is most important when a tree has to be felled. In describing the ritual felling of a cedar tree to serve as "cannibal pole" for the annual Winter Ceremonial, the lead participant cautions that, if the ritual is not properly carried out, "your life will be made short by the supernatural power of the cannibal pole."[68] Before chopping down the tree, he addresses it: "You will be the cannibal pole of [the] great supernatural power" of a neophyte "cannibal" in the Ceremonial; and he adds, "I mean this, you will just protect us, friend." (We'll come back to the question of who the "cannibal" is and who and what is cannibalized. In brief, the cannibalizing could be seen as the incorporation of protective, and dangerous, forest power in Kwakiutl life. The point here is the intensity with which that power comes alive when a tree is killed.) In one customary ritual a canoe-builder enlists the tree's help in ensuring that it falls in the right direction. After he has determined that direction, the canoe-builder begins chopping and then pauses to throw four wood chips where he wants the tree to go, asking them to follow where their "supernatural power" leads, and finally addresses the tree as a whole: "O, friend! now you will go where your heartwood goes. You will lie on your face at the same place."[69] Then he voices the tree's agreement, which protects him from the danger of what we would call an accident.

The "cannibal pole" suggests that some pretty hairy people in-

habit the big trees. In one tale, a girl is carried off by one of these—
Dzonoqua, the Wild Woman of the Woods, who (whether portrayed
as solitary, or as one of a tribe) haunts the deep inland forests (she
eats children, but she's not, strictly speaking, a cannibal, because
she's not human). The girl has been crying, and to frighten her into
silence her grandmother says: "Go to sleep, or else the Dzonoqua
will pick you up in her arms."[70] Shortly thereafter, the child goes
out into the night and the forest monster appears. "It looks like a
big person with a hairy hand," she cries. The Dzonoqua takes her
away, first "down" underground and then "upward" and "inland,"
to her house in the forest. The child throws down hemlock branches
along the way, so that she can find her way home if she can escape.
When the Dzonoqua spies the girl's ear ornaments and wants to borrow them, she asks the girl to pierce her ears. This the girl does,
with large branches—and "the branches went right through the ears
of the Dzonoqua, and she was nailed to the floor." The child thus
kills the Dzonoqua and then pushes her into the fire. Unlike the witch
in "Hansel and Gretel," this forest demon turns into a dead tree before
burning. After the child finds her way back home, the tribes go inland to the Dzonoqua's house and carry away all her food provi-
sions and dried skins. The girl's father can then give a potlatch for
the whole tribe. He becomes a chief because of "the magic treasure
that his child had obtained." The potlatch here signifies the ambiguously demonic and sacred wealth of the forest, its human incorporation and its human relinquishment.

Another character—the dominant figure of the Kwakiutl world,
and a chief actor in the forest and Winter Ceremonial—is Man Eater.
His presence there shows just how strange the Kwakiutl forest could
be. He lives,

> with wife and children, [in] a house in the woods. Dwelling in
> mountainous forests, a spirit region in opposition to that of sea
> and sky, he has his closest associations with forests beasts and
> flesh-eating birds. . . . The mountainous forest is a special do-
> main of spirits; it is not a human habitat. When the myth people
> were still in animal form [in one version], . . . they lived as peo-
> ple do now, on the beach. The interior was a dangerous zone,

which people entered to seek for *nawalak*. The forest was also
the ancient cemetery, where the dead were draped in trees.[71]

According to one family history, he has a cannibal pole—his "own
tree that connects him with the sky"—carved with his associated
animals: Eagle, Raven, Grizzly Bear, and Wolf. In the elaborate
dances and rituals that formed the Winter Ceremonial, Man Eater
is met, (provisionally) tamed, and incorporated into tribal power,
hierarchy, and continuity. In the traditional way of "burying" the
dead (placing them in boxes in tree branches), one could say the
reverse takes place: in trees the dead are devoured. But in narrative
and ritual, humans have an ally in "a woman who is actually human
who is deeply rooted" in the floor of Man Eater's house. Man Eater
himself is part tree, though also "hawklike, beastlike, . . . humanoid,"
covered with mouths. In one ceremonial dance, one of his female
attendants proclaims: "*I am the real tamer of* [Man Eater]*/I pull
the red cedar bark from* [Man Eater's] *back*."[72] Man Eater is Death's
strong cedar tree.

   Man Eater and related characters show how living in the neighborhood of a forest where trees live on other trees, where the forest
devours and grows big on itself, works over time on the soul of a
culture. The forest is not the home of the Kwakiutl but is located
"down," "upwards" and "inland," hence very much *outside*, the place
of estrangement. But everything depends intimately on trees and their
use; from them, "almost all of Kwakiutl material culture is derived,"
and their soul pervades the material.[73] Life in that sense is firmly
rooted in the house of the chief forest spirit.

At times, the deep woods and supernatural power of the trees are
more benevolent, but even then death remains near. For example,
a person may go into the woods to commit suicide in despair over
mistreatment by a cruel father or other inescapable pain, or to seek
a cure for bewitchment or other illness. The "suicide" is also a
metaphor for initiation or shamanistic death, in which trees play
a helpful role and lend their restorative power. In this partial reversal of the usual cosmological order, the human world becomes a
place of anxiety, death, and estrangement; and the spirit world of

the forest becomes a "long-life maker" and a "Healing Woman." Then one goes to the woods and drapes one's human death in trees.

One such narrative was enacted in a Winter Ceremonial dance. In it, a young man is beaten by his cruel father, a chief, during a terrible argument. Afterwards, the son escapes into the woods, having resolved: "I will kill myself in the woods and die."[74] A search party subsequently fails to find him, but that night his tribal group's "ancestors . . . all come out of the woods"; the ghost world irrupts into this one. The young man's death is revealed to be a shamanistic initiation, and as shaman he proclaims, "I have been led further along into the woods by the magic power. . . ." In the ceremony that memorializes the story, the reach of soul-ancestors extends further; even members of the audience "were the souls of the trees and bushes and . . . birds and . . . small creeping animals. . . ." The house of ceremony has become the forest.

The Kwakiutl Winter Ceremonial was not a pure and primary rite of shamanistic communion with the supernatural forest, not a harmony shattered by the arrival of white settlers. The Kwakiutl didn't idealize the forest. Even before the whites' arrival, the Ceremonial strongly emphasized violence, portraying rage, murder, suicide, abduction, cannibalism (the "cannibal dancers" would actually bite people in their frenzy, though they then didn't swallow the flesh or, if they did, vomited it up), and acts of war such as house-burning and canoe-breaking. The ceremony was quite closely connected with war, serving to ritualize and metaphorize it (at different points in Kwakiutl history, it seems both to have strengthened habits of war and to have attenuated them by providing a dramatized and *actively imagined* alternative to actual fighting). In any case, the Ceremonial is not only upwardly spiritualized but also goes downward, into the soul of the forest. There are ways in which the Kwakiutl psychology of trees seems to favor this downward direction over spiritualized ascent.

Though alienated from the forest, the Kwakiutl also recognized the potential for intimate solitude in the woods, where the search for *nawalak* and for nonhuman companionship can meet, however rarely. Deep and direct communion with those same trees whose ire is so dangerous is possible. One man relates that

when a man thinks that he has been bewitched by . . . his enemy,
then [he] . . . goes into the woods where different kinds of trees
grow, and when he comes to the middle of a patch of different
trees, he sits down on the ground and . . . says, "Oh, friends, turn
your faces to me, look through me, Supernatural-Ones, because
I have been bewitched, that I may die. I beg your help, Supernatural-Ones, O Life-Bringers. . . . I ask . . . that you may take
away the power of witchcraft against me, Supernatural-Ones, to
whom nothing is impossible. . . . I mean that you will let me
dream a good dream this night." . . . [after praying] he comes out
of the woods, goes into his house and lies down on his bed . . . he
wishes to dream of what was told him by the supernatural spirits
of the trees. Now the sick man does not think of anything but
the supernatural spirits of the trees. Many men say that the dream
comes from the spirits of the trees who give instruction to the
bewitched man how to cure himself. . . .[75]

There can be times of chaos, threat, and disarray when nothing is
more crucial than trees, and something in one thinks only of them.

In 1970, a thirty-two foot tall Memorial Pole was raised in honor
of Mungo Martin, a noted Kwakiutl artist and pole carver who had
died eight years earlier.[76] There are four crest figures carved in the
pole, Martin's mythic ancestors. At the top is the great bird Kolos,
with wings outspread, which lend the pole a more treelike contour.
He is painted, like all the figures, in rather subdued tones of red,
yellow, black; his cheeks are green and his round black eyes gaze
penetratingly ahead. Below him, with that same steady gaze, is Cedar
Man, or "Chief-with-Talking Stick." He is standing and grasps with
his left hand a talking stick carved with crest figures. In his right
hand he grasps, from the bottom, a beaten copper sheet with the
crest of Killer Whale. Originally a large cedar tree, Cedar Man was
transformed into a man and a chief. Beneath him is Raven, and
Raven's large taloned feet perch on the head of Dzonoqua, with her
traditional puckered lips and pendulous breasts.

In accordance with tradition, the pole-raising ceremony com-
memoratively proclaimed the family's history and mythic ancestors.

(It is the inheritance, and not the order of figures on the pole, that powers the Kwakiutl sense of hierarchy. The phrase "low man on the totem pole" is thus a misnomer, but it does reveal the verticalizing spirit of trees outside of Kwakiutl society.) In that sense, crest poles are Witnessing Trees that see human events and gather mythic memories. The souls of the cedars from which they are wrought are understood to be captured in these "symbol[s] of the geographic and political entity which is the present Northwest Coast."[77] The figures, essentially a pictorial narrative of how a family or tribal division was given the right to the crests of animal and spirit (and sometimes earlier human) ancestors, are therefore doubly *alive*. The soul of the tree infuses the spirit presences; the animal spirits, in particular, are alive in their own right and so infuse the soul of the tree. Not only do the animal spirits see (and the trees see through animal eyes); they speak, making their characteristic sounds. One might hear the jaws of an image snap while walking past a pole. They are *active imaginations*, in Jung's sense of the phrase, figuring the conversation of human and spirit worlds at the core of Kwakiutl tradition; such psychological presence accounts for "the extraordinarily dynamic and restlessly animate" character of Kwakiutl carvings.[78] The sentient trees "are forms of life that undergo transformations, becoming all other forms . . . one does not speak of images carved in wood, but of wood transformed." Crest figures, like all wooden figures, "always appear as living creatures but, like trees, are rooted in place"; "the house posts come alive but cannot move. The doorways snap their angry jaws at guests but are stationary like devouring plants. . . . Animals and trees join their forms and qualities."

Animals and trees join together in the living, dying forest as well—and in the larger spirit of the Pacific Northwest coastal ecosystem that is mirrored in Kwakiutl tree stories. Consider the story of one young man, a hunter and trapper, who was hurt by a falling log in the forest. When he got home he had a powerful dream; in accordance with it, he bathed and "found many land otters in his traps," as well as "an animal with human head."[79] Actually it was a salmon, an animal of great power, as he found out after he had killed it. Following further necessary rituals, he went hunting in his canoe "by torchlight. . . ." Then he saw someone, a "woodman," emerging from the trees. At first he was "almost paralyzed" by the presence; "whenever the woodman moved, it sounded like the crackling of sparks." Impulsively, the hunter "jumped out of his canoe, pursued the woodman, and shot and killed it." As when he had killed one of the Salmon People, the hunter got scared and so showed his grandfather "the body of the woodman, which appeared like that of a human being with a little, thin face." Having killed the woodman, the young hunter had for a time a special power. He "claimed that he had been revived after his first accident by the woodman, who made him a shaman." The falling log was no accident after all, for, as Franz Boas remarks, "the supernatural helper who is about to initiate a person [as a shaman] makes him sick or comes to him while he is sick and cures him." Though he was "killed" by the hunter, the "woodman" lived in him.

A close relationship exists between the human hunter, the salmon person, the woodman, and the psychological power of the forest—a link between the peopled worlds of the Kwakiutl: human, animal, plant, and supernatural. This interlinking manifests in a particular way "the total community of life"—its "dependent and interactive realms."[80] The connection is sensual as well as metaphysical, as suggested by Annie Dillard's image of salmon in *The Living*: "They glistened with life, dark and spotted, tough-skinned, like the land's trees."[81] In addition to vitality, salmon and trees have in common supernatural power—the power the shaman was given. In that sense he became himself a soul of tree and forest, or "myth person." His initiation in woods and dreams and ceremony involves encounters with death—and a kind of ire. His power, however, was not inherent in him; he could lose it.

Power does inhere in the "woodman" he meets. "Woodman" is Bukwis or the Wild Man of the Woods, who appears every year during the Winter Ceremonial season, signaling the irruption into the human community of dangerous forest forces. Facing the community through ritual masks, Bukwis is pretty scary. His wooden mask may bare a large set of reddened teeth and his face have a ghostly pallor. His nose is "similar to a bird's beak"; he stares at you with "non-human eyes" through rounded, "hollow . . . sockets" accentuated by angrily slanted eyebrows arching down on his forehead; and he has "cheek ridges emphasized with lines of carving that call atten-

tion to their nonhuman, almost skull-like form."[82] It is Bukwis who
comes for the bodies of drowned people, taking them into the forest.
If he has carried you away, a canoe might appear to take you home,
but it turns out that its crew "are land otters, the paddles are minks,
and the canoe is a skate."[83] "His body is cold as ice," Boas says, and
his is the forest's lower realm. He feeds on toads, lizards, snakes,
rotted wood, and the bodies he appropriates.

"His salmon" itself "is rotted wood," says Boas—a detail that
shows how deep, and deeply sensual, is the link between Bukwis
and the salmon. Salmon which is rotted wood is really ghost food;
Bukwis wants to feed it to you so that you'll belong to his world,
a pattern reminiscent of Hades, who gives Persephone the pome-
granate to eat so she will belong to the dead. But the image of salmon
as rotted wood is quite particular to the house of Bukwis. Imagine
you're walking in the deep, moist old-growth forest. You grow hungry.
Then a section of rotted log catches your eye; you pause and examine it, noting its tawny, grained appearance and soft porous texture. On an impulse, you poke at it with your foot and pieces flake
off. You now have the sense of how the Kwakiutl could link the rotted wood with dried salmon—traditionally one of their most important winter foods. In a way, it's a trick, an illusion, but more
importantly it is a metaphoric image, one that embodies with exactitude the life–death symbiosis and inmost working of such a forest,
its ecological soul. Rotted wood *is* salmon for the trees, other plants,
and small creeping animals; the powerful person of Salmon is not
in the actual animal only but pervades the forest floor. Salmon, then,
is not only a force of life and plenitude but also of devouring death—a
mask of Bukwis, spirit of the hungry forest.

CHAPTER 5

Trees of Pain and War

Gatherers of Pain

GASTON BACHELARD says: "The suffering tree is the epitome of universal pain."[1] For instance, the "accumulation of pain" in Jane's apple tree. Or the difficult witnessing of the tree that "writes" of mass murder in its roots (the Kurdish poem discussed on pp. 114–15). Or, in another way, the power of wounded and devastated trees after a great storm. Conversely, we may ourselves suffer varieties of fear, estrangement, and death amidst trees. In such ways, we are animated by trees of pain.

When I first drove northeast out of Charleston on Highway 17, I went straight into this pain. Highway 17 cuts through the eastern edge of the Francis Marion, in the area hit hardest by Hugo's 140 m.p.h.-plus winds (the hurricane made landfall over Charleston itself, but the most intense part of the storm, its northeastern quadrant, passed over the Francis Marion). As I continued northward, low clouds and fog that had shrouded the landscape burned off, and the sun revealed a desolate scene. Many ruined buildings were still boarded up, though I saw several people emerge from small wretched houses. For miles on either side of the highway, the forest, mostly pine, was flattened. A few tall, scraggly trees remained, most with few limbs or needles and bent toward the southwest, away from the hurricane wind. All other forest trees (the loblolly pines) over about twenty feet tall were either snapped off or uprooted, with the trunks and limbs falling in the same direction. In the hardest-hit communities on or near the coast, like Awendaw and McClellanville, oaks and other hardwoods stood without limbs, or with half of their crown dangling and dead; others lay sprawled, having pulled up huge clods of earth as they fell over.

There was sun where shade and shadow should be. I passed a field of broken trees on my right where the ground had been blackened by fire. Men in heavy work clothes were gathering piles of limbs together and burning them. White smoke wafted over the highway. I felt faintly nauseated. I understood now what Susan, a secretary with whom I had spoken by phone, had told me. When she got up the morning after the storm and looked out at the downed trees, "it just made me sick to my stomach. I felt on the verge of going into shock." Dangling, twisted limbs in too much sun assaulted me on all sides. Various images of war—from Vietnam and of the leveled cities of Hiroshima and Nagasaki—came to mind: images of rubble, of dead trees, of blast-bent smokestacks. The tangled limbs and branches—"rough," in foresters' parlance—especially reminded me of bombed-out ruins, even of human remains. These images and more general ones of a polluted industrial wasteland somehow merged in my overall impression of miles of tree trunks snapped off at between fifteen and twenty feet from the ground. It still disturbs me, this image of a blasted forest of smokestacks.

Susan's home is in the Francis Marion. In her mother's yard was a white flowering dogwood tree that had been blown over by the storm. Since this tree still had roots in the ground and was small enough to be handled, Susan propped it back up and tried to reroot it. As she said when we met, "it was nice to be able to . . . save something like that. Or even try." A friendly, worn-looking woman in her thirties, Susan was reluctant to directly voice her emotions. When I asked how she felt just after she had propped the tree back up, she hedged: "You really didn't have time to think about it." But then she responded with an image: "when that tree . . . flowers out" in the spring "I'll feel a lot of satisfaction." I asked how she might feel then, standing by the tree while it is flowering, and Susan replied, "I'd probably want to hug it or something." Her spirit flows kinaesthetically into the righted tree, and its spirit into her. But, though the image was one of hope and beauty, it also evoked deep pain, which I felt at the moment as a sudden wave of sadness. It seemed that Susan was about to cry, but she stopped herself: "Well—

sometimes it doesn't pay too much to think about all this stuff, you know? You can't really concentrate on . . . a few single things too much, because you'll be disappointed, maybe, you know?"

The commingling of beauty and pain is not unique to Susan. Trees can elicit tears, as they did in David. And we can compare the sequence of David's narrative to Susan's image; each amplifies the other. In David's case, helpers arrived to right his three palms, "and they stood 'em up for me. Started cryin'. I couldn't help it, . . . it was pretty to see 'em come up . . . those guys helped put me on the track . . . because a tree's comin' up, all the sudden we're goin' again." In each case, it is the *righting* of the tree, combined with a prospect of beauty, that releases pain. The human–tree analogy becomes emotionally and kinaesthetically embodied; Susan and David get in touch with a human grief, but equally they are in touch with something nonhuman—or are momentarily transformed into tree spirits.

We can learn about this grief–beauty connection from "The Ecology of Grief," to use the title of an article by Phyllis Windle, a plant ecologist and hospital chaplain. Windle notes her own response to reading that a blight could annihilate dogwood trees. This "stunned" her, and "memories of dogwoods came flooding back. . . . I remember my first wild dogwoods. Across a southern Illinois field, a few gloriously white-blooming trees stood against a backdrop of dark pines. I was doing field work with the man I loved, and those wild trees blossomed in my heart, too."[2] She realizes that "I am in mourning for these beautiful trees." She reflects on environmental scientists' deep love for "their organisms" and how in a time of massive species loss this poses particular difficulties. "Notice how quickly developers accuse us of caring more for spotted owls, snail darters, and wildflowers than for people. Our guilty backpedaling suggests we know they are right, at least about our love for the organisms and places in which we invest our life's work, if not about how people rank in our affections." Remember that Will complained that some people in the Earth First! movement seemed to care more about trees than human beings. But then he, too, was susceptible to the love of dogwoods. Also, as the experiences of David and Susan suggest, one need not have invested one's life work in ecology in order to feel deep grief over ecological loss.

What also makes it hard, whether one is a biological scientist or not, is that societal assumptions "may make environmental losses difficult to grieve. We have almost no social support for expressing this grief." Indeed, one staff member at Fairchild Tropical Garden said that "a lot of us were ashamed to admit how depressed we were" over what Andrew did, as though such grief were somehow inappropriate. Frank, a South Florida botanist, struggled not to cry as he reassured me (and himself) that nature would "come back." But he couldn't contain his tears when thinking of the remaining trees coming back into leaf and flower—like freshly unfolding pain. He seemed profoundly uncomfortable about being so emotional about what his training told him would renew itself; but the logic of his loving attachment to what he wanly referred to as "my life's work" follows a different grain. In Frank's case, his botanical knowledge made mourning harder. It was an ecological image that made it nonetheless possible—the releafing of the trees, the spirits in the leaves.

Fortunately, Dan, the South Carolina forester, worked in a setting where there was support for grieving. Dan became tearful as he recalled driving back through the forest with his wife and children, after having taken shelter from Hugo in the western part of the state:

> When I got into the national forest and saw the areas, the stands that I was familiar with and worked in—well, I just cried. 'Cause it was just devastating to see this 100-year-old longleaf [pine] just laid flat just as far as the eye could see. . . . I really did have to just pull off the road for a minute, it affected me so much I . . . just couldn't continue drivin'. And everybody I met those first few days was like that—it gets me choked up to start thinkin' about it. . . . I'd gotten to a point where I'd adjusted to the idea [but during] the first few weeks [when] I'd have to drive right back through the forest and look at all of it, I'd find myself cryin'. . . . But everybody I talked to, the guys that work on the forest, the timber markers, the guys like that—these rough, tough guys— they all had tears in their eyes. They loved this forest—as I did.

Pamela, who didn't work in such a congenial setting (but in a car rental agency), seemed to say obliquely that the destruction made her want to cry when she remembered walking in the woods as a child: "What gets me about the trees is that—I actually used to start to cry when I saw the sun shining through the trees, like on summer days or spring days, . . . just seeing the sun shine." In each case, the words of a curator of an English botanical garden after the October 1987 storm apply: "I can think of nothing so heart-breaking for a gardener that [*sic*] to sit indoors and hear the sound of trees going over one by one."[3]

One of the first things we learn, then, from Trees of Pain is that our grief over ecological loss has to be taken on its own terms and that the general lack of acknowledgment of such grief in our culture may cost us dearly. In our era of global ecological concern, it is worth taking seriously what Dan says of the destruction of the forest: it "is almost like a death in the family, it's the same kind of feeling. It takes the same period of time and all to work your way through it, it's not somethin' that you can get over in a week or somethin'." Or when Steve likens the destruction of Fairchild Tropical Garden to "hearing that someone you were really close to died, because it's sort of like a living organism—everything's alive here." That's why, on the morning after Andrew, Steve and his girlfriend, on seeing "sticks and no order," "got choked up and started to cry." He called this "just like an instinctive reaction; it was like an overwhelming loss." Trees of Pain tell us we love far more than we know.

Because we love far more than we know, we do not grasp the full power of trees in regard to pain if we go no further than to say that people can cry or feel genuinely heartbroken over the loss of trees that, in Susan's words, "you get attached to." For there are times "when loss leans like a broken tree," times when trees, broken or not, have the power to evoke unexpected depths and reaches of loss in us.[4] Trees can elicit the felt images of brokenness in all their forms. Susan's imaginative contact with the dogwood tree drew out the whole of the loss she felt in connection with the hurricane, including prior family losses. For Dan, the forest's devastation was also an uprooting of his family's deep attachment to their home, an attachment dating back to their Revolutionary War ancestors—and it intensified his sense of dislocation in the human and bureaucratic world. Pamela keenly felt a basic loss of her early connections with nature.

Jane started to cry when she related her favorite old apple tree, with its "accumulation of pain," to the depth of estrangement she perceives between human and nonhuman life (trees, she said, are like "strangers in a strange land"). Afterwards, she added that the "tree knows there's a threat" to the ecological future. That is, the imaginal power of the tree brings to awareness the threat Jane feels and knows. The power of trees evokes a heightened awareness of pain and the knowledge that comes from such awareness. This is not a new insight; after all, the author of Genesis 2 knew that trees of knowledge can be trees of pain.

Particularly revealing of the reach of Trees of Pain is the way Lewis, the Homestead plant physiologist, juxtaposed his response to the trees hurt by Andrew with a more personal wound—his recent divorce. Lewis described how he had begun to try and reconstruct his life after the divorce, when "here comes this hurricane. And I was *just* getting things started and *WHAM!* it's all wiped clean." And, said Lewis, "it's so amazing—the thing that really upset me, almost more than anything," was the loss of a particular grapefruit tree he had recently planted. This destruction led Lewis to angry words with Andrew: "'You could have wiped out everything, but maybe you coulda left me that one tree.' . . . it just means I have to start over again. And I've been startin' over again too much," he said, with a tense laugh. Lewis recognized something important in his attachment to "that one tree," the way "it just symbolizes," as he put it, the way his life is back on hold. The felling of the tree *brought up* in a very immediate way Lewis's frustration at the thwarting of his life goals—the growth of "my tree."

Lewis insisted that the native trees of the area can "handle" hurricanes. But "it was devastating to me to see everything just missing leaves." Immediately—like David and Susan—he imagined recovery: "Now one of the therapeutic things was when you actually started digging through your trees, and you could lift up a tree, and underneath it there'd actually be a small tree that had made it because of the big one [that] fell on it." And "a few leaves make you feel so much better" because "they hide the damage . . . the jags and the metal." As with David and Susan, the image of tree recovery serves to quicken pain: "First thing I did was get all the metal out of the trees, 'cause that was the real [disturbing thing]. . . . I'd see that metal in the tree and that—that really affected me. *Didn't* like it. It, uh,

I don't know what it made me feel, it just made me think of destruction." For "twisted metal" in leafless, broken trees "just makes you feel *so* horrible. . . ."

Like David and Susan, Lewis then imagines vertically: "Even when a tree's laying on its side, you get it set up and you feel better 'cause at least then you've tried to do somethin' and the tree then has a chance." Lewis, like David and Susan, struggles for a kind of efficacy, for doing something—in an arboreal way. The tree is upright and, kinaesthetically, that also gives the human self a chance at new vitality. But once again pain also increases. Lewis next spoke about his first trip out of the Homestead area after Andrew. As he drove northward, looking at the destruction, "I started to cry—which is interesting," he added, perhaps in part to keep a handle on his emotions right then. After he had driven beyond the area of greatest damage, he found himself realizing how important it was to again see leaves on the trees. "I thought to myself, This is *Paradise*, compared to where I just came from." Then more grief begins to leaf out: "It was interesting because I hadn't really been e—emotional" about the storm before. His subsequent struggle for words was painful to listen to: "And still, though, the hurricane emotions on my indelible—I mean, on my, uh, unevenness about my emotionalness, you know, or getting—getting emotional about things—I know this hurricane will not affect me as much as my divorce. I *still* get emotional about my divorce, *constantly*. You know, I'll be—I'll be just driving home, and suddenly I'll get hit with it." Of course, the hurricane and the divorce are psychologically very much connected and intensify each other; Lewis's grief over his divorce makes "the hurricane emotions" more difficult—but in their own way, those also are "indelible." Both are heightened by trees.

Lewis's predicament and his personal psychological style differ from David's and Susan's, but the way in which trees reach complexities of pain is remarkably similar in all three. It is the precise joining of broken trees and "hope for a tree," to use the words of Job (14:7), which joins human and nonhuman loss. The felt pain is the resurgent power of the trees' bodily spirits.

Trees need not be utterly devastated in order to evoke shared pain and social concern, as literary images make clear. When Miss Amelia and her hunchback Cousin Lymon, the principal characters in Carson McCullers's short novel *The Ballad of the Sad Café*, go upstairs to bed after their first meal together, the lamp Miss Amelia holds "made on the staircase wall one great, twisted shadow of the two of them."[5] This is McCullers's way of illuminating and foreshadowing the twists and deformities of love and of morality in the South that is the subject of this and her other work. Miss Amelia and Cousin Lymon are very much at one, it transpires, in their mingled capacities for love and for ruthless exploitation of one who loves them. Miss Amelia first brutally spurns a man's love for her and then milks him for everything he's got during a marriage that lasts ten days. However, she loves Cousin Lymon. But Cousin Lymon doesn't return her love. Instead, he exploits Miss Amelia's love for him and eventually participates in her ex-husband's revenge against her. The story is about "one great, twisted shadow" of love.

The story holds other shadows. As Cousin Lymon first arrives one evening, "the moon made dim, twisted shadows of the blossoming peach trees along the side of the road." Introduced in the novel's first sentence, the peach trees mirror the course of the narrative. Their blossoming, "light as March clouds," is coincident with Miss Amelia's first flush of love for Lymon: her love *is* that beautiful, and her character mirrors the complexities of the peach trees themselves. The café that flourishes for a time, and inspires a heretofore lacking sense of community among the townspeople, is also like the trees. At the time of Miss Amelia's marriage, over a decade before the arrival of Cousin Lymon, "the peach trees . . . were more crooked and smaller" than when the café flourished. But now, years after the tragic conclusion, mirroring the decaying town and a now aged Miss Amelia, "the peach trees seem to grow more crooked every summer, and the leaves," seen in the merciless August sun, "are dull gray and of a sickly delicacy." They portray the broken-down spirit of the place. Imagistically, these sickly trees can be compared to the "stunted, smoke-blackened tree" with "new leaves of a bilious green" that anticipates the tragic resolution of McCullers's novel *The Heart Is a Lonely Hunter.*[6] The stunted, stifled peach trees figure Miss Amelia's biogaphy and the history of a mythic town—the suffering and decay (and also the tenacious life) in the rural American South which McCullers's fiction probes.

A still starker illustration of the power of trees to evoke social pain is a particular chokecherry tree that was "planted" on the back of Sethe, the former slave woman and protagonist of Toni Morrison's *Beloved*.[7] You don't see the tree at first, and Sethe herself didn't know it was there until, fleeing slavery after being brutally beaten, and now about to have a baby, she was found in the woods by a white girl who briefly cared for her. The girl unfastens the back of Sethe's dress and describes the wound:

> It's a tree. . . . A chokecherry tree. See, here's the trunk—it's red and split wide open, full of sap, and this here's the parting for the branches. You got a mighty lot of branches. Leaves, too, look like, and dern if these ain't blossoms. Tiny little cherry blossoms, just as white. Your back got a whole tree on it. In bloom.

Morrison here reverses the conventional association of trees with flourishing life, so that planting a tree embodies flourishing pain and oppression. But these grimmer embodiments are as ancient as are trees of life; and the chokecherry tree in American lore is often unwanted, a weed tree. At the same time, though, Sethe loves trees. Even where she had been enslaved, there were "the most beautiful sycamores in the world"; and the trees "beat out [her two runaway] children every time and she could not forgive her memory for that." She treasures the woods that shelter a clearing in which her mother-in-law would preach, that "green blessed place" where "woods rang" when the assembled sang. And Sethe is about to give birth—another way of planting a tree—to a daughter who at one point sleeps outside so that "she smelled like bark in the day and leaves at night. . . ." (Sethe's tree-daughter would appear to take after an image of Janie Crawford's mother in Zora Neale Hurston's *Their Eyes Were Watching God*. Janie's grandmother, during her escape from slavery at the conclusion of the Civil War, at one point "wrapped Leafy," as she called her newborn daughter, "up in moss and fixed her good in a tree" until sure that "all of us slaves was free.")[8]

Part of what makes for Sethe's pain, after being discovered by the white girl and later on when she is caressed by her lover, is what brought whelming sadness to Susan, Dan, Jane, Ted, Pamela, and Lewis. In the white girl's words, "anything dead coming back to life hurts." The way trees gather pain is the way they raise the lost and the dead into new life but also figure irrevocable wounds. Loss lives in trees. That is why Sethe, years later, began to cry when her lover "rubbed his cheek on her back and learned that way her sorrow, the roots of it; its wide trunk and intricate branches."

Trees of Death

Not only can the dead come to life in trees, but also the living can go to death. This may take an oblique form, as in Annie Dillard's images of Beal Obenchain as a *piling driven into sand*, and of a local Indian fatally wounded—a "stake had been driven into the ground, and he had been driven onto the stake."[9] The stake had been driven deeply into the ground, and the man rooted there, as it were, like the "Rooted Woman" of Kwakiutl mythology who inhabits the house of Man Eater or, in another way, like Christ on the *tree* of the cross.

Further, trees *secure* life's connections with death. Death's images are inherent in the memory of woods. All our persisting fantasies of Dantean "dark woods" indicate how death flourishes among trees. William Styron, in his account of his suicidal depression, can think of no image more apt than Dante's lines that introduce us to the *Inferno*, when "I found myself in a dark wood." This tells us something about the depth to which depression can take one, and also about Dante's exquisite artistic ability—his words which "still arrest the imagination with their augury of the unknowable, the black struggle to come. . . ."[10] But it also tells us about the psychological nature of dark woods.

Think again of Will's Old Folk Trees and the ranks of Trees of Fear. Think of certain yew trees Sally recalled, which grew outside of her parents' kitchen, "very dark"; nothing could grow beneath them, and when you went out there you noticed a "strange smell." Their "kingdom" had a "sinister" quality that "sort of sucked you in." And "the tree trunks were strange"; they "had [a] sort of flaking bark which, if you rubbed against, you'd get green. . . ." The trees deposited a thick carpet of needles, "and you'd get the kind of strange feeling that things were buried there, and you didn't quite know what it was." What might these things have been? I asked. Sally replied, with a slight gasp, that "it could've been cats." Then she added: "I never felt bodies. And I tended not to dwell on those sorts of things anyway."

Yew trees, in part due to their dark quality, have legendary associations with death and cemeteries.[11] But death among trees is far more pervasive than that. The Kwakiutl forest was also a cemetery. The woods may evoke involuntary anticipations of death. Will imagined the wooded hills of his childhood home that way (chapter 3, p. 66). And David Rains Wallace writes about nearly getting lost in a Florida woodland, when he noticed a large orb weaver spider that "had caught a young anole lizard in its web, had wrapped it in silk, and was eating the flesh of its head. The lizard's white skull gleamed strangely from the gray web."[12] Shortly thereafter, he "saw myself lying beneath a fallen branch, my skull gleaming like the anole's." Wallace's own mortality gleams whitely in this vision of woods as *the web of death*. We find another such figuration in a story about soldiers on patrol in Vietnamese mountains during the war—in the "jungle, sort of, except it's way up in the clouds and there's always this fog . . . everything's all wet and swirly and tangled up and you don't see jack, you can't even find your own pecker to piss with. Like you don't even have a body."[13]

There are no limits to ways in which trees can prompt an encounter with deaths. Every tree grows posthumously.

Sally was fifteen when her mother died. She remembered that "I was asked if I wanted to go in and see her body. And I chose not to, because it was too painful." But her still-incomplete mourning (she "didn't . . . so openly explore" her pain at the time of her mother's death) was re-evoked when Sally spoke of her deeply felt horror "when you see, like on television, . . . one of these giant forest trees in the Amazon or something just being felled . . . crashing down and destroying stuff below and all the life above. . . . all these trees could be crying out in unison and most people do not . . . hear. . . ." Sally did hear "the sound of the forest, the sound of the cry and the crash, [and] the silence afterwards," adding that this "silence after the destruction of the forest that has gone on forever—as we know

it—is quite horrifying, you know?" When I asked if she could recall
any other times when she felt such horror, Sally paused. Her response
showed what else the tree spirits, speaking through a television language, could say:

> Well, in a strange way—I suddenly got this thought that it related
> to the way that I felt when my mother died. That there was a lot
> of activity in our home, there was a lot of life in our home. There
> were people coming and going. There was nourishment and nur-
> turing. . . . and life that just . . . revolved around her, and out
> from her. And when she died—and I have this very very strong
> image that I'll probably carry to my grave—the door to her
> bedroom was closed (and I didn't go through because I didn't want
> to see her dead). That door shut on that life there. And there was
> a palpable silence about the way the life revolved within the house
> after that, or . . . it was cutting off the mother . . . it was the
> silence of death. And I believe that's what the silence is when they
> cut the great trees down in the forest.

The trees, Sally's mother's life, and something in Sally and in her
family's life are in their mirroring way cut off and cut down.

Trees hold together death and survival. The uncanniness of trees
of death has to do with the way death not only ends life but survives in it. Life grows on death, and death grows on life. The
multifarious traditions linking death, burial, and trees reflect this
awareness. They show love but also the persistence of death. Jan,
a young woman, described the funeral service for her mother, who
had died recently. She was cremated and, at Jan's suggestion, the
family buried her ashes under a tree in the family's small cemetery
plot. But if her ashes were buried under the tree, Jan reasoned, the
tree would take them up and make them part of its life. To Jan's
surprise, her whole family embraced this idea. Her father, whom
she thought would not be receptive, added that he would like his
ashes placed beside his wife's. Here is a memorializing and witnessing of human life, but not exactly its immortalizing. In a contemporary rural Greek lament, the author wonders: "My beautiful
cypress tree, where would you like me to plant you?" and then
resolves: "I will plant you in the graveyard, / so that you can spread

out your boughs and branches."[14] Death lives in trees, where it becomes the heartwood of survival.

Partly because every tree has roots in the posthumous, it can be particularly important for people to know that trees will survive them or their loved ones. The Illinois man's urgent desire to retrieve his family tree from the flooded house of his newly dead mother testifies indirectly to the link between trees, death, and survival. The response of people to the sudden loss of trees gives more direct evidence. That evil wizard whom Treebeard let out made his way to the hobbits' homeland, the Shire, where at his "bidding [trees] had been cut down recklessly far and wide"; Sam, one of the main hobbit protagonists, "grieved over this more than anything else. For one thing, this hurt would take long to heal, and only his great-grandchildren, he thought, would see the Shire as it ought to be."[15]

Just about everybody I talked with after Hugo and Andrew pondered the *lasting* quality of the destruction of trees. In South Carolina, people's responses were typified by the first Charleston newspaper editorial after the hurricane: "Never in our lifetime will the city of Charleston look the same. Neither will much of the surrounding Lowcountry. . . ."[16] Pamela told me with wistful sadness that "it will *never* grow back again—not the way it was." Especially painful for many was a sense of shared, *generational* loss. Said Dave, the wildlife biologist: "Our generation will never see it the same. . . ." Dan, the forester in the Francis Marion, spoke for many, in the Lowcountry and South Dade County, when he said that "you don't realize that people who live through things like this have to live with it for years. . . ." Ted observed with quiet frustration that "houses can be rebuilt . . . but you can't rebuild a forest. It will not be back the same in our lifetime." Kevin, summarizing what many Charleston-area residents told him about the loss of trees in their yards, said they would have preferred that houses and not trees be gone when they returned after the storm: houses can be repaired. "But they will never live to see the trees in the same condition they were in. There just is not enough time left in their lives to have . . . sixty-foot pines back in their yard, or oaks. . . ."

For some people around Homestead, the trees had receded into the background of concern. Frank, for instance, reversed Ted's statement, saying, "You can grow trees but you can't grow houses." Reconstruction had been agonizingly slow, and the less-tangible, but no less traumatic, psychological effects of the storm were taking their toll. And for three months it had been, as one woman made homeless by the storm put it, "hot and stinky." Yet, as Frank's remark suggests, the trees were still psychologically present—or absent, despite new greening. Despite the difference between Frank's and Ted's responses, both connect trees, houses, and shelter. Further conversation, as in Frank's case, often revealed that the loss of trees made other things that much harder to bear—more "foreign," as Lewis said.

When the fallen trees appeared more or less plainly personified—as in images of an "injured" or killed "friend"—that also reflected a loss of shelter, familiarity, companionship. For instance, Dan's job requires he be "out there with it [the devastation] day after day"—walking "day after day over the bodies of all those prostrate trees out there." It "has affected me in a way that few other things have." Dan later elaborated on the image of "bodies": "A wildlife technician who . . . does some contract work for us . . . came up with that image. He said it's like walkin' around over dead people. . . . It does give you that feelin'."

Trees of War

Susan phrased it another way: "It wouldn'tve surprised me . . . to see a bunch of dead bodies layin' out in the road every place around, you know? It looked like a war zone." Dan, regarding one of the barrier islands off the South Carolina coast, said: "The place looks like somebody dropped a bomb on it." Paul, a geographer, spoke of the forest of "dead people" over which Dan walked: "There are thousands of acres of the Francis Marion that look . . . like a war zone." I questioned Paul here, wanting to know what came to his mind in connection with "war zone." Paul's reply revealingly linked natural and social history: "Broken trees. Snapped off. Things like, you know, catastrophic damage . . . this is the first time I've ever seen pine trees broken off like this. . . . except in a tornado. So, that's . . . the 'war zone' image." Even broken trees bear historical witness, as illustrated by Paul's next thought: "I guess my historical impression of a war zone is just . . . photographs . . . beginning [with] World War I . . . I guess a lot of the war zone image of stark landscapes and shattered trees comes from images of World War I and World War II." Moreover, the association cuts both ways; it can move back from war to the trees: "It's just that those images of shattered trees are probably most easily brought to mind when you see pictures of war." And again, Paul continued, there were B-52 raids over Vietnam "where you just see a shattered jungle" or where vegetation was eradicated with Agent Orange. The South Carolina columnist who spoke of "a friend's funeral" in connection with the loss of trees in Charlotte went further back into history: "I thought of bleak battlefield photos of Antietam"—the bloodiest American Civil War battle (19–20 September 1862).

The assaults of Andrew and Hugo were indeed experienced as "shattering," as a near-death encounter, as fundamentally disrupting the psychological, social, and ecological order and the workaday sense of immortality (the belief that "you're protected by this major power," as Pamela put it). Any disaster can bring war to mind, and while it is important not to blur distinctions between actual war and other catastrophes, "posttraumatic" wounds, whatever their source, have much in common.[17] Ann, the staffperson at the Fairchild Tropical Garden, recognized both the difference and the commonality when she observed that "in Sarajevo you get mad at people; here you get mad at God."

Jane remembered a heavy wet snowfall in the Catskills one autumn that "caught everybody and all the trees unprepared." And, she said, "It was like after the bomb had dropped, because you saw trees down left and right." Jane used that metaphor twice more: "All over the area people were talking about trees. 'I lost,' you know, 'x number.' . . . Must've been just like in Europe, what happened, after a bomb dropped on a town. And 'I lost,' you know, 'this number.' 'I lost twenty trees.'" And: "The sense of desolation was like a bomb dropping." Evidently, tree spirits can speak through images of bombs, war, and destruction, independently of the severity of immediate trauma one has suffered.

Conversely, tree spirits can speak about war itself. To appreciate the psychological history behind "war zones" of devastated trees, we must remember that *Macbeth*'s Birnam Wood and the German forest Elias Canetti speaks of (chapter 4, p. 107) are not the only armies of trees. In general, says Canetti, "War has to do with killing. The enemy ranks are 'thinned'. It is killing wholesale; as many of the enemy as possible are cut down"—which is why "the forest has become the symbol of the *army*, an army which has taken up a position, which does not flee in any circumstances, and which allows itself to be cut down to the last man before it gives a foot of ground."[18]

We find images testifying to this sort of "thinning" from the Trojan War to the 1990s. In the *Iliad*, for instance, Hektor (the Trojans' best fighter) is wounded by a rock hurled by Aias (or Ajax): "As a great oak goes down root-torn under / Zeus father's stroke, and a horrible smell of sulphur uprises / from it, . . . / so Hektor in all his strength dropped suddenly in the dust. . ." (14.414–18). In Stephen Crane's *The Red Badge of Courage*, one fatally wounded soldier dies like a tree: "His tall figure stretched itself to its full height. There was a slight rending sound. Then it began to swing forward, slow and straight, in the manner of a falling tree."[19] The presence of the tree in Homer and Crane heightens the reader's sense of the magnitude and import of the event being narrated: in Homer's case, the mightiness of Hektor, of his fall, and of the awesome power of Zeus's stroke; and in Crane's, the shock of his protagonist's first close-up encounter with dying in battle. Moving forward again, we find an instance in which the presence of trees serves not to heighten awareness of war's impact but which acknowledges in a half-mocking, furtive, and numbed way Canetti's blunt point that "war has to do with killing." During the Vietnam War, the American military advertised its defoliation efforts with an amended version of Smoky the Bear's warning about forest fires: "Only *you* can prevent a forest."[20] And during the renewed fighting between Croats and Serbs in late January of 1993, a diplomat commented: "Our experience here is that once the fire starts, it burns through a large part of the forest before it stops."[21] At least indirectly, he would seem to be referring to the Bosnian holocaust.

In each of these cases, one can connect actual wooded terrain with actual war. But it turns out that, even in the untreed desert of the Persian Gulf War, there was a forest. An Iranian oil engineer, noting Saddam Hussein's hold on power in Iraq (in November of

1992) said that "[then-President George] Bush burned the forest but left the snake alive."[22]

The image of the forest can shade out the particularity of violence and death in war. By contrast, particular trees in the *Iliad* and *The Red Badge of Courage* (and also in Canetti) render more immediate one's sense of human injury and death. Yet all these images intimate a larger theme, that of a war against a Forest of Death, against spookishness. This war can take many forms, and Michael Pollan recounts one for us in his book *Second Nature*.[23] In it, he discovers the vigor of the New England forest when he happens, near his home, upon "Dudleytown," an abandoned nineteenth-century townsite, which has been overtaken by second-growth hardwoods: "It is a spooky place. I'm not talking only about the ghostliness of abandoned settlement, or the weight of the past one often feels among ruins. What makes Dudleytown spooky is the evident speed and force and thoroughness with which the forest has obliterated the place. In the space of a few decades it has erased virtually every human mark." Thoughts of death are near at hand. "To the gardener in me," he continues, "Dudleytown assumed a spectral presence," and its vanguard consisted of the animal and insect pests against which he has to protect his garden. Then, half-mockingly, Pollan starts using war metaphors, referring to "the advance guard of animals and bugs and weeds. . . ." He evokes the return of the forest, beginning with a reversion of garden to meadow. After a decade of neglect "the forest," he observes, "would be licking at my front stoop, while that dark conspiracy of microorganisms we call rot goes to work on the house itself. In fifty years: Dudleytown. A cellar pit with a sycamore rising through it."

Implicit is a concern about the course of Pollan's own mortality over the next fifty years: by the time your house becomes a cellar pit with a sycamore growing in it, you're as good as deadwood. No wonder Pollan is glad to say that in his garden "I think I've drawn a workable border between me and the forest." It is war: "Might it prove to be a Maginot Line? That's possible, but I think it unlikely." Not a bad image for the border of life and death: "a Maginot Line."

War against, or amidst, the trees combines intimacy with and estrangement from the forest. Another such war is related in John Haines's aptly titled "Out of the Shadows," the account of his confrontation with a grizzly bear in the Alaskan wilderness. When the bear rushed him, he shot and wounded it. The animal turned and fled, leaving Haines (and his dog) in great anxiety about whether they might again be attacked—by a wound-maddened bear. He felt he had to make sure the bear was either dead or nowhere near them before proceeding on his way. So he traced its path across a bank and into the woods. And "once up the bank and into the woods, we stopped. It was spooky as hell under that shadowy, sun-broken canopy of leaves." This atmosphere deepened as he searched the woods further downstream: "As quiet as it was, as eerily still, I felt that somewhere in that dim tangle of alders, willows and dwarf birch the bear must be lying and listening to our movements. As in an episode of warfare, a pervasive uneasiness seemed to divide the shadows and the sunlight. I had that acute sense of being watched and listened to by an invisible foe. Each twig-snap and wave of a bough seemed a potential signal."[24]

Notice the spooky aura in both Pollan's and Haines's episodes of warfare. In both cases, there are threats and anticipations of death. And spirits of trees, which (bearing in mind Jung's observation about the "spookishness" of spirit) attend that death.

War amidst trees can, of course, be an actual human-against-human war, as in the following story by Tim O'Brien, set in the tropical rainforest during the Vietnam War. "How to Tell a True War Story" recounts, in several versions revealing psychological truths of the war experience, an accident that took place underneath some towering trees "in deep jungle":

> . . . I still remember . . . those giant trees and a soft dripping sound somewhere beyond the trees. I remember the smell of moss. Up in the canopy there were tiny white blossoms, but no sunlight at all, and I remember the shadows spreading out under the trees. . . .[25]

Two buddies, Rat Kiley and Curt Lemon, are goofing around under these trees, but "didn't understand about the spookiness." The narrator wants to distinguish the spookiness of war from that of a "nature hike," but it is a spookiness nonetheless embodied in the atmosphere created by the giant, flowering trees with their spreading shadows: "The game involved smoke grenades, which were harmless unless you did stupid things, and what they did was pull out the pin and stand a few feet apart and play catch under those huge trees." Then, Lemon steps on a booby trap, and the narrator sees his face in sudden bright sunlight: "When he died it was almost beautiful, the way the sunlight came around him and lifted him up and sucked him high into a tree full of moss and vines and white blossoms."

The story concerns the author's struggle to express the truth in Lemon's death (and by implication the nature of death in the Vietnam War generally), and the image of the event is played over and again in various forms. In one version, Lemon "was playing catch with Rat Kiley, laughing, then he was dead. The trees were thick; it took nearly an hour to cut an LZ [landing zone] for the dustoff." Death comes, and the trees grow thick. But their beauty, stressed in the first version of the accident along with that of the explosion itself, expresses the author's half-ironic point that war is not only hell and horror; "in truth war is also beauty." The beauty has to do with the action of combat and also the intensity, the fervor of imagination of nature and of the conviction of one's own ideals—the feeling of being most alive when closest to death. "After a firefight, there is always the immense pleasure of aliveness. The trees are alive. The grass, the soil—everything. . . . your truest self. . . ." This experience, itself well-documented in war stories, is ironic: in the *true* war story, the trees most vividly alive are Trees of Death.

And then come the dreams and *their* truths. The author remembers, in his dreams, having to climb the tree with a buddy and peel off the pieces of Lemon's body. Horrible as this memory is, "what wakes me up twenty years later is [his buddy] singing 'Lemon Tree' as we threw down the parts." The "gallows humor" may reflect the dreamer's struggle both to gain some psychological distance from the horror and to fully grasp the hideous ridiculousness of the death, the *story of war itself*. But the image that structures the humor is an archaic one: in death, one becomes, if not a tree, at least the departed spirit of one.

Like so many Trees of Death, Lemon Tree *remembers*, takes on the human name—echoing the commemorative tradition of naming trees, as in the case of the General Sherman Tree (the largest living giant sequoia). The name this tree bears, however, is a bitter fruit. Recurrent dreams reveal the truth of the "war story" which O'Brien's veteran narrator carries in him—"Lemon Tree" locating the taste of death, and of the entire war, its bitter and inescapable fruit. This *truth* is buttressed by the word "tree" itself, cognate as it is with *true*. Lemon Tree is the Tree of Knowledge of the Vietnam War.

This tree reaches other mythological soils as well. Lemon's fate is strongly reminiscent of Dionysos, God of dismemberment—or his double, Pentheus, whom Euripides portrays being torn apart after being shaken from his perch in a tree. Dionysos and Pentheus are explicitly sacrificial figures, like the Norse God Odin, who hangs as a sacrifice to himself on Yggdrasil, the World Ash, for nine days and nights—and, again, like Christ crucified on his own tree. The company in *The Things They Carried* (the collection of which "How to Tell a True War Story" is a part) is, revealingly, led by a Lieutenant Jimmy *Cross*. The war stories the veterans carry with them are crosses they bear, the "sacrifice" of the war. In a sense, O'Brien's whole collection of stories comes under the sign and shadow of living Trees of War—amidst "ragged green mountains" or in a jungle that is "serious spooky," where "the trees talk politics. . . ."

Given these various connections between trees and war, and the deep historical and mythological impression such links have made on human cultures, we cannot doubt that under the right circumstances people may feel a desire to "prevent a forest," in the phrase of the Vietnam defoliation program poster. The desire needn't be literally genocidal. For Ed, animosity directed against the loblolly pine served as a means of venting violent feelings related to Hugo's traumatic aftermath. But it was Kevin, the urban forester who spoke in defense of the pines, who imagined an even more massive killing of trees, as an expression of *his* post-Hugo frustrations (including his irritation at people's animosity toward the pines).

Kevin's demeanor was restrained when we spoke; his pent-up rage emerged indirectly. For one thing, he did not even feign laughter or a smile when I made an ill-considered pun ("It sounds as though the pines are a 'lightning rod' for criticism"). "That's true," he said after a brief moment of silence; "They have not weathered the storm very well, I guess you might say, in more ways than one." Despite attempts to look at the situation philosophically and from a professional forester's vantagepoint, Kevin too was under difficult weather. And being a forester had particular disadvantages at the time. For one thing, "it kinda tears me in half" to hear so much animosity toward the loblolly; then at the local fair, while most people mourned their lost trees, a few, when walking by the exhibit on urban trees he staffed, would say things like, "Well, guess we don't need any of that any more, do we?" Kevin "got irritated about it to the point where . . . I would leave and just go walking around the fair for a while" because "it was the kind of thing that I wasn't really in the mood to listen to anyway."

Ironically, but not surprisingly, an image of cutting down a forest came to Kevin when he discussed the personal importance of "the connection with people in relation to trees" and of "using plants as a way to learn about interacting with people." When I asked him for more detail, Kevin said that

> when you talk about forest management, you're looking more at protecting the forest as a whole, rather than any individual tree, and the benefits that you get from the forest as a whole rather than the individual tree. In that respect when you . . . turn around and start looking at human population in the same way, . . . you may not have to have the same level of respect or good feelings for every individual in the population to be able to look and say, "Well, it's a good town" or "It's a good state. There's plenty of good people and even though there are a few trees that don't produce good fruit, so to speak, . . . it's not necessarily time to go clear-cut the whole forest."

The practically and emotionally intertwined difficulties of getting by in Hugo's aftermath led both Ed and Kevin to speak in juxtaposed images of violence against trees and violence against other humans—this despite their quite different feelings toward the loblolly.

Sometimes the juxtaposition does indeed become associated with *actual* mass human death, killing, or genocide. Such are the images of deforested war zones, from after Hugo to the Persian Gulf and the Balkans. And the Tiananmen Square massacre of Chinese protesters by troops in June of 1989. *The New York Times*, in its 1989 New Year's Eve editorial, noted that "a tree falling in an un-televised forest may or may not make a noise; when it falls before the cameras in Tiananmen Square, it echoes worldwide." Jane, who made the connection between snowstorm and bomb, also had a historical association to reports of forest decline in Germany: "Let's say in Germany they lost 60 percent of their trees, I don't know. Could I accommodate to the news that we lost 60 percent of our trees here? . . . And if I couldn't accommodate what would I do?" The animating link with ecological threat for Jane is one between the massive loss of trees and the Holocaust: "I just don't think I could accommodate to a big loss of trees in my immediate environment. It does remind me also of my thinking about, you know, what if I had been a Jew in Germany during the—you know, and this one and that one disappeared. And how long would I accommodate to it? Or deny [it and] say, 'Yeah, but everything's alright.'" For "I guess I have a pattern in my thinking based on the Holocaust." At this point, Jane spoke of some German friends who themselves seemed to associate the loss of trees to pollution in Germany with the Holocaust: the trees bespoke a humanely authoritative stance. For Jane and her friends, the losses of trees, of people, and of the planet are mutually reflective, historical and ecological images inseparable. Just as Jane sees "trees as a mirror of me" and vice versa, the massive destruction of trees can mirror human holocaust.

The Sacrificed Forest

David was one of three people in South Florida who compared Andrew's devastation to the bombing of Hiroshima and Nagasaki. As a military man, "I've been to Nagasaki and Hiroshima; I've seen what we can do, and like I say, it's very similar. . . ." David, on leave for a weekend when on duty in Korea in the early 1950s, had gone down to Japan "just to see what the stuff that I loaded could do. 'Cause

I worked with nuclear weapons and conventional weapons." As he spoke, it was clear that the experience of Andrew had re-awakened and deepened a sense of guilt over having handled nuclear weapons. Now, he said, "I think we can keep away from" war, as if to suggest a hope that his experience could be helpful to such a collective endeavor.

Trees do talk politics—through the trees of Hurricane Andrew, Hiroshima and Nagasaki could speak. Steve said that after Andrew, Fairchild Tropical Garden looked like "what I imagine a bomb dropping would be like. After seeing scenes of Hiroshima and Nagasaki—just the profile of the skyline, with trees barren of leaves and just the sticks . . . just the limbs sticking up in the air—that's what it looked like. And I guess the winds in nuclear blasts" would be comparable, so that "it just did some very similar things here." The destruction heightened Steve's awareness of the "possibility" of nuclear attacks; "it made you think more globally." "In fact," as he ruefully noted, nuclear attacks "did happen." This global thinking includes "the diversity of the species" at the botanical garden, which "represents tropical botany from all over the world . . . and this was a global disaster for botany . . . so the combination of the awareness that the bomb exists and the fact that things here were global— yeah, I'm sure that heightened the sense of what had happened." Even the defoliated trees ring with inescapable history.

Ecological loss, actual and anticipated, affects us more deeply than we often realize. The spirits of broken trees, of lost forests, and of Hugo and Andrew tell us that, by the same token, untimely and massive human death and suffering—in and of themselves—are ecological disasters. This is the painful knowing of trees. Facing the destruction of trees can prompt one to ponder human death and to recognize Canetti's observation that war, above all, means killing. It works both ways: when we go, spirits of trees go. And when they go, we go with them, ourselves their souls. They are talking politics. They speak in "The Election," a poem written by Leonard Nathan in the early 1980s on the nuclear threat:

> . . . the trees voted
> for slow growth

upward and a shedding
of dead dependents.

And the men?

They voted against
themselves again
and for fire
which they thought they
could control,
fire
which voted for blackened stumps
and no more elections. [26]

In his book *Discordant Harmonies: A New Ecology for the Twenty-First Century*, the ecologist Daniel Botkin remembers his involvement in research on "an experimental forest [at Brookhaven National Laboratory] that was being subjected to radiation as part of a study of the possible environmental effects of nuclear war." [27] From it, he learned much about the value of computer simulations for the study of forest ecology. But one can also see this "experimental forest" as a *ritual* place—a forest sacrificed for the sake of nuclear knowledge.

Nuclear threat has historically been a major and largely unappreciated source of general ecological concern; moreover, specific tree and forest images played a role in stirring nuclear concern in the 1980s. [28] These included juxtaposed images of a World Tree or Tree of Life and mushroom cloud, and the evocation of nuclear holocaust in the literature of Physicians for Social Responsibility (the doctors' antinuclear movement) by photos of the forest devastated by the 1980 eruption of Mount St. Helens. But what stands out most starkly is an image in one of the central documents of the 1980s antinuclear weapons movement, Jonathan Schell's portrayal of nuclear disaster in *The Fate of the Earth*. [29] Schell draws on the same study of the irradiated forest cited by Botkin. It turns out that

large plants are more vulnerable to radiation than small ones. Trees are among the first to die, grasses among the last. The most sensitive trees are pines and the other conifers. . . . Any survivors coming out of their shelters a few months after [a global holocaust] would find that all the pine trees that were still standing were already dead . . . and in a full-scale attack [deciduous trees] would die. Then, after the trees had died, forest fires would break out around the United States.

He goes on to describe the erosion and land degradation that would follow these and other effects of a global holocaust (including the death of "virtually all animal life") and concludes that, given the arsenals of the time, "a full-scale nuclear attack on the United States would devastate the natural environment on a scale unknown since early geological times. . . ."

It was the sacrifice of the Brookhaven forest that made it possible first for Schell, and then others in the antinuclear movement, to speak of the postnuclear world as "A Republic of Insects and Grass."

CHAPTER 6

Trees of Solidarity and Peace

I VAN, THE HOMELESS man we met earlier (chapter 3, p. 56), reverses the direction taken in the last chapter: he goes from images
of planet-wide violence back to trees. God "knows all the shit that's
going on," said Ivan—and He just might decide "to have us burn
up, who knows?" More likely, "we're going to destroy ourselves"
before God can do much of anything. Yet Ivan finds solace here on
Earth, "around trees." And to trees his imagination returns. "It's so
nice to be able to go to Central Park and sit in greenery. I was born
in the country," near Baltimore. "I was born around trees, you know,
apple trees, pear trees, you know, go to a cherry tree. . . ." Unlike
the parents in W. S. Merwin's poem "Native Trees," who "didn't know
the names of the trees / where I was born," Ivan, though uprooted,
knows his trees—where he was born.

Freighted with history and evolution, Ivan's spontaneous imaginative trek from "all the shit" to "trees" echoes the social and cultural
evolution of greenhouses during the Industrial Revolution. The
greenhouse (also referred to as glasshouse or hothouse), with its "primeval" tropical forest, has roots in the sociocultural conditions of
the nineteenth-century European industrial city. This transparent
structure was built as a way of escape from oppressive, dark, polluted
atmospheres like Dickens's London, with its squalid working conditions and social inequity. Urban planners thus sought to shelter
trees and to create human sanctuaries in imaginations of the forest
where we were born. "The existence of the glasshouse," as Georg
Kohlmaier and Barna von Sartory say, "is inconceivable without the
reality of the cities created in the nineteenth century, with their colos-
sal masses of masonry and their menacing human swarms."[1] In the
case of the greenhouse, the image of Eden is a powerful motivator
(see next chapter, pp. 212–13). But what also impels Ivan and green-

house visitors is something far more archaic than Eden: the psyche's tendency to seek restoration amidst trees—the reforesting of the soul.

Recurrent images and themes emerge when Ivan and others speak of restoration in arboreal company. For Ivan, there is nourishment: "I mean fresh baked goods, fresh baked bread . . . that will always be a part of me, you know?" The trees provide him with something important as he speaks; for "if I'm . . . tense or upset, I can go to a park, I can go to a nice body of water and sit and watch the water, and it relaxes me, calms me." Trees, food, and water give Ivan a moment's vacation. "There's nothing else on this earth that can do that that's natural, and . . . being in the outdoors among trees, green grass, birds, squirrels [is] relaxing, believe me."

Ivan is not alone in moving from planetary devastation to images of trees. Carol, a peace activist who participated in the study of the American self, discussed nuclear destruction in terms of deforestation, picturing a realm of "stumps . . . with no life existence." Perhaps, she speculated, something could survive a nuclear or other global catastrophe. "Maybe there'd be . . . a few trees, pine trees." This leads her to a question about trees: "Is a pine tree called a 'conifer'?" The pines in mind are particularly adept at weathering forest fires. Carol thinks of arboreal regeneration: "Something like that would come out of [it], would regenerate from a seed that was just so deeply buried." The planet might be destroyed, but then again "there might be one pine tree that kind of starts" up again and leads "finally, at last, [to] peace and tranquility." Carol, a liberal Christian, speculates: "Maybe that's the whole idea of the second coming, the chance to start over again." Trees re-establish peace, reconstitute the world.

Trees can be tough devils—capable, at times, of psychologically counteracting the anguish associated with planetary violence; capable, even, of colonizing collective imaginations of treelessness. Though Ivan and Carol, in different ways, live estranged from mainstream society, this generative tenaciousness is a mainstream power, one that in conjunction with our evolutionary imagination can affect almost anyone—including David, who once loaded nuclear weapons aboard bombers, and Will, the antagonist of environmental "extremism" and a strong proponent of nuclear energy.

In Will's case, an imaginative movement from nuclear weapons to trees took the form of his own career. He had been talking about growing up in a family of engineers when he volunteered that one of his cousins, also an engineer, had done work on nuclear weapons at a major laboratory. Will struggled with uneasy feelings about the weapons. His cousin is devoutly religious, and his weapons work was "a reverse parallel if there ever was one." Will figured that his cousin "doesn't get to sit back and enjoy looking at the bomb that he's designed," that "you can't get any satisfaction out of that." For nuclear weapons engineers are "good at what they do," but don't exactly "enjoy . . . the fruits of their labor."

At that point, having somewhat ironically employed an agricultural and arboreal metaphor, Will's imagination takes him into trees and toward renewal. For as a forester, by contrast, "I can see a good job in the woods, in silviculture, and see the new trees regrowin' after work," and he can "know"—that is, imagine as he speaks—"what it's going to be in twenty or thirty years down the road," how "aesthetically pleasing" it will be. Growing trees becomes a matter of conscience for Will. In going from nuclear weapons lab to forest, Will indirectly says (as he had before, with regard to life–death issues and the difficult aftermath of Hugo) that forest management is psychologically very important to him. The way trees help him manage is another expression of their larger restorative power—one of those things, in fact, that links him with radical environmentalists (as well as people like Ivan and Carol).

Tree Spirits and Psychological Vitality

I will never forget Danny, a disheveled and hospitalized schizophrenic young man I once worked with. Danny was God, as he once—inadvertently—let slip, and that God rarely loosened his grip on Danny's mind. But when Danny was Danny, he had a good sense of humor and rapport with others. No matter who Danny was, he loved trees. I never found out the extent to which trees entered into his elaborate system of religious delusions, but certainly there were God-trees and Christ-trees. But among the trees that weren't delusional was an especially good spirit. It appeared one day when we were walking back to his on-grounds residence and were talking about actual trees—which, I had noticed, could sometimes help lessen his entrapment in fear and delusion. Danny had in fact done some camping and was fairly familiar with the local forest terrain. In the midst of this conversation, we met one of the other male patients. Danny, smiling playfully, nodded in his direction and knowingly identified his fellow "tree": "That's an old shagbark." This wasn't a hallucination, but a moment of wry, good-natured humor, much in the spirit of the sort of tree that was there.

In fact, there was slightly more irony than Danny may have intended—his own appearance was consistently messier than the other man's. His long hair and shaggy clothes took after the bark of the Shagbark Hickory, whose long strips peel back somewhat untidily from the maturing tree trunk. While it would thus be clear to his compatriot that Danny meant no insult, also present was an inadvertent self-mockery. Underneath his perception of himself as a venerable (and immortal) being was not only Danny's terror but his despair, his sense of self-decay. Just for a moment, though, that decay was captured and transformed by the image of the tree, so that Danny could relate perceptively (and in the same breath) to a forest and to a fellow human being. For a moment, he was freer and more lively than usual. Fleetingly, Danny could experience psychological vitality—in this case, that of an old, decaying, but still funny tree.

The psychoanalyst Harold Searles, in his book on the importance of *The Nonhuman Environment* in psychological development, describes a similar experience in which a tree infuses a human relationship with vitality and signals a measure of liberation from a static psychotic pattern.[2] For about two years, Searles met with one schizophrenic man "in almost totally silent sessions. During these many months he dressed untidily and rarely made any sounds except for grunts, belches, and the frequent passing of flatus." Not surprisingly, comments Searles, "I could not help reacting to him as being more an offensive animal than a human being. . . ." But Searles began to find some sessions, though silent, "deeply enjoyable and enriching to me." The *enriching* image is thematically parallel to the sustenance Ivan imagines among trees. For while Searles did not initially know what was sustaining these sessions, he realized he was also reacting to his patient as being a beautiful tree:

> We both sat gazing out of the window much of the time, and on several occasions I found myself, while looking at a very tall and luxuriant tree which towered nearby, to be feeling an unusually keen appreciation of its beauty, an appreciation poetic in quality and foreign to my usual nature. I saw the tree as being infinitely fascinating; its foliage formed, I realized, a tapestry of endless variety, but nonetheless the tree formed a wonderful wholeness of light and shadow, form and color—a wholeness far more alive than I had ever realized a tree could possess. . . . I began to wonder if [this experience] was saying something about my relationship with the patient. I sensed that my experience was probably a reflection of the patient's . . . own poetic feeling for Nature; he had made two or three remarks, over the months, which revealed such a capacity in him. . . .

Later, Searles surprised himself by recognizing that it was also "my way of vicariously appreciating the beauty of the patient himself." The man's appearance had in fact improved considerably, as other staff people corroborated, but the response was not "simply to some superficial beauty of his appearance, but . . . to the beauty of him as a whole personality," by which Searles ultimately means the "tapping of . . . profound and long-repressed lovingness in the patient." For the tree, however, Searles now found an "inordinately keen" appreciation, which grew out of his initial inability to recognize the *patient's* psychological beauty (which was then attributed to the tree).

However, perhaps the psychological presence of the actual tree "was saying something about my relationship with the patient"; perhaps part of their relationship involved the "deeply enjoyable" experience of the tree. Trees, because of what *they* are, can say something about human "lovingness"—in fact, inspire it, help make it possible. And if, as Searles says, a poetic appreciation of trees is "foreign to my usual nature," that foreignness reflects the psychological nature of trees—a nature that is not ours. There remains a foreign side to the reforested soul.

At difficult moments, we may be especially open to the trees' tonic power. As Roger Ulrich observes, "restorative influences of unspectacular natural scenes, compared to urban views, may be most pronounced when the observer's initial state is one of stress and excessive arousal."[3] Studies in environmental psychology and geography consistently show a more general preference for treed settings, urban as well as rural. People tend to find them, in Searles's phrase, more "enjoyable" and "enriching" than treeless environments.[4] One of Ulrich's studies found that patients in hospital rooms looking out on "a small stand of deciduous trees" recuperated faster from gallbladder operations than did those patients looking out on a "brown brick wall."[5]

Sitting for long periods of time with schizophrenia can certainly be difficult—both for therapist and patient. I would guess (considering my own experiences in work with psychotic people) that Searles was pressed toward an unusual appreciation of the tree by his emotionally trying hours. But one needn't be in that situation to realize, with a degree of surprise, the psychological vitality and beauty in trees. Ed, for instance, though he raged against the loblolly pine, also said of the devastated forest around his workplace that "you just don't consciously appreciate it until after it's gone"—a statement echoed by many people after Hugo and Andrew. In the case Searles describes, the conscious appreciation emerges under conditions that prompted a meditative concentration on a tree. The "lovingness" of tree spirits themselves can be, in Searles's phrase, "long-repressed."

Peace and Solidarity

Jaime struggled to capture his response to being among the massive rainforest trees. Their sight is "very awesome . . . very majestic. . . . I would imagine myself really feeling close to nature, very close to life itself." And "having a sense of *peace*, . . . of contentment, something like that." Going up and touching the trees, he remembered, would give him "this feeling of—some kind of presence." Jaime seemed to be saying this presence was a quality of the tree, a kind of "serenity" or "a different kind of presence of mind." In that presence, "your mind is not cluttered up" as it usually is. The presences of tree and of mind, brought together, render each other more acute.

Jaime also juxtaposes Trees of Solidarity and Peace with psychic difficulty, and so joins the company of Ivan, Carol, Will, Danny, Harold Searles, and his patient. The sanctuary that was lost with the trees in South Florida and South Carolina, as already noted, contributed much to the difficult aftermaths of the two hurricanes. Dan spoke of his troubles with bureaucracy and his sense that contemporary life and "development" were getting out of control. With these pressures, his times in the woods were vitally needed. Alone in the forest at work,

> I just feel a sense of peace. When I'm out in the forest, . . . all the clutter is gone . . . all the aggravatin' paperwork that I have to put up with here, and the deadlines and all that sort of stuff. I'm very much focused on . . . my immediate surroundings. . . . it's maybe one time in my life when I'm sort of in control of things. . . . I think we all have this feeling in modern life that things are out of control. . . . when I'm out in the woods [I feel like] . . . it's a situation that I can handle. . . .

Pamela spoke of her longing for deliverance from "daily deeds"— and, no doubt, the psychological difficulties brought by Hugo's aftermath—quietly remarking on how the sun-dappled woods used to be: "So peaceful. Such a peace." Liz, a cleaning woman, told me in her shy and soft-spoken way that she loves to walk in the woods behind her house. "It's peaceful. If I wanna get away from the kids or whatever, I just walk, you know?" Echoing Dan's sentiment, Dave, the wildlife biologist, mentioned that after a busy day involving time on the phone, on highways, at McDonald's, he likes to go climb out on a limb of a live oak "and watch egrets and waterfowl . . . it gives you a different attitude."

Peace, then, is often found in the presence of trees. A Japanese writer, Wakayama Bokusui, says, "When I think of the most various phenomenon of the world of nature, I always feel silence. I am overcome by the yearning of peace. But I feel it most intimately when I observe trees."[6] As he grows older, one of the men in Annie Dillard's

The Living finds "himself seeking the company of gulls and fish crows, young children, and the tolerant trees. . . ."[7] Jane finds drawing and being among trees so "refreshing," "reassuring," and "so peaceful." Sally remembers the huge oaks of her childhood as "welcoming you to sit" amidst their root systems, so that "you become part of the tree and are not noticed as separate from the tree"; so that "you . . . partake of the stillness of the tree. . . . Its slow-growingness. Its patience. Its peace. Its tolerance. Its allowingness."

The experience of a vitalizing peace among trees can move in overtly religious and mystical directions, as described by Hale White, a turn-of-the-century English writer:

> One [springtime] morning when I was in the wood something happened which was nothing less than a transformation of myself and the world, although I "believed" nothing new. I was looking at a great, spreading, bursting oak. The first tinge from the greenish yellow buds was just visible. It seemed to be no longer a tree away . . . and apart from me. The enclosing barriers of consciousness were removed and the text came into my mind, *Thou in me and I in Thee*. The distinction of self and not-self was an illusion. I could feel the rising sap, in me also sprang the fountain of life uprushing from its roots; and the joy of its outbreak at the extremity of each twig right up to the summit was my own: that which kept me apart was nothing.[8]

Though such experiences are the exception, they illuminate what many feel among trees in a quieter, more everyday manner, even when "conscious appreciation" is missing—a reconciliation, though partial and impermanent, between "distinctness and union," to use Jessica Benjamin's characterization of "the most intense experience of adult erotic life. . . ."[9] This feeling is, in fact, psychologically related to erotic life; and erotic life, as we've begun to see, can be very much related to trees.

To make such appreciation of the presence of trees conscious does not mean to idealize them; we've found that trees can help energize things which would best be left unrestored. But I do question the point at which we habitually decide that our love (or that of others) for trees, or for any nonhuman being, is "inordinately keen," for we may not be giving the trees—or ourselves—their due.[10] I do question the way we often exclude or isolate a keen love for nonhuman nature from the sphere of human relationships, for our habit of giving human relationships priority over all others may needlessly limit possibilities for relationships of all kinds—including the human.

To illustrate, let us imagine a "conversation of trees" from two different worlds of ecological and cultural experience—the Russian and the African-American.

In looking at the tenacity of human violence, we focused on the destructive potential of tree "armies." They may have a peace-giving potential as well, which stands out if we juxtapose images of pine trees that Mischa and Pamela shared. Mischa brought to our meeting his anger over military destruction of Russian forests, while Pamela—the daughter of a career military chaplain—brought to our conversation her anger over racial discrimination. They both spoke of trees using military language.

Pamela, we'll remember, indirectly connected the downed "forest-like" trees that "you used to admire," that "used to stand so tall," with her hopes for a time of renewal in which "black and white" could come together, where "there is no type of segregation," and where "I can see those trees standin' tall again. . . ." The phrase "standin' tall" is of course a traditional military metaphor, and given Pamela's background we can fairly infer a military presence in those trees, a militancy—a way of standing for ecological and social renewal. Mischa was more explicit, stating emphatically that "the pine tree's a *warrior* . . . that stands baldly. . . . Stretching into the sky." We had been talking about his boyhood love of the woods, which came into Mischa's mind as he recalled the devastation near Vladivostok he had seen. There is irony in this, given that Mischa unsparingly criticized Soviet and Russian militarism ("You can't restore [the] environment without renouncing . . . militaristic ideology, . . . in every sense of this word"). This "warrior" pine suggests a nonmilitaristic ecological militancy. It inclines Mischa away from a narrow nationalism toward thinking about the possible contribution of Russian experiences of nature to global ecological concern—and vice versa.

The psychological parallels between the southern United States pines and their Russian kin are striking—especially considering geographical, cultural, racial, national, and gender contrasts. For both Pamela and Mischa, the pines rise, like David's palms, from a scene of devastated trees that bears within it a history of private and public anguish. For Pamela and Mischa, the tall pines figure a striving for personal revitalization, peace, and renewal amidst chaotic circumstances. African Americans living in the hurricane-affected South Carolina Lowcountry and Russians living through post-Soviet turmoil have in common profound collective pain, and Pamela's and Mischa's images variously express a struggle for a regrowth of collective and cultural life. The particularities of pine trees join history and myth—and Pamela and Mischa.

We can hear a parallel conversation between trees in the life of Fyodor Dostoevsky, imprisoned in 1849 in the Peter-and-Paul Fortress of Petersburg, and that of Paul D, the principal male character in Toni Morrison's *Beloved*. A former slave, he was imprisoned before the Civil War in Alfred, Georgia.

Dostoevsky's crime was being part of a group associated with a French socialist. In July of 1849, he wrote his brother Mikhail (who had been incarcerated with him during the spring): "Do you remember how they sometimes took us out to walk in the little garden in May? The greenery was just beginning. . . ."[11] This memory made Dostoevsky "sad"; he remembered previous walks with his brother in another garden and also wondered if his brother, free but living in a treeless area, would "ever see green leaves again." Dostoevsky was surely also wondering about himself, since he wrote before his mock-execution, when he had reason to think he would not live to see another summer. At the time he was in solitary confinement. But a little over a month later things changed. He wrote: "My *private* life is monotonous, as before; but I've again been allowed to walk in the garden, in which there are almost seventeen trees. And that's a great happiness for me."

An arboreal setting that made Dostoevsky sad, but then again brought him "great happiness": here are Trees of Pain and Trees of Solidarity. As is often the case, the Trees of Pain evoke memories of human loss and love—memories that leaf out in new foliage. And yet, Dostoevsky's vitality was tenacious; he "clung mentally to the patch of sky visible through his cell window and to the . . . trees . . . outside."[12] The rejuvenating power of trees during difficult times would also seem to be implied in a later letter to Mikhail, written around the time of Fyodor's release from imprisonment in the Omsk Fortress in Siberia. "Omsk," he says, "is a vile little town. There are hardly any trees."[13]

In Morrison's *Beloved*, Paul D sustains himself partly by loving trees. For "trees were inviting; things you could trust and be near; talk to if you wanted to. . . ."[14] There was one tree at the plantation where he had been enslaved that he often talked to and ate lunch under. He called this large old tree "Brother." Paul D's owner was a kind man, as slaveowners went, and Paul D was "in love with the look of the world, . . . alive in a place where a moon he had no right to was nevertheless there." After his owner died, things got much worse and Paul D found himself imprisoned in Georgia. And there, "His little love was a tree, of course, but not like Brother—old, wide and beckoning. . . . an aspen too young to call sapling. Just a shoot no taller than his waist. . . . He sang songs that murdered life [one of the few ways imprisoned slaves could vent their rage and despair], and watched an aspen that confirmed it." At the time, that one little tree counted for everything—for the world, for all that Paul D could possibly love, for the survival of his own lovingness.

Courage

Aldo Leopold says: "I love all trees, but I am in love with pines."[15] He speaks with gratitude of their presence in another kind of difficult season:

> It is in midwinter that I sometimes glean from my pines something more important than woodlot politics, and the news of the wind and weather. This is especially likely to happen on some gloomy evening when the snow has buried all irrelevant detail, and an elemental sadness lies heavy upon every living thing. Nevertheless, my pines, each with his burden of snow, are standing ramrod-

straight, rank upon rank, and in the dusk beyond I sense the presence of hundreds more. At such times I feel a curious transfusion of courage.

Paul D holds Brother in similar regard. He has been thinking about a fellow man enslaved at Sweet Home, whom he admires and who also loved Brother. Years after attaining his freedom, Paul D continues to doubt his manhood, on one occasion thinking back on Brother and his friend, now dead: "Now *there* was a man, and *that* was a tree."[16]

The image gets at our theme—the restorative vitality of trees—from the angle of African-American experience, in which racial discrimination or insult and consequent self-doubt can make it harder to affirm oneself as a man, a woman, a tree. ("Oh, he did manly things," thinks Paul D regarding himself, "but was that [his former slaveowner's] gift or his own will?") What Paul D can take from Brother is limited by such doubt. Lying with Sethe after their rather unsatisfying first sexual encounter, he laments: "Himself lying in the bed and the 'tree' lying next to him didn't compare." The implication would seem to be that the aspect of him he struggles against identifies more with Sethe—a wounded tree woman. He was not a *real* tree, he thinks, not like Brother, not like his friend. But Paul D, in part due to the psychological power of the aspen for him, turns out to be a tree in spite of it all; even his struggles show it. For "he wanted to take root"—and eventually does. (The tree pattern in Paul D's life is highlighted by the way the narrative sequence, reflecting Paul D's ruminations, moves from Brother, the genuine tree [versus Paul D], to the diminutive aspen that confirms his life, and finally to his desire to take root.)[17]

As we found earlier (chapter 3), trees easily constellate our sense(s) of ourselves as men and women. They can transfuse *both* with equal courage—tree courage, that is. All of us, in Thoreau's words, could benefit from "an infusion of hemlock spruce or arborvitae in our tea."[18] Black men and women have won racial self-affirmation through drawing upon the recuperative power of trees; and trees can also figure their reach beyond racial differences. Langston Hughes—who called forth winds of anger to fell "trees" of racial oppression (chapter 4, p. 87)—also recognizes a very different kind of tree. He desires, in a poem titled, suggestively, "Dream Variation,"

> To whirl and to dance
> Till the white day is done.
> Then rest at cool evening
> Beneath a tall tree
> While night comes on gently,
>   Dark like me—. . .
>
> Rest at pale evening . . .
> A tall, slim tree . . .
> Night coming tenderly
>   Black like me.[19]

The "dream variation" embraces Hughes's self-affirmation and his transformation into the spirit of the tree. Standing in a similar way is the tree of the poet Mari Evans in her poem "I Am a Black Woman":

> I
> am a black woman
> tall as a cypress
> strong
> beyond all definition still
> defying place
> and time
> and circumstance
>   assailed
>   impervious
>   indestructible
> Look
>   on me and be
> renewed.[20]

For Pamela, the trees "standin' tall" concentrate in themselves both her hopes as an African-American woman and the potent image of her father, whose religious values she relies on for her sense of herself as "a decent person."

Like Hughes, Pamela could see destructive wind as an equalizer. She "didn't know there was such a segregation" in some parts of the Lowcountry until Hugo, but "I mean, it's just amazing how it brought those people together, even with the locals down here. Sorry," she added wryly, "it took a hurricane to do that but. . . ."

Like Pamela, who goes on to speak of "black and white together" among the renewed trees and flowers, Hughes, in the poem after the "wind [that] . . . uproots trees," talks of "Daybreak in Alabama" in a way that integrates trees and interracial solidarity. In Hughes's poem, the ecological feeling takes the form of a sentient Earth: "when I get to be a composer" and write music about his vision, "I'm gonna put some tall tall trees in it / And the scent of pine needles / . . . And I'm gonna put white hands / And black hands and brown and yellow hands / And red clay earth hands in it / Touching everyone with kind fingers. . . ."[21] Like Pamela and Hughes, Gordon Parks sees interracial connections in a treed setting: his friends comprise "a pastiche of hues. . . . The closest of them could hardly be called homogeneous—a black, a Chinese, a Frenchman, a German, a Jew, an Irishman, and a white Southerner from Louisiana. Altogether they are like one big sheltering tree with different colored leaves."[22]

In these various instances—in the wilderness experience and solitary communion with nonhuman nature, but also in the context of the nuclear age, the consulting or hospital room, the prison, the city, experiences of collective injury here and abroad—the imagination's way of moving into and among trees vitalizes the self with their power. We rarely recognize how heterogeneous are the forms of ecological restoration going on (or at least being attempted) every day that require a presence of trees. We rarely acknowledge that some of what we think of as human courage comes from a courage of trees. A "curious transfusion," as Leopold says.

The Tree Lady of Bed-Stuy

On Lafayette Avenue of the Bedford-Stuyvesant section of Brooklyn grows a *magnolia grandiflora* tree, and its spirit is no shy woman.

She had become attached to the tree in the 1960s, "adopted" it "as her own," and then, together with other local people, prevented the city from cutting it down.[23] Hattie Carthan died in 1984, but "her generous spirit is with us still, just as surely as the Magnolia Grandiflora at age one hundred eight still flourishes, tall, graceful and ever green." The tree, about forty feet tall, grows two doors down from the entrance to the Magnolia Tree Earth Center, a bustling place which sponsors numerous environmental, artistic, and cultural education programs for neighborhood children and youth, as well as activities for older citizens, and which she and other residents founded in 1973. "Bed-Stuy" is mostly poor, though it has some well-kept sections; its inhabitants are largely African-American, but include a number of Asian, Latino, and, more recently, Arab immigrants. The magnolia tree, brought from North Carolina by a man in the 1880s, is very well-tended. I found it, with its large dark-green leaves shining on a gloomy December day in 1992, to have shaped itself in accordance with its home on the south side of a brownstone row, which protects it from the winter's north winds. It leans slightly away from the building, and its branches grow alongside of the walls and out toward the sidewalk. Its foliage is luxuriant, but the tree is slender, as though expressing not only the constraining conditions of its climate (the *magnolia grandiflora*, as noted earlier, is native to the South and would not be able to survive without help in Brooklyn), but also the ongoing communal struggle for renewal amidst extreme urban desolation.

A quote from Hattie Carthan in the Center's photographic exhibit on "The Lady and the Tree" captures her spirit: "We've already lost too many trees, houses and people—your community—you owe something to it. I didn't care to run" when her block started going downhill in the 1960s. One of the first black women to be employed by a major area market research firm in the 1950s when she moved to Bed-Stuy from Virginia, Hattie Carthan planted herself there. Her treeish spirit is depicted on a mural, painted by Maulana Bengazi, adorning the wall of the building just to the right of the tree. Her face, broadly smiling, with her white hair and her earrings that look like the flowers the tree bears in season, is set against a crown of vividly drawn leaves, fruits, and flowers. Near the bottom of the mural is a slender tree trunk, enclosed by a protective iron grating and attended by ten children: metal and human shape, and are shaped by, the tree. The semi-circular mantle of cloud-flecked blue sky above tells us that this magnolia is really a World Tree. Photographs of Hattie Carthan, taken when she was in her seventies and eighties, show how treelike she really is—her expressive face is weathered, kind, determined.

Sophie Johnson, the Executive Director of the Magnolia Tree Earth Center, had known Hattie Carthan and spoke with me about the importance of her spirit and tree. For "it was principally Mrs. Carthan who drew me in[to] closer" association with the Center. Young people who come to the Center "can see living proof that one person can make a difference in a community"—that is, the living tree. For in Bed-Stuy, "markers for difference," for "change for the better," are hard to come by. Hattie Carthan is "a community person that they should know about," and introducing the young people to her "persona" has worked well. As we spoke, our images moved back-and-forth between the Tree Lady and the tree itself. Johnson, with obvious appreciation, said that often from inside the office they could hear people on the street stop "and they'll talk about the tree," saying things like "'That's the famous magnolia tree,' you know, 'Mrs. Carthan saved that tree.'" Children and parents teach each other about this part of the "neighborhood history."

In multiple ways, the tree, the spirit of Hattie Carthan, the community, its history, and ecology came together as Johnson spoke. As the photo exhibit puts it, Hattie Carthan's spirit "captured our hearts and engaged our best efforts to assist people, especially children, to respect, love, and enjoy the natural built environment." This phrasing is not the usual way we distinguish between tree and person and between "natural" and "built" environments. What we need is an environment at once *natural* and *built*; without that combination, in fact, the magnolia of Bed-Stuy would not have survived. It was city buildings, preserved, that preserved the tree. And the tree, in turn, "is a sign that the community has survived," that "it's a survivor" like the tree, which "wasn't expected to live when it came here. . . ." The magnolia says something about "us as a community."

The Center was also host to a summer 1991 project called

"PeaceTrees," which brought young people from all over the world to Bed-Stuy to plant trees within a new urban park which includes a memorial to African-American war veterans. It was, said Sophie Johnson, gratifying to see a "kid from Bed-Stuy make friends with somebody from Leningrad [before it was renamed St. Petersburg later that year]." That project, like the Center's role in drawing together diverse people from the local community, shows that though the neighborhood will continue to change, "there are certain things that are going to hold us together. . . ." And when the tree was threatened, it brought "together people from all races" in the effort to save it, and that inclusive spirit remains an important part of the Center. The tree and Hattie Carthan have "brought into being" not only the Center but a larger communal orientation toward "preservation and conservation." Various "developments," such as a nursing home and medical center, evolved at the same time and through communal involvement, added Johnson (tacitly subverting another usual distinction, that between "nature" and "development"). It is easy to see why she had once said: "That tree is an old friend and an inspiration to people in the neighborhood."

Friends, Relatives, Loves

"An old friend": we've heard people talk about trees like that before—people from Florida, South Carolina, England, Russia. William Klein, the director of Fairchild Tropical Garden—another place with a tree orientation that has become a metaphor for communal renewal—spoke similarly of trees not saved. For "after you've been around a landscape for a while, you become acquainted with these trees on a first-name basis, and they become friends." As with other friends, "you think about their struggle" and about their individuality: "a *particular* palm or a particular oak . . . [that] had become part of the rounds," that is, "familiar . . . and you watched it. . . ." With a greater estimation of the restorative power of trees, we can now understand why people so often recognize them as friends, relatives, even loves. We learn something more about the character of trees and of people, perhaps about the nature of friendship.

Andrea too thought about friendship and trees. She was working on a master's degree in forestry when I talked with her at the La Selva biological reserve in Costa Rica. She longingly spoke of the old-growth forests of the Pacific Northwest, where she lives. Most of all, she thought of the 1000-year-old cedar trees that grow on the Olympic Peninsula. She mused over how struck she is by the hugeness of their lifespans compared with those of humans, how the tree will have changed little from her childhood to her senescence. With those three images in mind—the *presence* of the great tree, her past as a little girl, and the anticipatory image of herself as an old woman—Andrea spoke of "the comfort" and "consolation" offered by "such a friend." In fact, she has a (human) friend back home who has confided to Andrea that, when she is depressed, she visits a particular tree. And so another image, another character, came into the picture. Through this character—the depressed or melancholy friend—Andrea continued to voice her own responses to the friendship of the trees. But like other characters we've encountered in the woods, such as Hillbilly and Swamp Rat, the two women and the girl are also their own persons; they are tree characters; they personify the trees and terrain.

They are really tree nymphs, or what the Kwakiutl call the "supernatural spirits of the trees" that bring healing to the bewitched. Through them the old great tree befriends the earth, hints at the life cycle, at death, and at what will outlast us—much as Hillbilly and Swamp Rat do for Will.

Other people describe particular trees in similar ways, their constancy being, as one woman recalling a birch tree of her childhood home put it, "like a friend" because "always, *always* there." Likewise, Sally emphasized the "friendly" quality of the English oaks in which she played as a child, and Jaime the "affinity" he felt with the guava tree of his boyhood. Valodya, a Russian psychologist, spoke animatedly of two walnut trees in the backyard of his vacation home in the Crimea: "They are my friends." With such friends we are most intimately familiar.

From the Russian forests to the streets of Bed-Stuy, from the Pacific Northwest to a Manila suburb, from the battered South

Carolina Lowcountry and South Florida to the English countryside we see the consistency with which trees are spoken of, or bespeak themselves, as friends. Such images address the abiding intimacy that can grow between trees and human beings—and perhaps the long evolutionary closeness between us and our arboreal compatriots.

For *trees are befrienders of friendship itself.* As Wendell Berry puts it in his poem about a dying elm tree: "Willing to live and die, we stand here, / timely and at home, neighborly as two men." Through trees' endurance, their steady hold, uprightness, and constancy of reach, they speak of the living and indestructible core of friendship. Their nonhuman presence somehow lays bare the human importance of friendship and love, its link with life, death, finality. Such presence—its utter continuity—allows, invites, and shelters one's own; it grows slowly and subtly into the depths of the human self, takes hold, and helps to shape our images and grasp of the deepest value of friendships. When Mischa and others describe the death of trees as the death of a friend, they acknowledge that in life too there is something uniquely instructive in the presence of trees. Whoever talks about the friendship of trees not only envisages but *becomes* the tree's personified presence, its face, its soul and spirit. It is we ourselves who then become souls and spirits of trees—*their* images. As images of trees we touch the ecological ground of friendship.

Much of this reciprocity of friendship is suggested by Alexandr Pushkin's poetic narrative of a return to his country house, where

> At the boundary
> Of the family land, at the spot
> Where the rain-riven uphill road begins,
> Three pines
> Stand: one apart, two close
> To one another. And when
> I rode past them, on moonlit nights,
> Their familiar rustling voices
> Greeted me. I take that road
> Now, and again standing before me
> I see them. They are the same,
> And their sighing sounds the same in my ears.

> But near their gnarly roots,
> Where I remembered barren ground,
> Now grows another grove,
> A new green family, huddled close
> In the shadows, like little kids. And apart,
> Still alone, stands their gloomy companion—
> An old bachelor, amidst
> The same barrenness as before.
> Greetings to you, young trees, my kin!
> I will not see you in your fullness,
> When you will have outgrown my old friends,
> . . . But let my grandson encounter
> Your wordless greeting when returning,
> In good humor, from a visit with friends,
> He also passes by you in the night—
> And, at heart, may think of me. [24]

Pushkin, like the trees, is speaking about what Robert Jay Lifton would call a sense of immortality—through both nonhuman nature and human family. [25] And he identifies with the trees in death too—imagines himself in another form of tree spirit.

Another poem, by Jim Peterson, concludes "I want to stand still forever." [26] Walking in a place going wild again (with "weeds overtaking" the "chain link gate" at its boundary) as night comes on, the narrator of the poem (itself titled "Stand Still") has "undergone the inspections of owls and deer / as mindless in the moment of watching / as trees. . . ." The poem does not say outright that the narrator becomes, among other beings, a tree spirit. This metamorphosis is implicit, though, in a subsequent "moment of watching" that leads the narrator to his or her desire for stillness:

> . . . never have I seen this place
> in the light of so much moon and stars
> leaves and needles shining on the ground
> and in the air.

Only a tree can "stand still forever," Daphne-like; the human narrator can only fleetingly become "as mindless . . . as trees," as in-

humanly mindful as the forest. Yet there is a treelike solidarity in
standing "beyond all definition still" (in the words of Mari Evans's
cypress woman). Because the spirits of trees inhabit us, we can "stand
still forever"—but just for a moment, because our standing remains
also human. We desire to stand "as trees"; in that desire intimacy
and estrangement become friends.

In 1973, the legal scholar Christopher D. Stone wrote a little book
titled *Should Trees Have Standing? Toward Legal Rights for Natural
Objects*, an essay composed in an attempt to influence public debate
on a case before the United States Supreme Court in the early 1970s.
(The Sierra Club had brought a suit to stop a development scheme
in a sensitive area of the Sierra Nevada forest—and the trees lost.)[27]
An important early foray into the more imaginative reaches of ecological concern, Stone's work argues for the value of *personifying*
trees and other nonsentient natural beings as a way of grasping their
importance and our solidarity with them: their standing in the soul
as well as the courts. While Stone contemplates actual legal rights
for such beings, his truer subject is not law, which, however important, remains instrumental. What he is really after is the cultivation
of love for nonhuman nature, for, as he says, "to be able to get
away from the view that Nature is a collection of useful senseless
objects is . . . deeply involved in the development of our abilities
to love. . . ."[28]
      Stone makes his assertion in contrast to Hegel's idea that a
nonhuman thing "has no end in itself and derives its destiny and
soul from [a human] will." Stone counterposes to this view a passage
from a short story by Carson McCullers—"A Tree • A Rock • A
Cloud"—in which an aging, broken-hearted vagabond and a news-
boy meet in a streetcar café.[29] Set in a poor Southern mill town,
the story begins: "It was raining that morning, and still very dark."
Like Coleridge's Ancient Mariner, the vagabond compels the boy's
attention and tells him how he developed a meditative "science" of
love for the world after his wife, who had been his first real love,
left him for another man. Sometime after his marriage had failed,
says the old man, "I realized what is wrong with us"—the way men
first fall in love: "Without science, with nothing to go by, they under-

take the most dangerous and sacred experience in God's earth. They fall in love with a woman." Excitedly he explains that men "start at the wrong end of love. They begin at the climax. Can you wonder it is so miserable? Do you know how men should love?" The man focuses on the boy, "his green eyes . . . unblinking and grave," and tells "how love should be begun": "A tree. A rock. A cloud." He developed his "technique" over a period of six years, so that now "I can love anything"—people in the street, birds in the sky, "a traveler on the road. Everything, Son. And anybody. All stranger and all loved!"

Stone reasons from this story that we all have the possibility of returning to a direct, unmediated love of the world. But the ecology of McCullers's tale has its complications. The vagabond's situation is hardly ideal. There is the dark predawn rain, the man's history of loss; his persisting debility, decay, brokenness; and even his physical features—those green eyes, for instance, and his old-looking orange hair. These elements of McCullers's story may give us some clues, however, as to what it means to cultivate the level of love Stone calls for—the beginning of love, of the greened seeing of a wooded, rocked, clouded world.

That greened seeing is worthy of a close focus. At one point, the old man's eyelids close "down with delicate gravity over his pale green eyes." Green in these eyes is surely the color of new, pale spring green—the beginning color of life; it also has a Venusian quality and is related to the man's orange, fired love—old flame though that is. However, it is not the literal, Edenic green often associated with the ecological imagination; it is a *saddened* green, a green attendant upon death and loss. Peter Bishop has brought out the many psychological hues of green, its "interior alchemy"—relating it to death and sickness and Saturnine decay as well as to hope and passion.[30] There is a vagabond green, which shows in the link between eyelids that close "with delicate gravity" and the *graveness* of the eyes themselves. This hue shows when the boy asks the man if he has been able to love a woman again, and the vagabond, "his green eyes" now taking on "a vague and scattered look," drinks the last of his "yellow beer" and replies that "I am not quite ready yet." So the green is *yellowed*, perhaps like the "bilious green" leaves of the stunted tree that appear toward the end of McCullers's *The Heart Is a Lonely Hunter*; and, as Bishop says, "yellow / green has been associated with bile, fear, with a sickly pallor. . . ."

As Bishop notes, this yellow green—the right response to threatened ecological disaster—also complexifies our more idealized hues of green. In the guise of the vagabond in McCullers's café, it is more precisely *characterized*, personified—it becomes a character in the background of Stone's response to the attitude that denies the nonhuman world its soul and our love. A systematic and meditative cultivation of love for the nonhuman world can infuse love relationships between humans.[31] But the ecological images *and characters* that ground and figure love have not had standing in themselves. Ecological love, moreover, can be imagined as a particular kind of yearning—one with a wandering, vagabond character—a companion to the estranged. And the green-eyed old man recognizes an original form of love only *after* his first loss of a love; privation and longing are necessary to his "science."

The vagabond's grasp of that love for the tree, the rock, the cloud parallels the way Paul D thinks in relation to his love for the aspen during his Georgia imprisonment. There "you protected yourself and loved small. . . . Grass blades, salamanders, spiders, woodpeckers, beetles, a kingdom of ants. Anything bigger wouldn't do. A woman, a child, a brother—a big love like that would split you wide open. . . ."[32] Certainly he couldn't risk loving a big tree like Brother, or the tree of a woman herself split wide open by a wound.

But maybe the depth of loss in each of these cases—in Stone's defense of the forest, in McCullers's old greened man, in Paul D's own treed eyes—opens for us the possibility of a depth of love that would give trees their proper standing, a standing inclusive of rocks, clouds, others. Estrangement and intimacy together: "All stranger and all loved!"

Metal and Machines

Metal and machines are not often thought of as friends of trees. Lewis, for instance, was especially upset by strips of twisted metal in the trees after Andrew hit. This anomalous association evoked the pain of his recent divorce; certainly, it is a peculiarly jarring and painful exemplification of Andrew's destruction (and its psychological aftermath). But there's more involved. I asked Lewis what he thought about this particular juxtaposition—metal and trees. "I don't like metal," he replied; "I don't think metal and nature mix. . . . metal is *human*" and "twisted metal in a tree just is a dead sign of destruction. . . ."

What Andrew did here was to violate an ingrained dichotomy between the organic and the metallic. Andrew struck a blow at a crucial way of relating to the life-power of the organic world, and that wound is part of what hurts Lewis. We understand his feelings; no metal object can have the character of a tree. And we understand Treebeard's feelings when he remarks of the tree-destroying wizard that "he has a mind of metal and wheels; and he does not care for growing things, except as far as they serve him for the moment."[33]

Treebeard's own origins tell us something else, however, about the relations between trees, metal, and machines. A recent biography of J. R. R. Tolkien quotes the author's son, Michael, on this subject:

> From my father I inherited an almost obsessive love of trees: as a small boy I witnessed mass tree-felling for the convenience of the internal combustion engine. I regarded this as the wanton murder of living beings for very shoddy ends. My father listened seriously to my angry comments and when I asked him to make up a tale in which the trees took a terrible revenge on the machine-lovers, he said, I will write you one.[34]

So this is how Treebeard and the Ents came into the world (and they do get their revenge). In a curious way, both tree-lovers and machine-lovers were their progenitors. In Treebeard's soul is a remembrance of metal. Perhaps that's why he can say of the metal-minded wizard, "Curse him, root and branch": the opposition between the arboreal and the mechanical depends, in several ways, on the encounter of tree and metal. The relationship between trees and metal may evolve twists and turns that confound our habitual dualities.

Consider one of Jaime's most important memories—one that still infuses his rainforest activism. As a boy, he got to fly with a "very experienced pilot" over the rainforest territory. Jaime guessed that they flew "at tree-top level, we were probably flying maybe fifty to a hundred feet," or not much more than that, "above the trees." Part of the pilot's experience in flying at tree-top level was in spraying chemical insecticides over plantations. That Jaime, who has had a considerable ecological self-education, did *not* at this point remark on the irony in that goes to show how caught up he was in his remembered flight. For he "could see miles and miles of rainforest, sprawling. Virgin forests." He became more excited as he reminisced. The flight was not so fast that the scenery was a blur, and the vibrantly colored features of the forest canopy stood out. "The leaves of the trees," said Jaime, "come in different hues . . . of green. Sometimes they would come in certain tints of orange or yellow . . . or red"; it was a "fantastic sight." This was for Jaime a moment of intense communion with the sensual world of the forest. But it was made possible partly by metal.

Metal can hold individual trees together as well as deface or destroy them. Consider the old mulberry tree in the garden of Sally's childhood home. Its three major limbs are chained together to prevent them from breaking off. Sally showed me a drawing of a limb whose bark was folded in at the point where the chain had been attached: "The chain [has] . . . kind of grown right in. . . ." If we think literally only, we'll think this description is wrong: of course it is the tree's growth after the attachment of the chain that envelops the latter. But if we think with the image, there is metal that has "grown" into the tree—the chain's presence allowed the tree to continue growing, to grow over it. In a solidarity between trees and metal, the metal takes on an organic quality and expresses human "lovingness" toward the tree (as it does in the mural depicting Hattie Carthan's Bed-Stuy magnolia tree). Sally feels that "trees in a garden need human help"; that "there's an arrangement made between the people and the trees. And they both give to each other." The metal vitalizes the tree, becomes part of its personified character, its particular way of giving. The metal has grown into the tree's interior, its soul. The image echoes the ecological understanding of a third-century Greek alchemist: "The metal gives and the plant receives."[35]

With this understanding in mind, let's ponder Will's characterization of "people that actually work in the wood business": it's "going to be a standard perception," he said, that "they love the trees. But, you know, an auto mechanic loves his cars, too. But you gotta tear 'em apart sometimes to fix 'em." If we look at that statement from a more usual point of view, an ecological voice in us might object: after all, trees and forests aren't cars. From that standpoint, Will's remark reflects everything that's ecologically wrong with industrial culture's mechanistic, utilitarian attitude toward land. If, however, we look at it alchemically, as an image involving a give-and-take of wood and metal, we can recognize several levels of solidarity.

Since Hugo had torn the forest apart, Will was surely hoping it would somehow get put back together. It is hard not to see in Will's image both a reflection of the rending experience of Hugo and a search for comfort, reassurance, familiarity. Moreover, the association between love of trees and Will's familiar images of engineering, mechanics, and technology would also seem to reflect one prominent way in which Will's particular love for trees comes across. Will, like Kevin, was upset about people's animosity toward the loblolly pine. One of the more discouraging things he'd noted since Hugo was that some people whose property had suffered tree damage said "they're never going to plant another tree." This is "another sad part. You know, we went from a love to a fear." Will was particularly upset about how local people tended to blame the loblollies—which tended to snap off at about fifteen to twenty feet above ground level in the storm—for being "weak"; even his son's "science teacher was talking about how weak the pine tree was."

After all, the first trees Will marked for cutting were loblollies. Even though it's "my business to cut 'em," he said of the pines he's harvested, "Basically, I identify with 'em. . . . A beautiful tree is a beautiful tree. And you hate to see one cut." When Will talks about "the entire life story of a tree," he means his story and that of the loblolly. Will explained: "The tensile strength of pine far exceeds that of any hardwoods. One of the reasons pines broke much more [often] than hardwoods [which lost limbs or were uprooted] is the

hardwoods lost all their leaves so the wind resistance was decreased."
This phenomenon was in spite of the fact that the "bending ability"
of pines is (relative to hardwoods) quite impressive. Will's language
is technical; he was giving me a lesson in "wood technology," as he
later characterized it. He was also speaking in defense of the pine,
in a sense taking it apart in his soul in order to fix its wounded reputa-
tion, to move a fear back into love, to reply to those who were saying, "'Boy, that's a poor tree.' It's not, you know?"

We might also note the gender-related contrast between Will's
machine–tree love and the combination of love, sex, and spirit that
trees evoke in Jane. But, surprisingly, her favorite apple tree is also
associated with a car, for near the tree "there used to be an old car
that the owners of the land had for sale, and the way they stick out
the car—they leave it out where people can see it," with a "For Sale"
sign, seems somehow like the way the tree sticks out. The car is "like
a 1950s Chevy or something. And I guess I associate the two of them."
Jane did not think of mechanical work itself in this connection,
though she does think a lot about roads, such as the one that enables
her encounter with the tree: "a very beautiful, winding road," "a
habitated road," "a road I travel a lot." A road ingrained in her. Moreover, Jane thought of a childhood game in which she would clamber
around the furniture trying not to touch the floor, the furniture
representing the treetops. The idea was "to travel through trees," of
"somehow the trees being a road and it'll go where you want to go."
In this image, *Jane* is the car traveling on winding arboreal roads.
Or the car is her tree–animal spirit.

Though Jane's and Will's ways of linking trees and cars differ,
they both challenge the usual way we distinguish trees and the
machine world. We can discover through our imaginations unexpected, and perhaps salutary, combinations where before we saw
only opposition.[36] Aldo Leopold, for instance, combines organic
and mechanical images in his description of communities of land.
His noted essay on "The Land Ethic" sees land as "a fountain of
energy" whose upward flow bears an analogy to that of "sap in a
tree. . . ."[37] But at the same time, he says that "an ethic to supplement
and guide the [dominant] economic relation to land presupposes
the existence of some mental image of land as a biotic mechanism."
And there is love: "It is inconceivable to me that an ethical relation

to land can exist without love, respect, and admiration for land, and a high regard for its value." As with Will (though Leopold would doubtless disagree with much of Will's philosophy), and as with Jaime and Sally and Jane, there is a kind of solidarity, a kind of peace, between the spirit of a tree, human ecological love, a land ethic, and the metal, mechanical, and technological realms.[38] The traditional Kwakiutl would probably recognize the soul in "wood technology."

The Solidarity of the Tree-Feller

Involvement in felling trees can be a form of solidarity with them, as well as estrangement from them. This is perhaps clearest when the tree-feller, as in Kwakiutl tradition, first acknowledges and thanks the spirit or soul of the tree. Less obviously, but no less powerfully, Will and Jane feel a deep, and deeply disturbing, connection between themselves and trees they marked for death. Walt Whitman records a similar experience in "The Song of the Redwood-Tree," which he describes as "a chorus of dryads fading, departing" and a "voice of a mighty dying tree in the redwood forest" while he watches a logging operation. This "in my soul I plainly heard."[39] Though there is pain—"the muffled shriek, the groan"—as the tree falls, what Whitman wants is to evoke the exuberant unfolding of America to which the trees gladly sacrifice themselves—the implication perhaps being that they will live on in Americans who could "here tower proportionate to Nature," like giant trees, or in the great tree, or forest, of the country itself.

American cultural history manifests a long-standing pattern of what Catherine Albanese refers to as "communion with nature through conquest"; this can include communion with the nonhuman in nature through conquest *of the same*.[40] Though Whitman is of more than one mind about it, his poem does portray an infusion of tree-power into the work of destroying a forest.

But *the appropriation of tree-power* through felling trees is a theme with resonance well beyond American history and cultural myth. Robert Pogue Harrison, in discussing "the paradoxical attitude of reverence and hostility toward [forest] origins," traces this theme from Virgil's *Aeneid* to Giambattista Vico's *New Science* (1744) and in the history of scientific thought itself.[41] For "where a primeval forest has already colonized the earth, the first human families had to clear the oak trees in order to plant another kind of tree: the genealogical tree." This refounding would seem to be one of the implications of the scene in Annie Dillard's *The Living* where the felling of a tree corresponds with the cry of a newborn baby (chapter 3, p. 62). What inevitably follows is

> the appropriation of the forest as a metaphor for human institutions. Human beings have by no means exploited the forest only materially; they have also plundered its trees in order to forge their fundamental etymologies, symbols, analogies, structures of thought, emblems of identity, concepts of continuity, and notions of system. *From the family tree to the tree of knowledge, from the tree of life to the tree of memory, forests have provided an indispensable resource of symbolization in the cultural evolution of humankind,* so much so that the rise of modern scientific thinking remains quite unthinkable apart from the prehistory of such metaphorical borrowings.

We can understand those "metaphorical borrowings" as also a way in which we remain in solidarity with trees even when alienated from the forest. And, likewise, as an expression of the tenacity of tree spirits, even when their trees are gone.

William Dietrich, in his account of *The Final Forest: The Battle for the Last Great Trees of the Pacific Northwest,* describes the felling of huge old-growth cedar trees. "There is," he says, "a terrible beauty in this. The fall of a great tree is as instinctively satisfying as a Fourth of July fireworks explosion."[42] The allusion to the *national* image, the celebration of American fire-power and independence, is very much in keeping with the story he witnesses. It echoes Whitman's celebration of the clearing of forests and building of America in his poem "Song of the Broad-Axe"; of the iconic "weapon shapely, naked, wan"; of "the beauty of independence, departure, actions that rely on themselves. . . ."[43]

There is, however, another and more uncanny presence in

Dietrich's account. When the loggers tackle one of these trees, it comes curiously alive. The tree cutter, perched precariously on a steep slope, must first "cut a bite out of the tree" with its center "marking precisely which direction he wants the tree to fall." That "bite" then subtly transforms itself in Dietrich's narrative. Two incisions must be made, a horizontal one and a diagonal one which meet at the center, leaving the shape of a "carved mouth," but the wood remains wedged in between the two incisions because "the tree tends to settle on its wound a bit." So a second logger helps "with this monster" by handing an ax to the cutter, who uses it to knock out the wedge. "The cut leaves a mouth in the cedar tree opened in an expression of mute surprise." The tree has become a *monster*, ambiguously sentient. The tree's "mouth," one senses, could possibly close on its destroyers; and it expresses something. The tree, being old, turns out to be rotted out inside, so the loggers are not able to control the direction in which it falls. The sawing continues until they hear "an ominous crack." The cutter "scrambles in a quick retreat uphill, eyeing the top of the trunk for signs of its intentions. There is another crack and another, a succession of internal snaps of woody tendons like a chain of firecrackers. The effect is eerie. The tree is not moving and yet from its interior are coming all those pops and bangs, as if there were a strange machine inside its bark."

This tree, then, has *intentions,* woody *tendons*—and an interiority that is at the same time a *strange machine.* Consider that machine the estranged soul of the tree; the firecrackers the "crackling" power of a forest spirit like those sensed by the Kwakiutl and other Pacific Northwest coast tribes; the woody tendons the organic medium of machine-soul and forest-spirit; and the intentions of the tree the emergence of our connection with its persisting sentience. For the soul of this tree, which is also its rottedness, has other-than-human intent; as it starts to lean, it "swings a bit, as if considering whether to fall as intended or launch itself straight downhill," which would mean it would shatter and be unsalable. Then "it twists further as if to choose the latter." *As if*, repeats Dietrich, as if to bracket his not quite voluntary suspension of disbelief in independent intentions of trees. For "the effect is eerie." Like anything haunting, it gets stranger as it gets nearer.

The solidarity of the tree-feller can also play an intimate role in biographical woodscapes. Jeff, a tall nineteen-year-old I interviewed in a New York City jail as part of the study on the American self, struggled with his intense violence. The violence was understandable as part of his reaction to a life which he understatedly characterized as "a disaster." He had seen his mother and baby sister die of AIDS contracted from the former's boyfriend, an intravenous drug-user. Jeff hated the violence of the ghetto environment, hated to see "little kids walking around the streets with AK47s." But, warding off his own rage against his mother for the many ways in which she had abandoned him, he told me heatedly that he would kill any of his fellow inmates who said anything bad about his mother. "And that be from my heart."

Jeff mentioned some good job experiences he'd had, so I asked him more about these, wondering if he had any sense of his own possibilities of growth—and hesitant to talk about issues of planetary destruction with him unless I felt he had something to hold on to, something that could affirm life. He replied animatedly that "I used to weld and whatnot. Landscaping was my thing, you know what I'm saying? Chopping down trees and cementing the ground." This was Jeff's only direct reference to trees during the conversation (though he spoke longingly of visits to parks), but it was a revealing one. However briefly, he had found some solidarity with the world, and with the life in himself, through welding, landscaping, chopping down trees. Doing so, "and cementing the ground," moreover, didn't contradict his excitement over times spent in a more rural area north of the city. "It's beautiful up there, man. Everything grow fast. You grow, get big up there because it's like being in the country. . . ." As with David after Hurricane Andrew, there is an indirect but powerful connection between the growth of vegetation, with its arborescent implications, and Jeff's human growth. He immediately went on to talk about the importance of combining "fun" and "responsibility," and his desire to take hold of his first responsibility, "my daughter," born when Jeff was sixteen. In a setting of extreme loss, violence, and social fragmentation exists a kind of underground root system connecting "chopping down trees" and growing "big" like them.

It was not coincidental that Jeff, right after speaking of his landscaping work, criticized the pettiness, as well as the deadliness, of the violence in jail. I think the peace of trees was there, in the dingy jail, as a steadying presence in Jeff. I think it was there when, in talking about the importance of his own growth, Jeff made an assertion with a self-referential element he probably could have recognized: "Life is short, man. You know what I'm saying? So we got to get as much done as we can 'cause we don't never know when we going to go."

The movement in Jeff's story is, despite the despair, not entirely dissimilar from that of an old Alaskan trapper and wood-cutter who says: "When I cut wood, I always look for a tree that is already hurt, got something wrong with it. I don't like to cut down a healthy tree. I think maybe they feel like we do."[44] Jeff could imagine growing big like trees through doing things like chopping them down. Felling trees itself can involve an ability to feel like they do.

Good Humor

A certain kind of humor comes with trees. The "old shagbark" that enlivened Danny exemplifies that humor—a droll, ironic, playful spirit that plays upon our combination of intimacy with trees and estrangement from them. It celebrates the oddness, power, and persistence of trees—and often allows for their personified appearance. In the person of Treebeard, for instance, we hear humor in his comments to his hobbit friends, as when he tells them before going to sleep: "You can lie on the bed. I am going to stand in the rain. Good night!" In this way Treebeard sharpens the contrast between himself and the hobbits, asserting *his* character and at the same time implicitly mocking their estrangement from undomesticated nature. But he can also mock himself, as when he says, "I am not very, hm, bendable," which may imply a wish that he could be more like the hobbits than he is. An ironic humor inheres even in Treebeard's reference to the evil wizard ("Curse him, root and branch!"). Even the enemy of trees—the person who is most different from them— is nonetheless, as we've already suggested, peculiarly treeish. Even when Treebeard is angry, his humor is good.

The short, seasonally based essays in Aldo Leopold's *A Sand Country Almanac* are often particularly masterful in their employment of tree humor. In one essay, he offers a loving description of "my pines" which he has planted on his Wisconsin farm. Noting that pine shoots each spring store all the rain and solar energy to be used for the following year's growth, Leopold says: "If you are thriftily inclined, you will find pines congenial company, for, unlike the hand-to-mouth hardwoods, they never pay current bills out of current earnings; they live solely on their savings of the year before. In fact every pine carries an open bankbook, in which his cash balance is recorded by 30 June of each year."[45] The power of these pines—and Leopold's admiration for them—comes through in his humorous, but ecologically precise, description of them; and the humor in turn depends on the human–tree analogy. Yet it can be as serious as the pines themselves. "Hard years," he says, "are recorded as shorter thrusts, i.e., shorter spaces between the successive whorls of branches"; and one can date a hard year by subtracting "one from the year of lesser growth. Thus the 1937 growth was short in all pines; this records the universal drouth of 1936. On the other hand the 1941 growth was long in all pines; perhaps they saw the shadow of things to come, and made a special effort to show the world that pines still know where they are going, even though men do not."

In an article called "Root and Branch in the Groves of Academe," the science writer Stephen Young notes: "Trees are indispensable to science. From physics to physiology, they serve as metaphors, expressing in a word details that would otherwise occupy a paragraph. They range from the momentous to the prosaic, from Charles Darwin's great Tree of Life to a layout for distributing cable television. In science, the intellectual landscape is everywhere a veritable thicket."[46] A survey of the history of science trees leads him to conclude: "If trees did not exist, scientists would have to invent them." The humor helps us to feel simultaneously the power of the tree and the provisional nature of metaphor. Its celebratory character comes through because it remains indirect, restrained. We do feel in some way restored by it, reminded of the *persistence* of trees in life and in science; yet at the same time that persistence is rendered less abstract, categorical, spiritualized.

The celebration in the humor, and the multifaceted metaphoric nature of trees, is perhaps a bit clearer in a couple of articles dating from after the October '87 Gale in England and after Hurricane Andrew. In the *London Sunday Observer* of 1 November 1987, we read of "budding hope as expert maps out new root" in the study of dendrology.[47] The hope is released by the pun, which becomes a manysided mirror of tree and human continuity. Similar to this is a subheading in an article written about the righting of trees in South Florida's gardens and preserves: "Getting a lift."[48] The psychological resonance here is immediately apparent (remember David's response to his trees being righted)—a playful way of combining great pain with hope. In a discussion of the evolutionary value of trees, there is a heading with an unwitting yet similar kind of play on the human–tree parallel: "Human Roots in the Forest/Savanna."[49]

The good humor of trees proliferates in bad puns—for instance, in titles of articles about trees.[50] They may evoke culture, as in "Roots" (about TreePeople, a highly successful Los Angeles-based urban tree-planting organization); "Leaves of Gas" (on the contribution of trees to photochemical smog in Atlanta); "Sex and the Single Tree" (about the propagation of tulip trees); and "A Tree Grows in Manhattan" (on a 102-year-old Chinese elm that has produced 2,000 seedlings—count them). These, of course, are all trees of memory, like those in another title: "Woody Witnesses: Tree Rings Provide Evidence of an 1812 San Andreas Quake." Then there are tree spirits of everyday sayings and clichés: "How the Wind Rubs Trees up the Wrong Way"; "Top This!"; "Searching for a Breath of Clean Air"; "Turning off the Maples"—the latter two on the effects of pollution and acid precipitation on trees. Even air pollution can personify itself (as a tree, that is): "Ozone Needles Loblolly Pines . . . and Saps Sequoia Seedlings." As well, we share with trees economic concerns: "U.S. Cities Axe Tree Budgets"; "How to Avoid Being Clipped by a Tree Trimmer." Some trees wage defensive war, as in "Tree Tactics" (how trees defend themselves against insect herbivores), or become aggressively expansionistic, as in "The Trees Are Taking Over" (about exotic colonizing tree species in the Everglades). There are happy and not-so-happy titles, like "Happiness Is a Green Tree" and "Would You Like to See a Grown Tree Weep?" (on "training" trees to grow weeping branches).

Finally, some good advice: "Go Ahead, Hug a Tree: It's Good
for You" and (for dendrochronologists and other lovers) "Make a
Date with a Tree."

Tree humor can also come spiced with eeriness, an evocation of Trees
of Fear. There can be "haunted-house trees," as one woman put it.
Or twilit trees that, as she said, with a playful gesture of her arm
and a mock menacing tone, wave hello to you: "Hi, there!" A 1987
Spanish film, *El Bosque Animado* ("The Animated Forest"), takes
this spirit in the direction of an unsparing, yet compassionate, depiction of the picaresque lives of Galician villagers that becomes a biting
but humorous commentary on oddness, loneliness, the contradic-
toriness of the Catholic church, class, sex, and sudden death. In the
forest adjacent to the village lives a man who decides to become
a bandit, only to encounter a ghost that scares away potential victims. After his own initial fright, the wannabe bandit befriends the
ghost, but only to get him to leave the forest. But, as the latter tells
him, "every forest has a right to its ghost."
    Treebeard's humor can be similar, as in the hobbits' initial en-
counter with him. Standing on a hill by the "old stump of a tree"
that turns out to be Treebeard, the hobbits survey the "frightfully
tree-ish" forest in fleeting sunlight. "What a pity!" says one to his
companion. "This shaggy old forest looked so different in the
sunlight. I almost felt I liked the place."[51] Whereupon they are startled
by the stump's response: "Almost felt you liked the Forest! That's
good! That's uncommonly kind of you."

Finally, of course, trees themselves can be just plain funny—or
awkward, or foolish-looking, almost self-mocking. It's in their nature.
Jane could laud this in her recognition that certain of the trees in
her paintings were "funny presences." But when that funny presence
took a more awkward form—the cartoon-style God, "kind of funny-
awkward," it became harder to reconcile with what she wanted to
focus on—even though she was reminded of "my own slapstick sides."
Yet, as suggested earlier, that God, "long-limbed," in a contorted
predicament, is in his way a faithful mirror of the shape of the tree,
its own more vulnerable character. The tree is like the old mulberry
whose aging paralleled that of Sally's father, "leaning more strongly

on its support. . . ." In another way it is like the palms a botanist at Fairchild Tropical Garden calls, affectionately, "caricatures in a way" of "real trees" like an oak or an elm—"comical in a certain way." Mischa, likewise, noted that, "sorry to say," in Russia an oak can be a "metaphor for 'stupid man,' . . . thick, stout, and in a sense clumsy." When we think of trees as funny, their specific oddities have grown intimate with us—and, perhaps, our own oddities intimate with them. It is because of how trees are that they so acutely mirror the world's foibles. We can learn from them about the art of self-caricature. They figure an ecology of laughter. They *should* be in cartoons sometimes, because they help create them. If trees did not exist, humorists would have to invent them.

Trees, Water, Manatees

There was one endangered species of marine mammal, very "friendly," that Jaime was compelled to mention, even though "it's not connected to the forests," and he hasn't even seen one firsthand. Certainly it is not associated with forests and Jaime's feeling for them in any obvious way, though the indirect links are the impulses toward preservation and toward friendship. In the Mediterranean, Jaime said, they're "called manatees . . . I think there's one species that's native to Florida and it's protected."

Trees, water, and manatees do somewhat more directly connect the Filipino rainforest activist to Will, though they have never met. Will was quick to tell me, in December of 1989, that he, his wife, and teenage son had gone on a crucial Thanksgiving vacation: they "went to North Florida to [scuba-]dive in some of the springs." The trip had been a profound moment of renewal—because of manatees, as well as water and trees. Manatees, explained Will, "winter over in the fresh water springs" of North Florida, and the family had swum with them. Will described them with reverent enthusiasm: "They're a calm, gentle giant. I mean" they weigh "tons, and you're just dwarfed by 'em in the water." The "elephant [and its] little calf" will "come up to you, and just nuzzle ya, and want to be petted." The encounter with the manatees was for Will a real "high point" of the trip. He contrasted it with going "crazy in the destruction and depression" following Hugo: "Doin' nothin' but snorkeling and layin' in the water and watchin' these big peaceful animals, you know, that was salvation."

Will had also been surprised by something his son had said during the ride home. Will had asked him: "What do you like best about" the vacation? And his son "said, 'Dad, there's trees.' And he'd thought about it. I mean, we'd gone to go scuba-divin' underwater, and his impression was, it was fun because there were trees." Will was in fact flabbergasted by this remark, not least because "that's an impression on a fourteen-year-old that you wouldn't expect to come out of their mouth." It was especially surprising because it came just after "swim[ming] with an animal that's been here for eons." I also think it moved Will because (though there is no reason to doubt the primacy of his feelings for the manatees) he himself was also greatly relieved to see trees, and in our conversation seemed to voice this feeling through his son's words. For his tale came in reply to a question about *his* response to what he had called "the massive destruction that's beyond any comprehension of what you can describe." His son's response echoes that of the pained Kwakiutl Indian who goes for healing into the forest and for a time "does not think of anything but the supernatural spirits of the trees."

If Will and Jaime were to meet, you can imagine a pretty heated discussion: Will scoffing at Jaime's defense of "virgin" forests and his anger toward loggers; and Jaime lambasting Will for his stress on the economic use-value of trees and his likening of radical environmentalists to Ayatollah Khomeini. And yet, the two men, different as they are—the "dyed-in-the-wool" American "hillbilly" who's never been to the big city (let alone out of the United States) and the ardent Filipino rainforest activist living half-way around the world from his home—have some things in common: a love for trees, water, manatees. When Jaime says, "Maybe I can do something" to help preserve the manatees, Will would agree with him on that point. And Jaime would have been united with Will in the latter's enthusiasm for swimming with "these big peaceful animals" that have "been here for eons" and will "come up to you, and just nuzzle ya, and want to be petted." Something about the friendliness of these animals, and their presence in water, would probably bring together the most different people in a common love. Water, of course, is also psychologically powerful; that's why Ivan got relief from a hard subject by going in his mind to the water, together with the trees, of Central Park.

Water also connects trees and manatees. Both need it; both are gentle, big, friendly. Both evoke the endangerment of species. Both easily suggest a massive solidarity between the human and non-human, a basic love. Water is not only around but *in* both trees and manatees—and Jaime and Will. The link between trees and water is deep, which is why trees so capably solicit tears, as well as our own more fluid, porous selves. And water can evoke trees: while Will's son didn't put it this way, it's probably fair to say that his time in the water with manatees helped him (and, in the narrative's implication, Will himself) to feel more deeply the presence and loss of trees. For trees and water are drawn erotically toward each other. And in the "water" of our talk of trees, so too Will, Jaime, and manatees. The arboreal imagination can flow anywhere in the world. Jaime and Will are joined by a swimming sea of trees.

CHAPTER 7

Walking in Aphrodite's Woods

TREES DISTINGUISH THEMSELVES in particular ways—characteristics that could sustain themselves in conversations with residents of Homestead, Florida, after Hurricane Andrew. The characteristics of trees reach us in myriad shapes—some obvious, some less visible, and some unexpected. Mythic and imaginative ramifications of trees can be further explored in a way that stays close to their distinctness and power. In both the most inclusive sense and in distinctly identifiable ways, this power involves desire, has an erotic life. The myth of "Aphrodite's Woods" we're about to enter contains and evokes, in subtly evolved ways, a widely various array of psychological patterns that thrive among trees. Amidst these woods are many possibilities for love, for the ecstasy that can be associated with sexuality, beauty, and religion—and also with rage and death. There are shelter and sanctuary and meditative solitude in these woods, but also shadows inclusive of terror. There are enduring grief and that human commitment which trees can call forth. There are pristine wilderness and cosmopolitan sophistication and the ways these are present in city and country and contemporary ecological awareness. There is a hint of primary oneness, but that remains only a part of the variegated woodscape. Aphrodite is a particular Goddess with a particular character, but at the same time a *perspective* through which we can evoke other characters, cultures, and places that are associated with trees.

The Trees, the Cocktail Lounge, and Nature's Temple

David Rains Wallace was about nine years old when he first discovered *Bulow Hammock*.[1] These turned out to be strangely cosmopolitan woods. "The hammock [a subtropical Florida hardwood grove] was . . . seductive"; and there was the smell, the "perfumey sweetness that reminded me of the hotel lobbies and cocktail lounges I'd occasionally been in with my parents." The human and forest worlds mingle in memory, are not apart. And that mingling is first through "a perfumey sweetness" that makes the forest so seductive. But "Bulow Hammock smelled stranger than liquor and perfume. It smelled intricately spicy, with a sweetness not so much of flowers as of aromatic bark and leaves. There was also an air of decay in the sweetness," and when the boy scraped the ground he uncovered "white sand and a network of fine, blackish roots like the hair of a buried animal." The smell and the seductiveness of this grove, continues Wallace, felt "dangerous, . . . inhibiting . . . to my nine-year-old mind." Death and humanity dwelled in the seduction, danger, and inhibition. This forest is not exactly a place of freedom from civilization, Wallace reflected:

> It is interesting to recall how *little* of freedom there was in my first perception of Bulow Hammock, how little of the unfettered feeling I got in . . . other open places that promised release from streets and classrooms. I wonder if the hammock inhibited me because there was more of humanity about it than a dune, meadow, or pine forest has; not of humanity in the sense of society and civilization . . . but of animal humanity. . . .

"Animal humanity" is both exciting and dangerous. It is excited by the beauty of the forest floor and "canopy of live oak, red bay, magnolia and cabbage palmetto"; but the hammock's "seductiveness was also a warning because it hinted at passionate entanglement more than freedom or tranquility."

We encounter a combination of sensual beauty, excitement, and strange familiarity among other trees as well. For instance, the Forest of Symbols in Charles Baudelaire's poem "Correspondences":

> Nature is a temple where living pillars
> Sometimes let out confused words.
> Man passes there through forests of symbols
> Which observe him with a familiar gaze.

Like long echoes confounded from a distance
In an obscure and deep unity,
Vast as the night or as clarity itself,
Scents, colors, and sounds respond to one another.

There are perfumes fresh as the flesh of children,
Sweet like oboes, green as prairies,
—And others corrupt, rich, and triumphant,

Having the expansion of infinite things,
Like amber, musk, bergamot, and incense,
Which sing the transport of the mind and the senses.[2]

Nature's temple, watching trees, a sensual spirit, an infinite expanse:
for Baudelaire, nonhuman nature is not unadorned but a seductive
pattern of correspondences between senses that discloses "infinite
things." As Wallace's reverie suggests, cocktail lounges and hotel lobbies can be part of Nature's temple. The later Baudelaire, as Robert
Pogue Harrison observes, could "speak of nature in wholly negative
terms."[3] But what he means by that is nature stripped of its own
imaginations, its infinitely sensual faces. In his essay entitled "In Praise
of Cosmetics," Baudelaire speaks of a beautifully adorned woman
as embodying nature's deeper correspondences, the symbolic density of the forest; of a mystical cosmetics that "restores to nature
its aspect of the temple, bringing the forests of symbols to a woman's
face." We need not follow Baudelaire's argument and tastes literally
to ask: Who is this curiously cosmopolitan Woman of Forests? This
question brings us to the "Homeric Hymn to Aphrodite."

Aphrodite's Woods

The hymn in question honors Aphrodite in what seems a strange
way. For Zeus has turned the tables on her. Usually it is Zeus who
is seized by Aphrodite's power, but this time he arranges for her to
be overtaken by her own desire, resulting in her love for Anchises,
a shepherd. With him she spends one night at his place on Mount
Ida, thereby becoming pregnant with Aeneas.[4] Ashamed over hav-

ing been drawn into a love affair with a mortal, Aphrodite wants it kept secret. She insists that the child be brought up at first by mountain nymphs and that Anchises claim that his son is one of their offspring. Aphrodite tells how these nymphs spend their lives: together "with the immortals they do [a] lovely, lusty dance, mingling in love with the Silenoi [men with horse tails and hooves—ritual dancers] and the sharp-eyed Slayer of Argos [Hermes] in the depths of dark caves." These nymphs are neither mortal nor immortal, but they are long-lived, says Aphrodite. And related to trees:

> at the moment of [their] birth pines and high-crowned oaks grow up from the nourishing earth: Beautiful trees they are, flourishing on high mountains. Their towering stands are called groves of the undying; men, who die, don't touch them with the axe. But when the fated time of death arrives, first the trees, so beautiful, wither upon the ground; all about them their bark dies and decays; then the branches fall away until, at the same time, the soul of the nymphs and of the trees leaves the light of the sun.[5]

Aphrodite, in this passage, reveals that she is an observant ecologist. While she is not talking about a vast primary forest, she is addressing remnants of one, where trees are free to die. Contemporary biological research on primary-forest ecosystems resonates with Aphrodite's words. Something of her voice and vision appears in the belated recognition of the richness of the old-growth forests in the Pacific Northwest, where the standing dead trees or "snags" and fallen (or "nurse") logs—in what used to be referred to as a "biological wasteland"—are now acknowledged, as they are in Kwakiutl mythology, as essential nourishers of the region's life. "Dead trees," in the words of one writer, "are what the forest grows on. . . ."[6] A recent volume on *America's Rainforests* describes the death of trees in words like Aphrodite's:

> The strong, tall trees of the ancient forest age and eventually succumb to the rigors of weather, disease, fungi and other devastating effects. Long before it is visible, life begins to leave an ancient tree. Its top broken or trunk diseased, an ancient tree dies slowly and remains standing for decades. Snags deteriorate from top to bot-

tom, and from outside to inside. Losing its bark, needles and branches, a three-hundred foot monolith eventually becomes a tall stump which crumbles to the ground, continuing the cycle of death into life.[7]

Aphrodite's words are amplified with more technical precision in an article on "Tree Death as an Ecological Process: The Causes, Consequences, and Variability of Tree Mortality," by a forest ecologist named Jerry Forest Franklin and two of his colleagues.[8] Franklin is the noted proponent of "New Forestry," a forest-management technique designed to mime the ecological cycles of an old-growth forest and thus avoid the kinds of devastation resulting from traditional logging practices; and he brings to his work decades of scientific study and close aesthetic appreciation of the forest.[9] His article can be appreciated as both a scientific account and an image of Aphrodite's woods—a meditation on "tree death as a rich ecological" occurrence illustrating "that many valid and useful perspectives on a single, presumably simple process exist."

A tree, "in its dead form, . . . continues to play numerous roles as it influences surrounding organisms." Its soul, though no longer in the light of day, persists. "Of course, the impact of the individual tree gradually fades as it is decomposed and its resources dispersed, but the woody structure may remain for centuries and influence habitat conditions." The soul is salmon, in the Kwakiutl image, because the decaying log may, paradoxically, contain a much higher proportion of living (fungal and other) cells than the standing tree and is "a major new resource for the ecosystem. . . ." The soul is machine, because "tree death . . . may do important mechanical work"—the work, essentially, of furthering the growth of the forest. The organic and the mechanical are interwoven with the beauty, the life, the sadness. Trees may be predisposed to die by many "biotic factors" ("old age, senescence, mechanical imbalance, starvation, consumption, disease") which contribute to "mechanical failure." Ecological science has come to see that, like the gradual fading of the "beautiful trees" of which Aphrodite speaks, "tree death . . . is more frequently a complex and gradual process with multiple contributors"—"an arbitrary point on a continuum." It is that point when soul goes under, which in the old-growth forest is all the time.

When Franklin hikes, he enters Aphrodite's woods in a different way. His wife, affectionately, says, "He's like a child. He whistles, he yodels, he names birds, he talks to the animals, he points out every new little flower. He expresses awe at every change of color around the seasons."[10] They had been married the year Franklin's article appeared; early on, he felt he needed to take his wife to an old-growth grove he especially loved. "He wanted to explain himself to his new bride. 'He wanted the trees to meet me,' she recalled." Franklin and the trees had met when he was a Boy Scout of eight; his first encounter with the grove was "a kind of epiphany." He explained to his wife that "he felt he received a mission . . . to speak for the trees." Though he subsequently became a scientific expert on old-growth ecosystems, the trees kept their spirit. "The scientist sat with [his wife] in the grove, explaining this mysterious thing that had driven him since childhood as the trees reared like pillars overhead. He cried a bit, she recalled."

Tree Deaths

The beauty of woods mothers the death of trees. When that death is part of the sort of process Franklin describes, we can, with Aphrodite, find beauty in it. The beautiful trees wither, their bark decays, and their branches fall away, and then, at the *same* moment—Aphrodite is very precise about this—the soul (*psychē*) of the nymphs and of the trees leaves the light of day. There can be an eeriness in this simultaneity, as in Jung's association between spirits and the souls of the departed (chapter 4, p. 98). And a respect, as indicated by Dave's, Jane's, and Will's affirmations of the importance of dead or dying trees. This more complex vision of beauty acknowledges the psychological and aesthetic presence of dead trees. In Aphrodite's woods, even they are spared the axe.

Further, *Death itself* is "spared the axe"; in these woods no one is cut off from death. The connection between dying trees and *human* aging and dying is highlighted in the hymn by Aphrodite's allusion, immediately before her descriptions of semi-mortal nymphs and trees, to the fates of two men, Ganymede and Tithonos, who are said to have attained deathlessness. Ganymede, abducted by Zeus, was nonetheless mourned by his father. Tithonos, with whom the Goddess of Dawn, Eos (a double of Aphrodite), fell in love, is granted freedom from death at the Goddess's wishes—but she forgets to ask for his freedom from "hateful" old age and senility. The immortality of these men is dubious at best, and Tithonos seems to have Alzheimer's Disease. Aphrodite could never take Anchises for her husband, she tells him, because unavoidable and deadly old age will soon be at his own side. The specter of the withering trees and their dying nymphs embodies this awareness. Will's concerns about the "mature" or "climax" (or post-Hugo) forest place him, perhaps against his will, within Aphrodite's woods. In objecting to the "huge, old, dyin'" trees, Will yet gives them a voice.

The slow death of trees, singly or collectively, is a primary way they make their presence known—in the old-growth forests, and everywhere around them. This is how the tree stories of Will, Jane, Sally, and others unfold. Aphrodite's tale echoes in different ways through contemporary encounters with irrevocable arboreal losses. Claiming public attention first were those forests, such as higher-elevation Appalachian forests in the United States and the Black Forest in Germany, which suffer from the effects of acid rain or other pollutants. Then came images of human-created desolation in tropical and temperate rainforests, in other old-growth forests, including the Russian taiga. The disturbing power of damaged trees is their way of making it harder for us to ignore or forget them. Their speech commands our closest attention. However disturbing and disheartening are the visages of dying and dead trees, they contain and evoke memories of beauty. They speak in Bill McKibben's description of what greenhouse warming could eventually do to the forests of his home in southwestern New York state:

> The trees will die. Consider nothing more than that—just that the trees will die. When I walk outdoors in the morning, instead of the slopes of trees, instead of the craggy white pines on the ridge toward Buck Hill, there may be yellowing and browning leaves and needles, thinning crowns, dead branches, and rotting stumps. [11]

The trees become their own coffins. The intimation carries us further, hinting at a coffin for nature, for the world itself.

Dying trees have come to prefigure a dying of the world. Ivan, for instance, is unable to sustain his image of being at peace among the trees of Central Park. For the destruction of the environment proceeds "slowly but surely as time goes on. You can look at the trees. That's something I notice each year. Less and less . . . there are less leaves on the trees." Perhaps Ivan is thinking of the London planes planted throughout the city, which are affected by a blight that begins to eat away at their leaves almost as soon as they sprout in the spring. Graceful trees, with lumpy trunks and mottled, peeling bark, these planes start shedding their leaves in late July. The fallen leaves give off an autumnal scent after rain in humid heat; walking over them at that time gives one an unsettling out-of-season feeling. For Ivan, the loss of leaves carries a planetary significance.

Jessica, a twenty-year-old Brooklyn woman, links the destruction of tropical rainforests, together with their animals and indigenous peoples, with nuclear threat and human mortality: "We can grow, we can live, just like the trees . . . and everything. So they're slowly dying. So are we."[12] The gradual dying of trees endures in imagination, speaking to the slow dying of ourselves in an ecological catastrophe that contains echoes of nuclear holocaust.

At the same time, Jessica's words hint at the older dimension of the trees' *slow dying.* Ted's injured friends, the live oaks, may die in the same incremental way. Hugo has left "live oaks that are just going to be . . . a skeleton of a tree standing there for a long, long time. They'll slowly rot and the limbs drop off." Their fate announces the inevitable outcome of life—arboreal, animal, human. Because of the long-lived resiliency of these trees as well as their noted beauty, their death, before Hugo and after, stands starkly in Ted's mind. "Occasionally," he continued, "one will die, be struck by lightning, contract some type of disease, just get weak and—perhaps they die from old age, I sort of doubt it." Even the trees felled by the sudden Andrew could die slowly. Thus William Klein, at Fairchild Tropical Garden, ponders "the slow kind of death that overtakes them. Are they conscious of the fact that life is seeping away? And [there is] a sadness, an extreme sadness, at that kind of loss."

Wendell Berry, in his poem on "The Old Elm Tree by the River," conjures the power in arboreal images of the dying and dead:

> Shrugging in the flight of its leaves,
> it is dying. Death is slowly
> standing up in its trunk and branches
> like a camouflaged hunter. In the night
> I am wakened by one of its branches
> crashing down, heavy as a wall, and then
> lie sleepless, the world changed. . . .[13]

Our biographical worlds are indeed changed, irrevocably so, when trees that have given them shape and shelter die off. No wonder contemporary concerns over the fate of trees and forests can give the desire to change the world a peculiar and intimate intensity.

We encounter the trees of Aphrodite's woods in many places and times; their psychological nature points beyond their narrower cultural context. In Aphrodite's sense of the links between death and beauty in the woods, for instance, Greek mythology comes close to the traditional Japanese grasp of natural beauty that also includes death and the dying. Old, dying, and dead trees, as well as deadwood and driftwood, find places in Japanese Zen gardens. With this meeting of cultural souls in mind, let us make a return trip to the postnuclear realms of Hiroshima and Nagasaki. For these places, as we saw earlier, also speak to us through ecological loss. Let us listen to their claims on us, articulated through a speech of trees. And to the trees that speak in turn through those claims.

Robert Jay Lifton, in his exploration of the psychological effects of the atomic bombing, noted the power of the dead trees of Hiroshima:

> That part of nature which had been destroyed—half-burnt dead trees throughout the city—made people uncomfortable until removed. A story is told of how Prince Takamatsu, the Emperor's brother, during a second visit to Hiroshima in December, 1945, noted with approval that the burnt trees were no longer visible; as the Prince made his comment, it is said, he playfully assumed

the posture of a Japanese ghost (by holding his two hands loosely in front of himself).[14]

Ghosts figured by trees: a stark counterpart to the withered trees in Aphrodite's woods whose soul leaves the light of day. No longer visible in that light, the dead trees of Hiroshima and Nagasaki stand still. Their spirits inhabit and move the prince's body. Such trees' "gestures," to borrow Jane's image, are indelible. And embodied as well are the *kami* and ghosts of the land. For just as the *kami* or sacred power originally descended to and dwelled in trees and forests, and constructed shrines later took their place, the Prince momentarily makes his body a shrine for the trees of Hiroshima.[15]

In "The Colorless Paintings," a story by Ineko Sata about the psychological aftermath of the atomic bombing, dead and ghostly trees adumbrate the emotional and physical death of a Nagasaki painter from what the survivors call "A-bomb disease." Narrated by a friend of the painter, the story is set in an art gallery where his last two paintings are hanging posthumously. The other gallery paintings are vibrantly hued, and the narrator recalls a colorful earlier oil painting by the artist hanging in her home: "It's a scene of the hilly part of Nagasaki, with bright sky and a pink Western-style house set among brilliant green trees."[16]

The colorless paintings are starkly positioned in this colorful background:

> They are . . . done entirely in shades of white tinged with gray. Both are landscapes. One, abstract in style, has a foreground with two trees in it, looking as if they were a sheet of stretched cloth. The other depicts three thin, withered trees painted in slight gradations of white and gray. They remind me of the dead trees standing in . . . swamps. . . .

The story conveys a longing for the brilliant green of trees—the psychological and physical life—taken away by the bomb, while suggesting a conflict-ridden attempt to "paint" over the horror (together with associated Japanese conflicts about Westernization) and the isolation of the survivors who cannot escape the ghosts that remain: dead trees of their souls. At the same time, there is a traditional sense and sensuality of sad beauty, what the Japanese call *mono no aware,* which pervades the whole and is exemplified by the juxtaposed images of green and of the dead, withered swamp trees. The dead trees, not without irony, hint, like the Prince's gesture, at the ancient sense of certain trees imbued with sacred vitality and presence—including all trees whose soul must leave the daylit world. "Framed in thin white pieces of wood, the pictures, surrounded by a world of bright colors, seem like softly moaning heretics." It takes hard listening to hear them.

These trees speak to us, who are all, finally, in Aphrodite's woods, where the dying trees and the dead are left to live. Such trees nourish moral and ecological concern. Again, the salmon of Bukwis comes to mind. As long as there are trees, we may be food. Says Will, who would want to die in "the woods," "I'd much rather a bear eat me than a hospital room." Remember that he has said to his family that, if he gets too old, "they ought to take me to the mountains or out in a swamp, and open the door, and tell me to walk that way." Thereby he evoked particular American placescapes, Southeastern forests of beautiful and dying trees (with their "biodiversity," he said), and their characters, Hillbilly and Swamp Rat. But not American only, for tree spirits belong to no single nationality and speak to us of many places. We're also in the territory of the man who painted bright green trees on Nagasaki hills and then, before he died, "dead trees . . . in swamps."

Shadows

The role of Hermes in the Homeric hymn suggests another dimension of death in Aphrodite's woods. When she first appears to Anchises, her beauty is such that she must convince him she *isn't* a Goddess before he dares make love with her. So she tells him, in an ironically humorous confabulation, that she was one of the girls playing in the train of the virgin Goddess Artemis and herself "without experience in love," but was seized by Hermes and carried first over domesticated countryside and then "shady dwellings" of wild beasts to Anchises' place. During this ecstatic journey, Hermes told her she should wed Anchises.

Hermes here acts curiously like Hades, Lord of the Underworld. Hades seized (or raped) the maiden Persephone in a similar situation, when she was playing with other nymphs, and carried her back with him to the realm of shades. (In another ironic reversal, in the story of Persephone it is Hermes who eventually comes to take the young woman *back* from Hades to rejoin her mother.) Aphrodite's "fantasy" hints at the true underworld context shading the background of her woods where tree nymphs mingle with Hermes in gloomy caves. Gloomy caves (in one of which Hermes himself was born after Zeus and his nymph-mother, Maia, made love) signify Hades. So do the "shady dwellings" Aphrodite mentions—though in a more indirect way. The Greek word for "shady"—or "shadowy" —comes from a noun whose secondary meaning is specifically the shade or shadows of trees, but whose primary meaning is "shade" in the sense of "ghost," an underworld dweller.[17]

We get a sense of both meanings in an offhand remark made by a businessman (and participant in the study of the American self) recalling his childhood trips in Europe with his father, a historian: "With his sense of history and all the things that he knew, . . . he brought the shadows out of . . . the forest and put . . . flesh and blood on 'em." In the shadows the forest gathers to itself, history and prehistory are remembered simultaneously.

There can be something more frightening in underworldly woods—shadows of trees of war. Going back to Vietnam mountains, we remember the setting in which Curt Lemon died (chapter 5, pp. 144–45)—in "deep jungle," beneath "the shade of some giant trees—quadruple canopy, no sunlight at all. . . . I remember the smell of moss. Up in the canopy there were tiny white blossoms, but no sunlight at all, and I remember the shadows spreading out under the trees. . . ."[18]

Just as in those shadows, there is a hint of death terror in Aphrodite's woods. For Hermes, lover from a gloomy cave, has quite a history of sex with pine and oak nymphs. One of his offspring is the goat-God Pan—panic, terror, and nightmare. In the "Homeric Hymn to Pan," Hermes is tending sheep for a mortal man when he is overwhelmed with an urgent yearning for the "nymph of Dryops" —*Oak Man*—with her beautiful (foliaged) hair.[19] When Pan is born, his goat-footed and horned appearance scares half to death the nurse

who attended his birth. A tree has given birth to fear. Pan, the nightmare God, embodies that presence of trees in Gordon Park's dream
of Southern terror (chapter 4, pp. 105–06).

That presence comes more clearly into view in another of Tim
O'Brien's Vietnam stories—a tale of the transformation of a soldier's
girlfriend, who comes to live with him at his medical detachment
amidst the mountains, into the "Sweetheart of the Song Tra Bong"—
"ready for the kill."[20] When Mary Anne, a pretty and innocent-look-
ing girl just out of high school, arrives, the soldiers are nonplussed.
She is curious about everything, like "What was behind those scary
green mountains to the west?" It happens that at the perimeter of
the detachment is a Green Beret outpost. "Secretive and suspicious,
loners by nature, the six Greenies would sometimes vanish for days
at a time, . . . and . . . late in the night just as magically reappear,
moving like shadows through the moonlight, filing in silently from
the dense rain forest off to the west." Mary Anne is drawn to them,
and one night her boyfriend is horrified to discover her sleeping there.
"I mean, in a way she was sleeping with all of them, more or less,
except it wasn't sex or anything. . . . Mary Anne and these six grungy
weirded-out Green Berets." Mary Anne and the Greenies are seven
spirits of the forest. "The wilderness seemed to draw her in. A
haunted look [was on her face] . . . partly terror, partly rapture."
She goes into the forest with the Greenies for three weeks, and then
one night "a column of silhouettes appeared as if by magic at the
edge of the jungle. At first [her boyfriend] didn't recognize her—a
small, soft shadow among six other shadows." At this point her eyes
"seemed to shine in the dark"—"a bright glowing jungle green."

These green eyes remind us of those of the vagabond in Carson McCullers's café, in that they are not the usual environmental
or ideal green. But they are deadlier; Mary Anne's love embraces
terror; she has become a killer. And, on patrol with the Greenies,
"she took crazy, death-wish chances" that were "played out in the
dense terrain of a nightmare." Finally, she takes off on her own, never
to be seen again. Except that the Greenies seemed to see her in the
forest. "Odd movements, odd shapes. Late at night, when the
Greenies were out on ambush, the whole rain forest seemed to stare
in at them—a watched feeling—and a couple of times they almost
saw her sliding through the shadows. Not quite, but almost. She

had crossed to the other side." Her estrangement from the human world was complete, and her intimacy with the forest consummated. "She was part of the land," its nightmare.

Erotic Loves

In Aphrodite's woods, terror is mostly hidden; but in the shadows it does remain, a disclosure of the woods' dense complexity. They can suggest forms of death and terror that are avoidable. But these woods also speak of deaths, and hint at terrors, that are inevitable, life-affirming, like death in the old-growth forest. Like the "hemlock" in Thoreau's "arbor-vitae." Like love.

Hermes' links with death have much to do with love, as his erotic dance with the oak and pine nymphs shows. It is the dance of mortal and immortal going wild amidst trees and dark cavernous places. The shadows of trees and trees themselves can move and dance in the imagination. Jane spoke of Trees that "are such dancers." "Trees in the wind, . . . I find so hypnotic. . . . also trees look like they're dancing when there is no wind. . . ." More, they can inspire a dance, stir our bodies to movement and celebration, move us briefly beyond the mortal.

Aphrodite can get us into trees in a very sexual way. The sexual dimension of "going into the trees," or of trees themselves, is in fact a time-honored literary convention. Wendell Berry evokes this sexual forest in "The Country of Marriage": "A man lost in the woods in the dark, I stood / still and said nothing. And then there rose in me, like the earth's empowering brew rising / in root and branch, the words of a dream of you. . . ."[21] Rainer Maria Rilke shows us that such images, however intimate and personal, are also archaic, impersonal, "immortal":

> . . . when we love, a sap
> from a time before memory
> rises in our limbs.[22]

Both sex and eros connect Carson McCullers's biographical woodscapes and her story "A Tree • A Rock • A Cloud." She wrote it in early 1942, when recuperating from wasting physical and psychological ills at her parents' home in Columbus, Georgia. She had been devastated by the breakup of her marriage with Reeves McCullers (whom she subsequently remarried). At the time, Carson was also deeply in love with a Swiss woman writer, but in the process of realizing that they would remain forever physically apart (so that fantasies related to her would grow, one could say, greenly exuberant in their correspondence and in McCullers's fiction). This frustrated desire may in turn have called forth one of McCullers's own greatest losses: in her late teens, her woman piano teacher had to move out of the area. Like the vagabond of "A Tree • A Rock • A Cloud," McCullers experienced the loss of a woman in a deep and enduring way.

Too, McCullers's love of nonhuman nature has its own intensely erotic consciousness. She especially loved to walk in the woods, as Virginia Spencer Carr, her biographer, says. At her writer's retreat in upstate New York, she walked in snowy woods, "for the rapidly falling flakes seemed to be [the] snow" of the woman she loved, "and the black firs, her forest." The predawn setting of "A Tree • A Rock • A Cloud" reflects in a more specific way its author's passion for woods. "To Carson," says Carr, "predawn was a wonderfully mysterious time." While in Columbus, each morning she "walked in the woods while it was still dark"; and this was "so that she might breathe deeply and more freely—absorbing, listening, scrutinizing, and becoming at one with the sounds and textures and hues of nature."[23]

Perhaps a suggestion of sexual nature is never absent from among trees, but it was plainest in the experiences of Jane, Jaime, and Sally. The "deep, hot" earth fires Jane's treelike sexual longing for a woman; Jaime imagines himself as rainforest tree, with many branches, "very lush," and "attractive to insects." And Sally, at sixteen, took the shape of a rather erotic tree feeling her way into spongy spring ground. A measure of modesty no doubt kept Jane, Jaime, and Sally from describing (if not consciously imagining) the particularities of this lusty tree-power.

For more complete and graphic accounts we may turn to Zora Neale Hurston's description of Janie Crawford's sexual blossoming in *Their Eyes Were Watching God* and Michel Tournier's description, in his novel *Friday*, of Robinson Crusoe's climb into a tropical (araucaria) tree.

Janie, at sixteen, first lets a boy kiss her after she had

spent most of the day under a blossoming pear tree in the back-yard. She had been spending every minute she could steal from her chores under that tree for the last three days. That was to say, ever since the first tiny bloom had opened. It had called her to come and gaze on a mystery. From barren brown stems to glisten-ing leaf-buds; from the leaf-buds to snowy virginity of bloom. . . . The rose of the world was breathing out smell. It followed her through all her waking moments and caressed her in her sleep. It connected itself with other vaguely felt matters that had struck her outside observations and buried themselves in her flesh. . . .

She was stretched on her back beneath the pear tree soaking in the alto chant of the visiting bees, the gold of the sun and the panting breath of the breeze when the inaudible voice of it all came to her. She saw a dust-bearing bee sink into the sanctum of a bloom, the thousand sister-calyxes arch to meet the love embrace and the ecstatic shiver of the tree from root to tiniest branch cream-ing in every blossom and frothing with delight. So this was a mar-riage![24]

Janie wished to be "a pear tree—*any* tree in bloom!" Despite the difficulties of her life, "she had glossy leaves and bursting buds. . . ." Robinson Crusoe also finds ecstasy in communion with a tree. He climbs,

doing so without difficulty and with a growing sense of being the prisoner, and in some sort a part of a vast and infinitely ramified structure flowing upward through the trunk with its reddish bark and spreading in countless large and lesser branches, twigs, and shoots to reach the nerve ends of leaves, triangular, pointed, scaly, and rolled in spirals around the twigs. He was taking part in the tree's most unique accomplishment, which is to embrace the air with its thousand branches, to caress it with its million fingers. . . . "The leaf is the lung of the tree which is itself a lung, and

the wind is its breathing," Robinson thought. He pictured his own
lungs growing outside himself like a blossoming of purple-tinted
flesh, living polyparies of coral with pink membranes, sponges
of human tissue. . . . He would flaunt the intricate efflorescence,
that bouquet of fleshy flowers in the wide air, while a tide of pur-
ple ecstasy flowed into his body on a stream of crimson blood.[25]

Written in the 1930s and 1960s, decades before the image of
breathing trees became current, these passages suggest something
of the erotic feeling for trees, the *atmosphere* of ecological intercourse which trees can create and which figures the background of
the image of trees as lungs of planetary survival. They portray the
ecological dimension of lust itself, crucial to Aphrodite's environment but also present, if often in the background, in the language
of human sexual desire. Commenting on the passage from Tournier, the philosopher Al Lingus notes that "lust is not a movement
issuing from us and terminating in the other. It is the tree that draws
Robinson, holds him, embraces him, caresses his breath with its
million fingers." Lust *is* that tree, actual and metaphoric, woman
and man, infinitely ramified.

Imagining the Tree of Lust as that in which we may participate,
and which is "in" actual trees as much as it is within ourselves, is
a kind of radical ecological movement, a way of holding together
ecological awareness and erotic and sexual desire. Aphrodite's woods
offer us the chance to acknowledge more generously and frankly
the extent to which trees and nonhuman nature really do turn us
on. The ecological importance of such an acknowledgment is worth
imagining. For something in us lusts after beauty. Beauty is, from
Aphrodite's perspective, a fundamental requirement of the soul.
Arguments for saving primary forests often state that aesthetic considerations are important but secondary to ecological, human, or
economic concerns. But Aphrodite would argue that the need for
beauty is second to none and is the lustful, empowering ground of
other considerations, however necessary in their own right.

Walt Whitman, in two entries of his memoir, *Specimen Days*,
speaks similarly about trees. The two entries come under the heading
"The Lesson of a Tree."[26] Under the first, dated 1 September (probably 1876), he reflects while standing before a tulip tree about ninety

feet tall and one of his favorites: "Science (or rather half-way science) scoffs at reminiscence of dryad and hamadryad, and of trees speaking. But, if they don't, they do as well as most speaking, writing, poetry, sermons—or rather they do a great deal better. . . . those old dryad-reminiscences are quite as true as any, and profounder than most reminiscences we get." Trees, Whitman says, teach us about being and endurance, so "palpably artistic," "so innocent and harmless, yet so savage" are they in their "tough and equable serenity." This lesson is a prelude to the next entry, dated 4 August, 6 P.M. of the following year:

> Lights and shades and rare effects on tree-foliage and grass— transparent greens, grays, &c., all in sunset pomp and dazzle. The clear beams are now thrown in many new places, on the quilted, seam'd, bronze-drab, lower-trunks, shadow'd except at this hour— now flooding their young and old columnar ruggedness with strong light, unfolding to my sense new amazing features of silent, shaggy charm, the solid bark, the expression of harmless impassiveness, with many a bulge and gnarl unreck'd before. In the revealings of such light, such exceptional hour, such mood, one does not wonder at the old story fables, (indeed, why fables?) of people falling into love-sickness with trees. . . .

Whitman's vision of "love-sickness" means being "seiz'd extatic" by the strength and beauty of the trees. This love is both sensual and mythological: a lovingly detailed attention to the forest's physiognomy and an arousal of imaginal "reminiscences." Being *seized* by "love-sickness"—itself a traditional nymphic power—implies being taken to another realm, another world, by a love whose arboreal strength overwhelms; a love which when fully revealed is scarcely bearable—sometimes sexual, always a wild desperate inhuman longing for beauty.[27]

Religion and Rage

In contemporary protests to save trees is an echo of the hymn's prohibition on cutting hallowed groves. Prohibitions on cutting trees in certain areas in ancient Greece could serve a pragmatic purpose, but the entwined sense of the sacredness and beauty of the trees in Aphrodite's woods is what gives the proscription its empowering force. More, when Aphrodite speaks of the inviolability of the Grove of the Gods, she implies that *the Gods and Goddesses themselves feel the sacredness of the trees.* This is not always what modern protectors of trees and forests intend when they feel and invoke arboreal sacredness. In Aphrodite's woods, humans do not touch the trees with iron—whatever they may feel about them. They avoid cutting them down because Another—the Great Goddess or other divinity—reveres, loves, treasures the trees.[28] Breaking the rule provokes Trees of Ire—as when, in *The Lord of the Rings*, Treebeard leads the Ents into war against the forces of the evil wizard.

The force of the rule that governs Aphrodite's woods is illustrated by efforts to save primary forests that have materially sustained communities over centuries (the forests defended by Chipko ["tree-hugging"] activists in India) or that are major cultural landmarks (such as the redwoods and other remaining old-growth forests). The intensity of the emotions involved becomes palpable in an image of "dedicated forest activists . . . engag[ing] in civil disobedience, stalling the impending massacre of old growth [California Coast Red-woods]."[29] I have witnessed this power firsthand in two very different communities: a Bronx neighborhood and McClellanville, South Carolina.

One day in late November of 1989, sixty-seven Norway maples lining a north Bronx parkway, planted in commemoration of World War I veterans, were cut down by the New York City Department of Transportation after their roots had been carelessly cut and exposed in a street reconstruction project. Residents watched as the trees' crowns were cut away, leaving several blocks peopled by ten-foot-high stumps. Imagine it: the community reacted with an outrage like that which gave birth to Treebeard.

I attended an energetic rally the following Sunday which flyers billed as a "wake" for the "murdered maples," a rally to save remaining threatened trees lining the parkway, and a celebration of community spirit. The event, attended by over two hundred people, took place on a bright but frigid and extremely windy day. Leaders passed out black armbands as various groups in the community, ranging from the Jewish Veterans of Foreign Wars to African-American junior high-schoolers, gathered. The spirit of the Tree Lady of Bed-Stuy was there. We marched past the still-standing limbless trunks of the dead trees to an intersection by the parkway where the rally was accompanied by songs and a few residents holding up and waving small branches from the fallen trees. The assembly was as determined and angry as any I have joined in or witnessed. The intensity of the communal feelings for the trees emerged when I spoke with one of the organizers who had been quoted in a New York newspaper as saying, "I never thought seeing trees cut down could make me sick to my stomach." After the rally, he suggested that I should take a walk up the street and see where, at about 3:30 P.M. the previous Tuesday, "the massacre stopped. . . ."

A week and a half later I visited McClellanville, a South Carolina community devastated by Hurricane Hugo. McClellanville is noted for its many companionable live oaks along and around the village streets and center, trees which before Hugo formed a dense, cave-like canopy. Many of the trees were still standing and, though of these a large number were hurt and had lost limbs, had long since begun putting out new leaves. I talked with Mark, a businessman and a native Texan, who had come to McClellanville twenty years ago and "was immediately met by this canopy of oaks. . . . I had never seen anything like that before—and I don't think I've seen anything like that since. . . . just as lush as can be. . . ." The storm damage was quite upsetting, but, expressing an upbeat attitude, Mark thought renewal would eventually come and the live oaks, his favorite trees, would thrive again. Anger was more evident when he recalled some earlier incidents in which the power company, installing new lines, had damaged some of the live oaks lining the road. It was widely shared; "I didn't know anybody that didn't get out of their car and verbally abuse the tree contractor who was chopping on these live oaks." When Mark stressed "*Everybody* in town, you know, took a shot at 'em," I wondered if he meant this entirely in a figurative sense. In fact, Mark added: "I can remember one person thinking that he would take a few shots at the side of the truck," not to "hurt anybody" but to let them know they were out of bounds in harming the trees.

This sudden movement of fantasy in our conversation toward

violent defense of the trees—or punishment for their being hurt—
is worth pondering. It reveals the intensity of an attachment to certain trees—their rootedness in sacred communal ground. Mischa also
spoke of an impulse toward physical violence in response to the scene
of forest destruction near Vladivostok: "I was furious. I had a simple impulse to hit some high-positioned military in the face, to punch
him." A love turns into real fury. Fury, that is, in the sense of the
archetypal Furies. As James Hersh notes, "The Furies are incited
to action by violations against the course of nature."[30] This archetypal
fury is at work in a general sense wherever anger and rage against
environmental devastation are roused. The rhetoric of the Furies infuses the slogan of the radical environmental group Earth First!: "No
compromise in defense of Mother Earth."[31] But even such opponents
of Earth First! tactics as Will can speak, however figuratively, as he
did to his son, of skinning his trees as "a capital punishment offense."

We can hold resolutely to a nonviolent stance in ecological protest while allowing a place for violent images and feelings. What
else do violently protective feelings about trees tell us? As Robert
Jay Lifton notes in connection with Vietnam veterans, a constella-
tion of violent images and rage may result and sometimes be acted
upon when an individual or group experiences a form of ultimate
threat to the self and its vitality. Hence, incidents of violence have
taken place *against* protesters of old-growth logging.[32] The imaginal
vitality that flourishes in the trees of Aphrodite's woods, and their
cousins in the Pacific Northwest, McClellanville, and the Bronx, also
has an ultimate dimension—one experienced differently by some in
logging communities and by forest preservationists.

It is doubtful that any nonviolent stance, however resolute, can
be at all times free from violent images when one is faced with
ultimate threats. Like Aeschylos in the *Oresteia*, we are confronted
with a finally impersonal claim, with finding a way to give a place
within a nonviolent milieu to the Furies and their point of view—
which can include images of violence. In the presence of *inviolable*
woods, such images can be envisaged as Furies of the trees and their
land, speaking in their frightening terms.

A way of healing that allows the violent image while renouncing violence itself can be found in the same precincts, through an

arboreal imagining that holds together fury and love. James Hersh, who writes perceptively of the social, ethnic, and national dimensions of the Furies' violence and of the need to grant these beings a locus in the democratic *polis*, quotes as an illustration of this therapeutics Nicolas Gage's account of his renunciation of revenge against the communist guerrilla leader who had ordered his mother's torture and execution in the Greek civil war in 1948. Recalling her special love for him and his siblings, Gage says:

> Like the mulberry tree in our yard, which still stands although the house has fallen into ruins, that love has taken root in us, her children, and spread to her grandchildren as well.
>
> If I had killed [the guerrilla leader], I would have had to uproot that love in myself and become like him—purging myself, as he did, of all humanity or compassion.[33]

The ecological dimension, also within the Furies' province, is vitalizing. Enduring fury and love, humanity and compassion, can be held together by trees. The Tree Lady of Bedford-Stuyvesant knew that, too.

Split Woods

Aphrodite's woods are not Paradise, but Paradise is always wooded. Having walked in Aphrodite's woods for a while, we can now grasp the distinctions and relations between their mythology and that of another place—"Eden," to use Jane's word for the wild apple orchard. The following words exemplify the paradisal imagination of the "New World":

> Its lands are high [with] very lofty mountains. . . . All are most beautiful . . . and all are accessible and filled with trees of a thousand kinds and tall, and they seem to touch the sky. And I am told that they never lose their foliage . . . and some of them were flowering, some bearing fruit, and some in another stage, according to their nature.[34]

These words, by virtue of being authored by Christopher Columbus, both conceal and reveal the ambiguity in a culture's yearning for the Trees of Paradise. As Richard Slotkin made clear in his exhaustive study on *Regeneration Through Violence* in the American cultural imagination, the Trees of Paradise have paradoxically contributed in powerful ways not only to the exploration but to the exploitation and deforestation of much of the world, in part because actual forests always frustrate the longing to create an Eden or New World. Some people, upon traveling to tropical rainforests on the strength of images of Eden, have been disappointed by bugs, uncomfortable conditions, and gloomy forest floors. The forest does not live up to Edenic standards. The idealized image of Eden too easily becomes its opposite, the "jungle" or gloomy Wild which must be defeated. The Trees of Paradise thus form one half of a split image.

Idealized imaginings of trees and forests can lead to their destruction. As Richard Grove notes, "The image of an untouched tropical island had long been associated with a Western utopia" and by the seventeenth century the world everywhere was "vulnerable to colonization by an ever expanding myth," figured by "the full flowering of what could be called the Edenic island discourse."[35] The consequences of this "discourse" included massive forest destruction, erosion, and diminution of local rainfall patterns in the colonized tropics. The split has sociopolitical consequences in the human exploitation and killing that often parallel the destruction of trees. Once again we are in the territory of the United States military alteration of Smoky the Bear's caution against forest fires during the Vietnam War ("Only *you* can prevent a forest").

The effects of the split woods within the Edenic imagination can be examined with reference to images of forest and climate management and of the greenhouse effect. There is power in the idea that logging keeps trees from dying. Even a managed forest is in a way a mythic, Edenic vision.[36] But we learn more about the shadow cast by Edenic woods by juxtaposing current fears about the potential harm to forests from the greenhouse effect, and the image of the greenhouse itself.[37] In the time when Darwin wrote about "Nature's hothouse," the greenhouse was an ideal place of restoration, of "distant forests of unknown continents," and figured as "the convergence point of all nineteenth-century social utopias"—a climate-controlled Paradise embodying "the often-repeated dream of setting up a Garden of Eden by artificial means."[38]

Partly because of this Edenic image, the "greenhouse effect" is often considered a profoundly misleading image for the devastating effects of rapid global warming. After all, as one man I interviewed on the subject put it, a greenhouse is "something that creates fertile things—allows trees to grow." In a similar interview with Jim, an energy-conservation consultant who is quite concerned about the greenhouse effect, I asked how he would describe a greenhouse by itself. He noted that the purpose of an actual greenhouse was "to try to change the climate of an area for a specific reason." He vividly recalled visiting a huge greenhouse or arboretum in Montréal, in which plants and trees from the tropics were being grown. I asked why tropical *trees*, in particular, were grown there. "Well," he said, "it was a botanical garden, a museum. That was the purpose. So people could see what the tropics look like, in Montréal. Maybe," he laughed, "we'll get to see that inadvertently, in about a hundred years."

Jim's humor suggests both his awareness of the power of that Edenic image and his perplexity over its emergence. For his main picture of "greenhouse" effects was of "everything getting hotter and"—he added with quiet emphasis—"forests dying and that sort of thing," places where "there are lots of trees and animals . . . wilderness getting scorched." The scene is imagistically akin to the nuclear "Republic of Insects of Grass" envisaged by Jonathan Schell. The laughter that rose with Jim's perplexed awareness was pained, an expression of the split between the cultural and mythological images of a thriving tropical forest on the one hand, and the massive dying-off of forests everywhere on the other. In this image, forests of dying and dead trees replace the dangerous wild woods (or "decadent" old-growth forest) as the "dark" side of the split Edenic imagination.

Mingling Woods

Yet, Edenic imaginings of trees, however idealized, have also helped motivate genuine concern for tropical rainforests and other threatened primary forests. "In truth, the roots of Western conservationism are at least 200 years old and grew in the tropics," as Richard Grove congenially puts it.[39] For the ecologically concerned, tropical "islands became allegories for the world at large." This trope becomes for us an echo of what we heard from Steve regarding Fairchild Tropical Garden after Hurricane Andrew (chapter 5, p. 131). In both cases (as in contemporary forest ecology and in Darwin's image of the evolutionary Tree of Life), essentially mythic imaginings combine with what Grove calls "rigorous analytic thinking" and "empiricism." Ironically, just as one variety of empirical experience led to climate-controlled greenhouses, eighteenth- and nineteenth-century scientific observers in the tropics became concerned about out-of-control climate change and desertification, particularly in semi-arid tropical areas, due to forest destruction. By the middle of the nineteenth century the possibility of the "general and gradual dessication of the earth and atmosphere" was discussed, and this discussion "presaged contemporary fears about global warming. . . ."[40] Then, as now, images of forest destruction were juxtaposed with those of Edenic woods.

While I argue for a different relationship to trees, for psychological travels in woods other than the Edenic, the image of Eden is not about to leave us, and it has not left me. Its trees continue to exert their hold on us. But the more capacious and variegated woods of which Aphrodite speaks offer a way beyond the split that has bedeviled Eden. Within us and about us, many woods can mingle. Eden's woods, the "lungs of the world," are touched by Aphrodite's erotic life. Her voice can be heard in Darwin's description of the tropical forest, the "great wild, untidy, luxuriant hothouse" he encountered in Mauritius during his voyage on the *H. M. S. Beagle* (see chapter 3, p. 72).[41] His use of "hothouse," a common nineteenth-century term for a greenhouse, suggests the erotic yearning for nature also contained in those structures. He wonders: "Who from seeing choice plants in a hothouse, can magnify some into the dimensions of forest trees, and crowd others into an entangled jungle?" The "entangled jungle" links Darwin's two evolutionary figures, the Tree of Life and the Tangled Bank, and there is an echo of David Rains Wallace's description of the Florida hammock as a place suggestive of "passionate entanglement." The vivid and synaesthetic sensuality of the forest is what impresses Darwin:

> Who when examining in the cabinet of the entomologist the gay exotic butterflies, and singular cicadas, will associate with these lifeless objects, the ceaseless harsh music of the latter, and the lazy flight of the former,—the sure accompaniments of the still, glowing noonday of the tropics? It is when the sun has attained its greatest height, that such scenes should be viewed: then the dense splendid foliage of the mango hides the ground with its darkest shade, whilst the upper branches are rendered from the profusion of light of the most brilliant green. In the temperate zones the case is different—the vegetation there is not so dark or so rich, and hence the rays of the declining sun, tinged of a red, purple, or bright yellow colour, add most to the beauties of those climes.

In Darwin's encounter, the sensual nature of the temperate forest is also heightened. Mischa shared a similar image of the Russian forest: "My favorite occupation is to watch pine trees in the sunset. . . . When the sun throws its light on the pine trees, and they're glittering with a red color, the bark . . . becomes suddenly red as copper, and glistening with tiny pieces of sap. This is one of the most beautiful sights I ever saw in my life, [and] that's what really . . . brings . . . enlightenment to our being human." And this echoes Pamela's description of her childhood times in the woods, "the shimmer" in the "forest-like trees" when you "see the sun shinin' through them and whatnot."

"Longing for Eden" encompasses not only the theme of separation, loss, and consequent desire for a "return" to origins, but also a yearning for nature's evolving erotic beauty. Edenic and Aphrodisiac woods can again mingle. Pamela continues: "It was like all this stuff was here from the beginning of time. . . . I never pictured anybody actually out there trying to plant a tree. . . . I'd always say, 'This is the way God put it here. It was like this, you know, from the beginning of time. . . .' I guess that's what hurts so bad." "The beginning of time" echoes the creation time of Genesis; so do the trees that in the primal garden were planted not by men but by God: "And out of the ground the Lord God caused to grow every tree that is pleasing to the sight" (Gen. 2:9). Yet Pamela also speaks Aphrodite's words: "Beautiful trees."

Artemis and Aphrodite

Since even Aphrodite has Artemisian fantasies, or a space for Artemis within herself (her confabulation is by no means a complete lie), our walk in Aphrodite's trees cannot conclude without a closer look at the relation between Aphrodite's and Artemis's woodland places. Artemis, in particular, lends us another perspective on the fantasies of apartness and separation between the natural and cultural worlds. Artemisian "pristine" woods also play a powerful role in the environmentalist imagination. Will is certainly right about that. Part of the reason is that beauty—Aphrodite's concern—is so important in the woods and in the imagination of pristine wilderness in general. That is, Artemisian and Aphrodisiac fantasies mingle in the woods.

Bill McKibben's description of dying trees brings us within the precincts of the linked theme of death and beauty so prominent in Aphrodite's description of the woods. However, in his book *The End of Nature*, he serves mainly as a spokesman for an Artemisian vision of woods and wilds untouched by and ultimately independent of the human world. By "the end of nature" McKibben means the end, due to inescapable human destruction of the natural world (mostly through the greenhouse effect), of "our sense of nature as eternal and separate," wild and pristine. Taken literally, the argument is at odds with the growing awareness of how, even prior to the greenhouse effect, the human and nonhuman have mixed and mingled in nature, in both psychological and ecological ways. [42] Moreover, Artemis is herself at times a cruel, death-dealing Goddess; an Edenic idealization haunts McKibben's perspective. But there remains a persuasiveness and importance in his words:

> Almost every day, I hike up the hill out my back door. Within a hundred yards the woods swallows [*sic*] me up, and there is nothing to remind me of human society—no trash, no stumps, no fence, not even a real path. Looking out from the high places,

you can't see road or house; it is a world apart from man. But once in a while someone will be cutting wood further down the valley, and the snarl of a chain saw will fill the woods. It is harder on those days to get caught up in the timeless meaning of the forest, for man is nearby. The sound of the chain saw doesn't blot out all the noises of the forest or drive the animals away, but it does drive away the feeling that you are in another separate, timeless, wild sphere.[43]

Artemis, who must stay "apart from man," loves "the high places," the mountains of her ancient topography of soul. The Artemisian feeling is bound, trapped by the sound of "chain" saws. In the presence of Artemis, one feels the necessity of the forest apart, of a free and separate community of trees, plants, mountains, animals. Something in us that can also be sensed in trees desires to be alone in the woods. The desire for such retreat, a separate place, the unique solitude of woods, can be as inhumanly fierce as any.

That fierceness can manifest as distance, coldness, withdrawal. Expressing that aspect of Artemisian woods, a poem by John Haines might be said to have something of Artemis, Goddess of the Hunt, in its title: "Ancestor of the Hunting Heart."[44] Its narrator explains:

> There is a distance in the heart,
> and I know it well—
> leaf-somberness of winter branches, ...
>
> Neither field nor furrow,
> nor woodlot patched with fences,
> but something wilder: a distance
> never cropped or plowed. . . .

The distance spoken here is an Artemisian aloofness from all things domesticated—and yet "the distance is closer than / the broomswept hearth"; it is in the autumn leaves that "lie yellow on the kitchen floor." As close as it is, it remains psychologically out of doors; "Snow is part of the distance, / cold ponds, and ice. . . ." Now the stage is set for the arrival of the hunter's distant and distancing heart—along with the severe trees of winter.

Trees that are black at morning
are in the evening grey.
The distance lies between them,
a seed-strewn whiteness
through which the hunter comes.

These trees don't make for intimacy or involvement as we usually
think of them. They make space—space, perhaps, for another form
of intimacy, intimacy with the wild, with a heart of coldness. There
is nothing in Haines's poem to suggest a moral judgment of this
distance. Rather, the words allow for it, like the trees.

Trees allow for something else as well, as this poem says: hunting, killing of animals. The virgin innocence of Artemis, of the
woods, is not the innocence of things before death; it can take the
form, rather, of an innocent *delight* in death, an ecstatic celebration of it—something whose place in the ecological imagination,
which in its more idealized forms would seek to expel death from
a vision of harmony, is highly problematic. But to the extent that
woods are Artemisian as well as Edenic, innocence and death coexist
in their shadows. Annie Dillard's portrayals (in *Pilgrim at Tinker
Creek*) of death in the woods, described with a kind of enthusiasm,
are more in the spirit of Artemis. In Charles Boer's translation of
the "Homeric Hymn to Artemis," "the forest / in its darkness /
screams / with the clamor of animals" whom Artemis is hunting. [45]
Artemis "darts in and out / everywhere . . . / killing / all kinds of
animals." Mary Anne, the woman who fuses with the Vietnam-War
forest, becomes in a different but related way a pure killer.

The killing power of the forest takes many forms, including a
"forest of difference" in human conflicts that stop short of war. That
case is less a retreat into the innocent or pristine than a withdrawal
from mutual hurt; a movement into an intimacy with woods that
expresses estrangement from a human partner (or group). This kind
of forest appears in Toni Morrison's portrayal of the split between
Sethe and Paul D in *Beloved*. Paul D has learned that Sethe had killed
one of her daughters rather than surrender to a cruel slavecatcher,
and in his anguish he demeans her; "right then a forest sprang up
between them, trackless and quiet." [46] In the silent moment, "the forest
was locking the distance between them, giving it shape and heft."

Paul D leaves without a formal goodbye. "'So long,' [Sethe] murmured from the far side of the trees."

We can hear forests of distance, and difference, in the words of Pamela and Will as they talk about their times in the woods. Pamela observed that "a lot of folks like to come here in South Carolina. They say it's like getting in touch with nature again," not only with trees "but—people." She had me in mind, as became evident when I wondered aloud if part of Pamela's feeling had to do with the slower pace of things in the Lowcountry. "A slower pace," she repeated, "especially—for you, you're from New York, my God. So you guys are like always going, going, going, right?" Pamela had once visited New York, and she didn't like it: the pace was impossible, and people didn't even take the time to say "hello."

The contrast Pamela wanted to highlight was between people in the city and people outside of it, who are in touch with nature. That distinction is already in part an Artemisian fantasy. But Artemis tends toward still more intense separation from the daily human world, toward privacy and solitude. I asked Pamela if she remembered from childhood any discrete experiences of being in the woods. That query prompted her to talk about times when she wanted to be apart from (human) people in order to get in touch with (nonhuman) nature. "I have always been the type of little girl" that preferred solitude. That little girl then entered the room and our conversation—"After school, here I am . . . sitting in class," where "I used to dream about pickin' flowers." She would go home, do her chores, but "used to basically look forward to going along the path, picking up flowers. . . . I was by myself a whole lot." She was slightly embarrassed to remember this: "My sisters say I was weird . . . at the time." But "as a young girl, I was very much in tune with myself"; she felt "mature," and picking the flowers (something she saw adults doing) "interested me more than just, you know, playin' with dolls and all that." This recollection is what brought to mind when "I used to actually stand up and cry when I saw the sun shining through the trees. . . ."

With Pamela's words in mind, listen again to how Will characterizes himself in relation to his family and his interest in forestry and the outdoors: "My father, my brothers and sisters are all engineers. I'm the black sheep in the family." Remember that in talking about "rural America's perception of a tree," Will ended up talking about the difference between himself and his little brother who wanted to cut down the "old gnarly dogwood" that "for me . . . was aesthetic" and that also had powerful links to the place where the family grew up "and all of the dogwood trails and all of that. . . . So I don't know that that wasn't a little bit different feelin'." Like Pamela, Will is uneasy about the sense of difference between him and other family members, but he also affirms it. One of his relatives, he told me, once said "that Will's the only one in the family that enjoys what he's doin'." As with Pamela, an attachment to trees reveals a distance, and a difference, between Will and others close to him. In the difference is the commonality, and in the distance the closeness, of trees.

Artemisian woods, finally, can help frame the debate around "the idea of wilderness," of pristine, nonhuman nature. The imagination of wilderness, as the mythology of Artemis suggests, is not merely a recent (post-Enlightenment) human construct or American conceit (though it often does posit a false dichotomy between human and nonhuman realms). We find wilderness imaginations in ancient Greece, among the Kwakiutl and other Amerindians, Africans, Amazonians, and, in fact, wherever and whenever an "other world," alien terrain, or Land of Life or Land of Death appears.[47] But Michael Pollan is right to say that "wilderness is . . . a profoundly alienating idea, for it drives a large wedge between [humankind] and nature."[48] One could say that, as image, wilderness *intends* alienation, figures the intimate depth that can be found in retreat, distance, and estrangement. That is the *desire* of wilderness, a profound mood of trees and forest.

Wilderness preserves in this sense are far from being only a modern and human invention; as in the stories of Pamela and Will, they also express qualities of woodland, the imperatives of trees that impinge upon our private minds, our narratives, and our public policies. Seen mythologically, they by no means rule out other ways of articulating the relationship between human and nonhuman nature. Artemisian precincts and the viewpoint of that most cosmopolitan of Goddesses, Aphrodite, coexist in the "Homeric Hymn to Aphrodite" and perhaps in our own imaginations in still undiscovered ways (even though such coexistence does not mean lack of conflict between the differing wooded images). E. O. Wilson, the eminent scholar and lover of the tropical rainforest, offers us an image of that cohabitation in speaking of "*biophilia*, the connections that humans subconsciously seek with the rest of life," from the Greek *bios*, "life," and *philia*, "friendship, love."[49] The love of woods steadies us and impels us toward solidarity, toward friendship with the world. And yet, "To biophilia can be added the idea of wilderness, all the land and communities of plants and animals still unsullied by human occupation," that which is "beyond human contrivance, . . . virgin land. . . ." Biophilia and the idea of wilderness have been part of our relationship to the world since we became human; and they continue to evolve. Passionate entanglement and apartness can live with each other. They do in one way for David Wallace in *Bulow Hammock*, and in another for Pamela amidst her shimmering "forest-like trees." Aphrodite would keep certain sacred groves virginal, untouched by the axe of the human. And in the deep woods of solitude we can find Aphrodite's desire, making love with trees.

Yet let us remember that the idea of wilderness is also the Ecological Pandaemonium; it is complex, paradoxical, contradictory. Though it is the ideal place of kinship and restoration, it also contains intricate varieties of death, fear, comedy, sadness, strangeness. Wilderness is part of the power of trees, wherever their spirits are. A power in the gnarled stoniness of ridgetop oaks, their leaves that seize the wind. In the bared branches of maples coming alive. In dancing hemlocks in blizzard conditions. In the vagabond lover's grave green eyes that see "A Tree • A Rock • A Cloud" in the sad café, the crowded street, the predawn rain. In old shagbarks and apples, dead and living, under the weather. In the foreign country of Homestead, Florida, after Hurricane Andrew.

Notes

CHAPTER 1

1. Catherine S. Manegold, "Alien Terrain Replaces What Was Once Home," *The New York Times*, 31 August 1992, p. A1.

2. Douglas Davies, in his article "The Evocative Symbolism of Trees" (Denis Cosgrove and Stephen Daniels, eds., *The Iconography of Landscape* [Cambridge: Cambridge University Press, 1988], p. 33), comes close to this approach, speaking of "the evocationist or evocative theory of symbolic thought" which recognizes that "I do not simply see the tree but am attracted to it by some inhering attribute whilst also conceiving it through cultural and historical precedent" and that "the attractiveness of trees lies both in their physical nature and in the creative metaphorical capacity of the human mind." I would go further, however, in emphasizing *psychological* attributes of *physical* nature, as do James Hillman and subsequent writers in archetypal psychology. See Hillman's seminal work on the world soul or *anima mundi*: "*Anima Mundi*: The Return of the Soul to the World," *Spring 1982*: 71–93; and his more recent book, *The Thought of the Heart and the Soul of the World* (Dallas: Spring Publications, 1992).

3. On the psychological, emotional, and spiritual value of trees, see John F. Dwyer, Herbert W. Schroeder, and Paul H. Gobster, "The Significance of Urban Trees and Forests: Toward a Deeper Understanding of Values," *Journal of Arboriculture* 17, 10 (October 1991): 276–84; and Herbert W. Schroeder, "The Psychological Value of Trees," *The Public Garden* 6, 1 (January 1991).

I am indebted to the work of James Hillman (see his *The Thought of the Heart*) and other archetypal psychologists who have, in the past decade and a half, emphasized and probed the imaginal and metaphoric presentation inherent in physical reality. See especially Peter Bishop, "Facing the World: Depth Psychology and Deep Ecology," *Harvest* 36 (1990):

62–71, and *The Greening of Psychology: The Vegetable World in Myth, Dream, and Healing* (Dallas: Spring Publications, 1990). In the latter work, Bishop develops valuable, iconoclastic perspectives on ecology. He deeply values it, stating that just as Freud and Jung drew on metaphoric systems of the natural sciences of their times, "I believe that a fundamental remetaphorization is required, that an ecological image of psyche should complement" earlier images (p. 2). Moreover, ecology per se is imaginal through-and-through. "The idea of *ecology*—no matter how sophisticated, how pertinent and 'right' it seems for these desperate times—is an imaginal fiction. Nevertheless, the creation of such a fiction, such an important symbol, is a major psychological event. Through this symbol, concern for images of the *Other* is becoming more important than concern for images of *Self*" (p. 3). And: "The fundamental and elemental foundation of human soulfulness in vegetative life still awaits full recognition, although its voice can be heard from within movements as diverse as depth psychology and Deep Ecology" (p. 27). For another Jungian—and iconoclastic—perspective, see Andrew Samuels, "Education and Ecology: Psychological Reflections," *Quadrant* 2 (1990): 75–79. Samuels astutely questions tendencies within environmental movements to unquestioningly idealize nonhuman nature. Robert Jay Lifton's "formative-symbolic" approach to the psyche has consistently recognized the importance of ecological images in the human need for "symbolic immortality" or connection beyond the individual self. See especially *The Broken Connection: On Death and the Continuity of Life* (New York: Basic Books, 1983 [1979]), pp. 22–23 and 342–45; and Lifton's most recent study, *The Protean Self: Human Resilience in an Age of Human Fragmentation* (New York: Basic Books, 1993), pp. 134–35, 218–19. Among more traditionally oriented psychoanalysts, Harold F. Searles recognized thirty years ago the intrinsic psychological importance of nonhuman nature. See Harold F. Searles, *The Nonhuman Environment: In Normal Development and in Schizophrenia* (New York: International Universities Press, Inc., 1960). More recently, Theodore Roszak (paralleling Bishop) has drawn on aspects of the Freudian id and the Jungian collective unconscious in his call for a focus on the "ecological unconscious," a fundamentally ecological view of psyche. See his *The Voice of the Earth* (New York: Simon & Schuster, 1992), pp. 301–05.

On deep ecology, see Bill Devall and George Sessions, *Deep Ecology: Living as if Nature Mattered* (Salt Lake City: Peregrine Smith Books, 1985); Michael Tobias, ed., *Deep Ecology* (San Diego: Avant, 1985); and Arne

Naess, "The Basics of Deep Ecology," *Resurgence* (January–February 1988). For able philosophical discussion of deep ecology, see Max Oelschlaeger, *The Idea of Wilderness* (New Haven: Yale University Press, 1991), pp. 301–09. In recent years, much thoughtful work has been done that brings together spiritual, psychological, and ecological concerns. See, for instance, Thomas Berry, *The Dream of the Earth* (San Francisco: Sierra Club Books, 1988). Drawing on modern cosmology, Berry asserts that "the human activates the most profound dimension of the universe itself, its capacity to reflect on and celebrate itself in conscious self-awareness" (p. 132). But also, "every being has its own interior, its self, its mystery, its numinous aspect" (p. 134). The experiential basis of deep ecology is developed in John Seed et al., *Thinking Like a Mountain* (Philadelphia: New Society Publishers, 1988). Seed, together with Joanna Rogers Macy and psychologically and spiritually oriented environmentalists, has developed "Council of All Beings" workshops in which nonhuman beings are given a voice in explicitly ritual settings. Warwick Fox, similarly, stresses the possibilities of human identification with nonhuman ("cosmological" and "ontological") forms. See his *Toward a Transpersonal Ecology: Developing New Foundations for Environmentalism* (Boston: Shambhala, 1990), ch. 8. Ecological concern impels a variety of activists, writers, and scholars to reflect in diverse ways upon *the interiority of the nonhuman.*

4.   Jessica Benjamin, *The Bonds of Love: Psychoanalysis, Feminism, and the Problem of Domination* (New York: Pantheon Books, 1988), p. 29; Liam Hudson and Bernadine Jacot, *The Way Men Think: Intellect, Intimacy, and the Erotic Imagination* (New Haven and London: Yale University Press, 1991), p. 133.

5.   Quote from Robert Pogue Harrison, *Forests: The Shadow of Civilization* (Chicago: University of Chicago Press, 1992), p. 69. "Foreign" comes from the Latin *foras*, an adverbial derivative of *foris.*

6.   W. S. Merwin, "Witness," in *The Rain in the Trees* (New York: Alfred A. Knopf, 1988), p. 65.

7.   Harrison, *Forests*, p. 201.

8.   Daniel C. Noel, "Soul and Earth: Traveling with Jung Toward an Archetypal Ecology (Part 1)," *Quadrant* 23, 2 (1990): 58, 72. Noel identifies crucial passages in Jung's work in Part 2 of his essay (*Quadrant* 24, 1 [1991]: 83–85). In various ways Jung stressed the interdependence and interpenetration of world and soul, and in his theory of archetypes he made the connection explicit. So that, as Noel summarizes, "archetypal images,

in other words, always tell an ecological tale, narrating not the one-way *mono*logue of projection, but the deep *dia*logue between soul and earth" (p. 83).

Notice that through his independent study, which extended over a period of several years, Noel articulates an inherently ecological image of the psyche. His conclusions thus parallel those of Peter Bishop and Theodore Roszak.

9. See Charles B. Strozier, Michael Perlman, and Robert Jay Lifton, "Nuclear Threat and the American Self," ms.

10. Hillman, *"Anima Mundi"* in *Thought of the Heart*, p. 122.

11. See Henry David Thoreau, "Walking," in *Thoreau: The Major Essays*, ed. Jeffrey L. Duncan (New York: E. P. Dutton & Co., Inc., 1972).

12. Most notable is Alan Bleakley's call for a re-emphasis on the aesthetic particularities of the world in ecological thinking. See his article on "Greens and Greenbacks," *Spring 52* (1992): 68–71. In an expanded version of his thoughts, Bleakley explicitly related his perspective to Aphrodite ("Greens and Greenbacks," presented at the Festival of Archetypal Psychology 7–12 July 1992, University of Notre Dame). See also Roszak, *The Voice of the Earth*, pp. 35–39 for a critique of an excessive reliance on ecological fears and guilt, to the exclusion of love and sensuality, as motivators of environmental action.

13. Robert Pogue Harrison eloquently discusses the relationship between Artemis and the forest in *Forests*, pp. 19–30. For a Jungian and feminist-oriented discussion of "Artemis and Ecology," see Ginette Paris, *Pagan Meditations: The Worlds of Aphrodite, Artemis, and Hestia* (Dallas: Spring Publications, 1986), pp. 109–15.

14. On forest destruction in preclassical Greece, see John Perlin, *A Forest Journey: The Role of Wood in the Development of Civilization* (New York/London: W. W. Norton & Co., 1989), pp. 58–68 and 75–82 and references. See also J. Donald Hughes, "Ecology in Ancient Greece," *Inquiry* 18 (1975): 118–19, 121. Plato (*Kritias* 111b–d) and others from the classical period lamented the effects of deforestation. Hughes cites and discusses the ancient literature in an article on "How the Ancients Viewed Deforestation," *Journal of Field Archeology* 10: 437–45.

A number of scholars, however, question the actual extent of deforestation in classical and preclassical Greece. For a summary of their position see Robert Sallares, *Ecology of the Ancient Greek World* (London: Duckworth, 1991), p. 35 and references. More important than the actual and literal extent of such deforestation is the unmistakable evidence of concern in classical authors. That is, the *image* of deforestation haunted Greek civilization from early on, as it did those of the Near East. It is a psychological and cultural phenomenon sui generis—and a primal call to ecological consciousness and relationship.

George Soutar, an Oxford scholar, made a parallel and interesting claim: "In Greek poetry we find no forest-sentiment, nothing worthy to be called forest-description. . . . Homer probably knew something of forests. In many of his similes in the *Iliad* he takes us to the wooded mountains; but they are the scene of the woodman's labours or of the ravage caused by fire or wind or wild animals." There are no evocations of great forests in the Greek sources as there are in English, German, Nordic, Hindu, or other mythological literatures (*Nature in Greek Poetry* [New York / London: Johnson Reprint Co., 1971 (1939)], p. 146).

While Soutar's observation is correct as far as it goes, we may say more precisely that there is nothing that corresponds to the *colonial/industrial-age image* of forest as "primeval." The ancient Greek imagination includes no overall "forest-*sentiment*" as is aroused by that image, but rather a multitude of discretely and sensually imagined feelings, atmospheres, and narratives set among trees or woods. We can discern these Greek antecedents in our more global—panoramic and romantic—contemporary senses of forest when these senses are attentively and imagistically studied. Also, Soutar curiously omits consideration of a characteristic Greek imagining of trees whatever their setting: an imagining of nymphs.

For another interpretation of the role of (nonhuman) nature in Greek mythology, see Mott T. Greene, *Natural Knowledge in Preclassical Antiquity* (Baltimore: The Johns Hopkins University Press, 1992). Greene emphasizes, though without considering psychological dimensions, the importance of physical nature in the formation of mythological images—an avenue largely neglected since the early twentieth century.

15. F. A. Jenkins, Jr., "Tree Shrew Locomotion and the Origins of Primate Arborealism," in *Primate Evolution and Human Origins*, ed. Russell L. Ciochon and John G. Fleagle (New York: Aldine de Gruyter, 1987), pp. 12–13.

There is disagreement in evolutionary biology about the degree of relationship between the Mesozoic tree shrew and our *primate* ancestors; it may be highly indirect, since it seems that "the separation between tree-shrews and primates must in any case be very ancient" (R. D. Martin, *Primate Origins and Evolution: A Phylogenetic Reconstruction* [Princeton: Princeton University Press, 1990], p. 710). But current evidence suggests a still deeper connection between most of the planet's mammals (excepting the marsupials) and the tree shrew: far from being "a 'model' for ancestral primates, [tree shrews] actually provide an indication of the ancestral placental mammal condition. . ." (Martin, p. 213).

16.   In the words of one Russian activist working with the Sacred Earth Network [SEN], which focuses on forest preservation and the establishment of computer networks between concerned Russians and Americans: "Using e-mail [electronic mail] I see now whole world in my computer. It's wonderful. It's new life, new mentality . . . I have not words." Alexej of the Astrachan Green Association, quoted in letter from Bill Pfeiffer to SEN supporters, November 1992. Groups working on preserving the *taiga* and other boreal forests include the Taiga Rescue Network, based in Sweden (see *Taiga-News: Newsletter on Boreal Forests* 4 [December 1992]).

17.   Harrison, *Forests*, p. 8.

CHAPTER 2

1.   J. R. R. Tolkien, *The Two Towers, Part II of The Lord of the Rings* (New York: Ballantine Books, 1973 [1965]), p. 89.

2.   Barry M. Blechman and Stephen S. Kaplan, *Force Without War: U.S. Armed Forces as a Political Instrument* (Washington, DC: The Brookings Institute, 1978), p. 2; quoted in Elaine Scarry, *The Body in Pain: The Making and Unmaking of the World* (New York: Oxford University Press, 1985), p. 287.

3.   Amplification in a more traditional Jungian framework is a process of "directed association" involving overt interpretative comparisons with other images from the individual and, at times, parallels in myth, folklore, religion, or other collective imaginative forms—but always closely attending to the particular image being amplified. In my psychological interviews, amplification takes the form of careful restatement of images as a way of prompting the person being interviewed to go into more detail. I avoid mythological or other collective amplifications. My interviews attempted

to amplify, from particular imagistic angles, the psychological power of trees.

4. Ralph Waldo Emerson, "Nature," in *Selections from Ralph Waldo Emerson*, ed. Stephen E. Whicher (Boston: Houghton Mifflin Co., 1957), p. 24.

5. See Lynn White's essay, "The Historical Roots of Our Ecologic Crisis," *Science* (10 March 1967): 1203–207, which assigns considerable blame to the biblical tradition; William Anderson, *The Green Man: The Archetype of Our Oneness and the Earth* (London / San Francisco: Harper-Collins, 1990), pp. 52–53 (for a discussion of antagonism against and incorporation of trees in medieval Christianity); and John Williamson, *The Oak King, the Holly King, and the Unicorn* (New York: Harper & Row, 1986), pp. 58–78 for a look, which relies heavily on the interpretative frame of James G. Frazer's *The Golden Bough*, at the interweaving of arboreal and Christian symbolism. More recent ecological thought has been critical of the assignment of blame to the biblical tradition, emphasizing its contribution to ecological concern as well as its destructiveness. See Christopher D. Stone, *The Gnat Is Older Than Man: Global Environment and Human Agenda* (Princeton: Princeton University Press, 1993), pp. 237–40; Max Oelschlaeger, *The Idea of Wilderness: From Prehistory to the Age of Ecology* (New Haven: Yale University Press, 1991), pp. 43–53; and Rosemary Radford Ruether, *Gaia and God: An Ecofeminist Theology of Earth Healing* (San Francisco: HarperSan Francisco, 1992), pp. 208–10. See also the collection of essays in Steven C. Rockefeller and John C. Elder, eds., *Spirit and Nature: Why the Environment Is a Religious Issue* (Boston: Beacon Press, 1990)—especially Ismar Schorsch, "Learning to Live with Less: A Jewish Perspective"; Seyved Hossein Nasr, "Islam and the Environmental Crisis"; and Steven C. Rockefeller, "Faith and Community in an Ecological Age" (pp. 158–61).

6. "In Milford, Finding Faith in a Maple Tree," *The New York Times*, 23 July 1992, p. B4.

7. Dr. David Bellamy, quoted in Geoffrey Lean, "Britain Can Be Green Again," *The London Observer*, 25 October 1987, p. 5.

8. Matthew L. Wald, "A Philosophy Built It; Solar Logic Keeps It Warm," *The New York Times*, 25 March 1993, p. C1.

CHAPTER 3

1. Thomas Pownall, *A Topographical Description of the Dominion of the United States*, ed. Lois Mulkean (Pittsburgh: University of Pittsburgh Press, 1949 [1784]), p. 24; as quoted in Daniel B. Botkin, *Discordant Harmonies: A New Ecology for the Twenty-First Century* (New York: Oxford University Press, 1990), p. 51.

2. Zora Neale Hurston, *Their Eyes Were Watching God* (New York: HarperCollins, 1990 [1937]), p. 8.

3. C. G. Jung, "The Philosophical Tree," in *Alchemical Studies, CW* 13, trans. R. F. C. Hull, Bollingen Series XX (Princeton: Princeton University Press 1977, [1967]), pp. 253, 272.

4. E. F. Hammer, *The Clinical Application of Projective Drawings* (Springfield, IL: Charles C. Thomas, 1958), p. 630. Following quote from Karen Bolander, *Assessing Personality Through Tree Drawings* (New York: Basic Books, 1977), p. 4.

5. Moshe S. Torem, Alan Gilbertson, and Vicki Light, "Indications of Physical, Sexual, and Verbal Victimization in Projective Tree Drawings," *Journal of Clinical Psychology* 46, 6 (November 1990): 900–06.

6. Gaston Bachelard, *Air and Dreams: An Essay on the Imagination of Movement*, trans. Edith R. and C. Frederick Farrell (Dallas: The Dallas Institute Publications, 1988), p. 207.

7. Wendell Berry, "The Elm Tree by the River," in *The Country of Marriage* (San Diego: Harcourt Brace Jovanovich, 1975), p. 3.

8. An interesting if indirect parallel to this occurs in Jacques Lacan's discussion of the "mirror stage," which he postulates as occurring in infancy between the ages of approximately six and eighteen months—a time during which, as observations show, the infant jubilantly recognizes his image in a mirror. In this image, the infant inchoately anticipates an overcoming of "a certain dehiscence at the heart of the organism, a primordial Discord betrayed by the signs of uneasiness and motor unco-ordination of the neo-natal months" (Jacques Lacan, "The Mirror Stage," in *Écrits: A Selection*, trans. Alan Sheridan [New York: W. W. Norton & Co., 1977], p. 4). That is, in the *actual* mirror image, the infant gazes upon the possibility of the coherence, integrity, and coordination of the body-self, which then symbolically ramifies in later development. Lacan doesn't mention

trees, but a certain treelikeness appears in his conception of the mirror stage as "the succession of phantasies that extends from a fragmented body-image to a form of its totality that I shall call *orthopaedic*—and, lastly, to the assumption of the armour of an alienating identity, which will mark with its rigid structure the subject's entire mental development" (emphasis added).

I would speculate that, very early on, actual trees can become mirrors in an analogous sense as an infant or small child discovers—often with considerable excitement—the trees' coherent, verticalizing (if often odd) integrations of form. This becomes an instance of the more general function of the mirror stage, namely "to establish a relation between the organism and its reality"—one's "relation to nature. . . ." It is a variation on the theme discussed in my text—the experience of vitality, renewal, and infusion of integrity in the presence of the upright trees. At the same time, as Lacan indicates, there is in this relation the potential "of an alienating identity," a treelike form of estrangement.

9.   George Nakashima, *The Soul of a Tree* (Tokyo / New York: Kodansha International, Ltd., 1981), p. 79.

10.   Edward S. Casey, *Spirit and Soul: Essays in Philosophical Psychology* (Dallas: Spring Publications, 1991), pp. xv, xvi–xvii, xviii, xix, xxi.

11.   Edward S. Casey, *Remembering: A Phenomenological Study* (Bloomington: Indiana University Press, 1987), p. 267.

12.   "Getting Placed: Soul in Space," in *Spirit and Soul*, p. 297.

13.   In William Dietrich, *The Final Forest: The Battle for the Last Great Trees of the Pacific Northwest* (New York: Simon & Schuster, 1992), pp. 278, 279.

14.   In W. S. Merwin, *The Rain in the Trees* (New York: Alfred A. Knopf, 1988), p. 64.

15.   Rilke, *Prose Fragments*, 109–10; quoted in Bachelard, *Air and Dreams*, p. 208.

16.   Donald Culross Peattie, *A Natural History of Trees of Eastern and Central North America* (Boston: Houghton Mifflin Co., 1991 [1948]), p. xii.

17.   The student thought of Martin Buber, who introduces his concept of the "I–You" (versus "I–It") relationship with a passage on an encounter with a tree. The movement from the encounter with a tree into reflective

thinking—the way the tree seems to *initiate* that movement—is worth noting. In different ways, all those of whom I've spoken so far move spontaneously from immediate experiences of trees into philosophically or ecologically reflective thought; the student's reference to Buber only makes more plain that these transits are all reflections of an old and near-universal association between trees, thought, philosophy, and knowledge.

But a look at Buber's words in *I and Thou* suggests that the particularity of the human–tree relationship shapes in precise ways his more general understanding of the "I–You relation." In contrast to the self that has objectified *experience* of the "It," "whoever says You . . . stands in relation." Prior to mentioning the tree, Buber's metaphor of *standing* prepares for the encounter. Imagining himself before a tree, he fleshes out the bodily and kinaesthetic images. First, "I contemplate a tree" and "I . . . accept it as a picture"; next "I can feel it as movement: the flowing veins around the sturdy, striving core, the sucking of the roots, the breathing of the leaves, the infinite commerce with earth and air—and the growing itself in its darkness." In a way that conveys admiration for the tree and partially contradicts the conclusion of this passage ("What I encounter is neither the soul of a tree nor a dryad, but the tree itself"), Buber's words envisage the tree as having specific qualities of sentience. After describing contemplating the tree as an It (which involves "overcom[ing] its uniqueness and form"), Buber describes being drawn into a relationship with the tree as a You (involving a "power of exclusiveness"—the particular tree as distinguished from abstract and objective categorizations). He stresses the tree's actuality with the assertion "it confronts me bodily and has to deal with me as I must deal with it—only differently." The tree confronts the human being as well as vice versa, and in a way that leads Buber, as his translator points out, to use a "most unusual" German construction to emphasize its bodily nature. For, continues Buber, "relation is reciprocity." He then must add that that does not mean the tree has "consciousness," but there would seem to be something of tree consciousness in his following discussion of the I–You relationship between human beings, which he introduces with a phrase meaning literally "I stand [*Stehe Ich*] . . . across from": a horizontal reciprocity between tree and human You-ness, as it were, embodied in the vertical standing. See Martin Buber, *I and Thou*, trans. Walter Kaufmann (New York: Charles Scribner's Sons, 1970); quotes from pp. 55 and 57–59, respectively.

18.   Carolyn Forché, "The Recording Angel," excerpted in *The Best American Poetry 1991*, ed. Mark Strand (New York: MacMillan Publishing Co., 1991), p. 50.

19.   Jane is joined in her interest by a number of recent writers in the academic and feminist communities. See, for instance, Elinor W. Gadon, *Once and Future Goddess* (New York: HarperSanFrancisco, 1989), especially chs. 8 and 10.

20.   For an acutely perceptive feminist psychoanalytic analysis of male / female, father / mother idealization, see Jessica Benjamin, *The Bonds of Love: Psychoanalysis, Feminism, and the Problem of Domination* (New York: Pantheon Books, 1988), pp. 100–23. Benjamin relates her analysis to ecological debates, questioning the polarization between destructive masculine techno-exploitation of nature and a unitive, utopic feminine merging with the ecological (pp. 158–59). A close consideration of trees shows that, no matter how polarized one's ideas of male and female, the dichotomy is inadequate to one's experience of trees—their psychological ramifications.

21.   C. Kerényi, *The Gods of the Greeks*, trans. Norman Cameron (London: Thames & Hudson, 1979 [1951]), p. 141.

22.   Quoted in Jung, "Philosophical Tree," p. 273; Alciata, *Emblemata cum commentariis*, p. 888b.

23.   Andreas Alciatus, *The Latin Emblems*, ed. Peter M. Daly with Virginia W. Callahan (Toronto: University of Toronto Press, 1985), Emblem 143.

24.   Hurston, *Their Eyes Were Watching God*, pp. 12, 15.

25.   Gordon Parks, *Voices in the Mirror: An Autobiography* (New York: Doubleday, 1990), p. 19.

26.   John Fowles, *The Tree* (New York: Ecco Press, 1983), pp. 7–8, 18.

27.   See *The Odyssey*, XXIV. 227, 231. Following quote from 336–41 (author's translation).

28.   In W. S. Merwin, *Rain in the Trees*, p. 6.

29.   Annie Dillard, *The Living* (New York: HarperCollins, 1992); following quotes from pp. 18–19, 17, 11, 34, 264, 310–11, 198, 275, 25, and 37 respectively.

30.   On the psychology of yellow, see James Hillman, "The Yellowing of the Work," paper presented at the International Congress of the International Association for Analytical Psychology, Paris, 1989; and at a workshop on alchemy at the Open Center, New York, 1992. See also Peter

Bishop, *The Greening of Psychology: The Vegetable World in Myth, Dream, and Healing* (Dallas: Spring Publications, 1990), pp. 15–16.

31. Buzz Eades, quoted in Timothy Egan, "Clinton Under Crossfire at Logging Conference," *The New York Times*, 3 April 1993.

32. See, for instance, William Dietrich, *The Final Forest*, ch. 6; William Booth, "New Thinking on Old Growth," *Science* 244 (14 April 1989): 141–43; and Richard E. Rice, "Old-growth Logging Myths: The Ecological Impact of the US Forest Service's Management Policies," *The Ecologist* 20, 4 (1990): 141–46.

33. The debate about forest, and forest-fire, management in Yellowstone continues (though observers have emphasized that such fires appear to be an important feature of the longterm ecology of the region). For detailed analyses of the ecological impact of the Yellowstone fires, see the articles on the subject in *BioScience* 39 (November 1989).

34. Will's argument is colored by the traditional viewpoint of American forestry, which over the past two decades has been radically altered to take into account ecological and biological work on the heretofore unnoticed or neglected forms of diversity in old-growth forests. At the same time, Will's experience of successful forest management in the Francis Marion carries with it its own validity, and to recognize the value of preserving old-growth forests is hardly incompatible with (and may indeed require) ecologically attuned forms of what Will would likely insist are human control and management.

35. See Howard E. Gruber, *Darwin on Man: A Psychological Study of Scientific Creativity,* together with Charles Darwin, *Darwin's Early and Unpublished Notebooks*, ed. Paul H. Barrett (New York: E. P. Dutton, 1974).

36. Howard E. Gruber, "Darwin's 'Tree of Nature' and Other Images of Wide Scope," in *On Aesthetics in Science*, ed. Judith Wechsler (Boston / Basel: Birkhäuser, n.d.), p. 123.

37. Ibid., p. 127.

38. Charles Darwin, *Origin of Species*, in *The Origin of Species and The Descent of Man* (New York: The Modern Library, n.d.), p. 85.

39. Gruber remarks that the diagram in the *Origin of Species* is fundamentally "the same . . . as his figure 3" in his unpublished notebooks (Gruber, "Darwin's 'Tree,'" p. 127). The tree figure is reproduced on p. 129 of the text.

40. In *Origin of Species*, pp. 99–100.

41. Gruber, "Darwin's 'Tree,'" pp. 134, 124.

42. From Darwin's description of his visit to Mauritius in *The Voyage of the Beagle* (New York: Dutton, 1959 [1860, 2d ed.]), p. 477. The following quotes are from pp. 484 and 416.

43. Robert Pogue Harrison, *Forests: The Shadow of Civilization* (Chicago: University of Chicago Press, 1992), p. 201.

44. "The idea is that a thing's essence is exhaustively determined by its relationships," says the environmental philosopher J. Baird Callicott; in fact, "it cannot be conceived apart from its relationship with other things." Certainly this is as true of trees as it is of human life. See Callicott, "The Metaphysical Implications of Ecology" in his compilation of essays, *In Defense of the Land Ethic: Essays in Environmental Philosophy* (Albany: State University of New York Press, 1989), p. 110.

45. See also Andrew Samuels, "National Psychology, National Socialism, and Analytical Psychology: Reflections on Jung and Anti-semitism (Part II)," *The Journal of Analytical Psychology* 37, 2 (April 1992): 135–39 for thoughtful post-Jungian reflections of "the psychology of difference." Samuels especially emphasizes "reconnecting to Jung's intuition about the importance of difference but being firm about staying unhindered by excessive dependence on complementarity, on the dogma of 'the opposites,' on oppositional thinking and, above all, on essentialism—the argument that things are as they are because it's only natural for them to be that way" (pp. 138–39). The recognition of intimacies within difference seems crucial both to the humane rethinking of (interhuman) cultural divergencies Samuels's advocates, and to the exploration of the range of divergencies between human and nonhuman actualities.

46. While working on a revision of this section, I received in the mail an offprint of an article by Jonathan Z. Smith entitled "Differential Equations: On Constructing the 'Other'" (Thirteenth Annual University Lecture in Religion, Arizona State University, 5 March 1992) that speaks precisely to the cultural importance of difference. Echoing Andrew Samuels's disentangling of difference from "the opposites" (see previous note), Smith values the fluidity implied by the concept of difference over the conceptual *absolute* of "the other." He highlights "the ubiquity of the construction of difference in human culture" and proposes "that culture itself is constituted by the double process of both making differences and relativizing those very same distinctions. One of our fundamental social projects appears to be our collective capacity to think of, and to think away,

the differences we create" (p. 11). While Smith is dealing with interhuman difference, one could think about the human / nonhuman (or human / tree) distinction in those words.

47. John Kleinig, *Valuing Life* (Princeton: Princeton University Press, 1991), p. 70.

48. Jane's phrase, "more light," is also Goethe's, spoken on his deathbed. For a sensitive literary discussion of the desire for "more light," for *clearing*, see Robert Pogue Harrison, *Forests*, pp. 9–11. Clearing the forest becomes a basic metaphor for the development of consciousness. Its persistence, and the estrangement from the forest that it implies, is evident in Max Oelschlaeger's conclusion to his study of *The Idea of Wilderness*. He wonders: "Have we so fouled this earth, so covered the green world beneath our second world, that no light can penetrate the world's midnight?" (p. 353). Such questions can only be dealt with by "the postmodern mind," by an "exercise of consciousness. . . ."

49. John F. Dwyer, Herbert W. Schroeder, and Paul H. Gobster, "The Significance of Urban Trees and Forests: Toward a Deeper Understanding of Values," *Journal of Arboriculture* 17, 10 (October 1991): 281; E. O. Wilson, *The Diversity of Life* (Cambridge: The Belknap Press of Harvard University Press, 1992), p. 350.

50. Herbert W. Schroeder, "The Psychological Value of Trees," *The Public Garden* 6, 1 (January 1991): 18.

51. Donald R. Perry, "Tropical Biology: A Science on the Sidelines," in *Lessons of the Rainforest*, ed. Suzanne Head and Robert Heinzman (San Francisco: Sierra Club Books, 1990), p. 29. See also H. Rolston, "Values Deep in the Woods: The Hard-to-Measure Benefits of Forest Preservation," in *Proceedings of the 1987 Society of American Foresters National Convention* (Minneapolis, 18–21 October 1987), pp. 315–19.

CHAPTER 4

1. Natalie Angier, "Warming? Tree Rings Say Not Yet," *The New York Times, Science Times*, 1 December 1992, p. C4. "The reason why trees are such an extraordinary barometer of the world around them is that they respond to shifts in temperature, rainfall or other environmental conditions by altering their growth," so that the widths of season rings vary.

2. J.R.R. Tolkien, *The Two Towers, Part II of The Lord of the Rings* (New York: Ballantine Books, 1965), pp. 82, 102, 87, 89, 105–06, 109, 97, 96–97.

3. For the quote from Aldo Leopold, see "Thinking Like a Mountain," in *A Sand Country Almanac: With Essays on Conservation from Round River* (New York: Ballantine Books, 1966), p. 138.

4. O. Henry, "The Last Leaf," in *The Complete Works of O. Henry* (Garden City, NY: Doubleday, 1953), pp. 1455–459.

5. Wendell Berry, "Planting Trees," in *The Country of Marriage* (San Diego: Harcourt Brace Jovanovich, 1975), p. 23.

6. In Gwendolyn Brooks, *The Near-Johannesburg Boy: And Other Poems* (Chicago: Third World Press, 1986), p. 14.

7. Langston Hughes, *The Panther and the Lash: Poems of Our Times* (New York: Alfred A. Knopf, 1979), p. 100.

8. Franz Boas, *Kwakiutl Culture as Reflected in Mythology* (New York: American Folklore Society, 1935), p. 169.

9. James Hillman, *Re-Visioning Psychology* (New York: Harper & Row, 1975), p. 13.

10. W.S. Merwin, "Touching the Tree," in *The Rain in the Trees* (New York: Alfred A. Knopf, 1988), p. 7.

11. Michael Pollan, *Second Nature: A Gardener's Education* (New York: Laurel, 1991), pp. 150–51.

12. Jessica Benjamin, *The Bonds of Love: Psychoanalysis, Feminism, and the Problem of Domination* (New York: Pantheon Books, 1988), p. 71.

13. See C.G. Jung, *Psychology and Alchemy*, CW 12, trans. R. F. C. Hull, Bollingen Series XX (Princeton: Princeton University Press, 1974 [1953]), pp. 257, 279.

14. This can serve as a psychological definition of nature, but one with philosophical implications. Implicit in the image of nature as Ecological Pandaemonium is presence, power, and contradiction. But I'm trying at the same time to avoid the pitfalls of *essentialist* definitions of nature or the natural, which conflate nonhuman nature and human cultural construction (see pp. 109, 110–11).

15. In *Pilgrim at Tinker Creek* (Toronto/New York/London: Bantam Books, 1975 [1974]), pp. 45–46.

16. Robert Jay Lifton, in his study of *The Protean Self*, notes that Proteus transforms himself briefly into a tree (New York: Basic Books, 1993), p. 5.

17. Peter Bishop, *The Greening of Psychology: The Vegetable World in Myth, Dream, and Healing* (Dallas: Spring Publications, 1990), p. 102.

18. Ibid., p. 122.

19. Ibid., pp. 136–37.

20. We do find considerable hostility toward trees at certain points in the monotheistic traditions (though it should be borne in mind that such hostility is hardly monolithic, and there is a great diversity of tree-related images and feelings in the Bible and Qu'ran). God means it, for instance, when he instructs Moses and the Israelites: "Justice, *and only* justice, you shall pursue"—which means, first of all that "You shall not plant for yourself an Asherah of any kind of tree beside the altar of the LORD your God" (Deuteronomy 16:20, 21), Asherah being likely a reference to a Goddess, possibly a Near-Eastern form of the one called by the Greeks Aphrodite. See also Exodus 34:13 for God's instructions to cut down trees, and the prophets Hoseah (4:13) and Isaiah (1:29) for further examples of divine antagonism toward trees.

Asherah, in the Bible, appears "to be a blending of several Near Eastern goddesses: Athirat (. . .), Astarte, Anat, and the Mesopotamian goddess Innana-Ishtar" (William J. Fulco, "Athirat," in *The Encyclopedia of Religion*, vol. 1, ed. Mircea Eliade [New York: MacMillan, 1987], p. 492). Astarte and Ishtar are love-Goddesses, and Ishtar is indirectly associated with the forest. This may be reflected in her response to being spurned by Gilgamesh after he and his friend, Enkidu, cut down the cedar forest (its monster, Huwawa) in the course of *The Epic of Gilgamesh*, she causes a drought (figured by an attack by "the Bull of Heaven")—perhaps an image connecting forest destruction and desertification. Ishtar's initial proposition to Gilgamesh includes the ironic line "in the fragrance of cedars thou shalt enter our house" (*The Epic of Gilgamesh*, in *The Ancient Near East*, vol. 1, ed. James B. Pritchard [Princeton: Princeton University Press, 1958], p. 51). Rikvah Schärf Kluger notes a variant of the story "which expressly confirms [a] connection between the cedar forest, Humbaba [Assyrian spelling], and Ishtar" (*The Archetypal Significance of Gilgamesh: A Modern Ancient Hero* [Einsiedeln, Switzerland: Daimon Verlag, 1991], pp. 94–95). On the relation between Gilgamesh and forest destruction, see John Perlin, *A Forest Journey: The Role of Wood in the Development of Civilization* (New York: W. W. Norton, 1989), pp. 35–39; Robert Pogue Harrison, *Forests: The Shadow of Civilization* (Chicago: University of Chicago Press, 1992), pp. 13–18.

Hostility toward trees as manifested in the Bible has pre-biblical, pagan roots.

21.   See Rafael Patai, *The Hebrew Goddess* (New York: Avon Books, 1978 [1967]); on contemporary women's spirituality see, for instance, Elinor W. Gadon, *Once and Future Goddess* (New York: HarperSanFrancisco, 1989). For a commentary on the importance of the Goddess image in American feminism, see Catherine L. Albanese, *Nature Religion in America: From the Algonkian Indians to the New Age* (Chicago/London: University of Chicago Press, 1990), pp. 178–85.

22.   Joseph M. Kitagawa, *On Understanding Japanese Religion* (Princeton: Princeton University Press, 1987), pp. 44, 45.

23.   Genichi Kato, *A Historical Study of the Religious Development of Shinto*, trans. Shoyu Hanayama (New York: Greenwood Press, 1973), pp. 119, 120.

24.   Dr. Sokyo Ono, *Shinto: The Kami Way*, collab. William P. Woodard (Rutland, VT/Tokyo: Charles E. Tuttle Co., 1962), p. 99.

25.   "Sotoba Komachi," in *The No Plays of Japan*, trans. Arthur Waley (New York: Grove Press, 1921), p. 151.

26.   Juliet Piggott, *Japanese Mythology* (London: Paul Hamlyn, 1969), p. 61.

27.   James Hillman, "Peaks and Vales: The Soul/Spirit Distinction as Basis for the Differences between Psychotherapy and Spiritual Discipline," in *Puer Papers*, ed. James Hillman (Dallas: Spring Publications, 1979), pp. 54–74.

28.   C. G. Jung, "The Phenomenology of the Spirit in Fairytales," in *The Archetypes and the Collective Unconscious, CW* 9, 1, trans. R. F. C. Hull, Bollingen Series XX (Princeton: Princeton University Press, 1977 [1959]), p. 210. The following quote in my text is from p. 209.

29.   Printed in *Poetry for the Earth*, ed. Sara Dunn with Alan Scholefield (New York: Fawcett Columbine, 1991), p. 31.

30.   One could contrast the role of idealization in Jane and Ted, noting that for Jane it may be an important motivating image in her current search for *women's* roots and her openness to sexual love between women. For Ted, the idealized image is primarily a hindrance, a reminder of his distant relationship with his father, an expectation no one can live up to. Both cases complexly mingle biographical and cultural psychological struggles; Jane and Ted are very different people, in very different life-locations; the

crucial *context* of idealization points to the divergent roles it plays in each life. But, in addition, each struggle takes a thematically similar shape when it comes to the tension that grows in trees. And in each case there is value in the less ideal image.

31. *Beowulf*, trans. Berton Raffel (New York: The New American Library, Inc., 1963); quoted in *News of the Universe: Poems of Twofold Consciousness*, comp. Robert Bly (San Francisco: Sierra Club Books, 1980), p. 263.

32. Zora Neale Hurston, *Their Eyes Were Watching God* (New York: HarperCollins, 1990 [1937]), pp. 17–18.

33. John Haines, *The Stars, the Snow, the Fire: Twenty-five Years in the Alaskan Wilderness* (New York: Washington Square Press, 1989), p. 167.

34. Maximo D. Ramos, *Philippine Demonological Legends and Their Cultural Bearings* (Quezon City: Phoenix Publishing House, 1990), p. 18.

35. Ibid., p. 55. Following quote from p. 53.

36. Annie Dillard, *The Living* (New York: HarperCollins, 1992), quotes from pp. 71, 206, 172, 173, 221, 187, 174, 197, 217, 265.

37. Gordon Parks, *Voices in the Mirror: An Autobiography* (New York: Doubleday, 1990), pp. xii, xiii–xiv.

38. Ibid., p. 165.

39. *The New York Times*, 25 May 1992, p. A18.

40. See the insightful discussion of the forest images in *Macbeth* in Harrison, *Forests*, pp. 102–04.

41. Elias Canetti, *Crowds and Power*, trans. Carol Stewart (New York: Continuum, 1981 [1960]), p. 173.

42. Robert A. Pois, *National Socialism and the Religion of Nature* (New York: St. Martin's Press, 1986), p. 26.

43. See Wilhelm Steckelings, "From the Oak Tree to Certain Victory," printed in George L. Mosse, *Nazi Culture: Intellectual, Cultural, and Social Life in the Third Reich*, trans. Salvator Attanasio (New York: Shocken Books, 1981 [1966]), pp. 288–90; quoted in Pois, *National Socialism*, p. 133.

44. Toni Morrison, *Beloved* (New York: Alfred A. Knopf, 1987), p. 6.

45. North East Thames contingency plans for a nuclear war, quoted in *The Guardian*, 14 May 1983; quoted as epigraph to Stephen Daniels, "The Political Iconography of Woodland in Later Georgian England," in

The Iconography of Landscape, ed. Denis Cosgrove and Stephen Daniels (Cambridge: Cambridge University Press, 1988), p. 43.

46.   See Robert Jay Lifton and Eric Markusen, *The Genocidal Mentality: Nazi Holocaust and Nuclear Threat* (New York: Basic Books, 1990), p. 3.

47.   Joan M. Welch, "An Assessment of Socio-Economic and Land-Use Histories That Influence Urban Forest Structure: Boston's Neighborhoods of Roxbury and North Dorchester," Ph.D. Dissertation, Boston University (1991), p. 24.

48.   Lewis Lapham, "City Lights," *Harper's Magazine*, July 1992, p. 6.

49.   Keith V. Thomas, *Man and the Natural World* (London: Allen Lane, 1983), pp. 219, 217–18.

50.   Michael Pollan, with reference to Thomas's discussion of English trees, speaks of the "Political Tree," but recognizes that the qualities of trees themselves affect the sociopolitical scene when he says of the old English trees that they "not only reflect the country's conservative traditions, they've probably helped to perpetuate them too" (*Second Nature*, pp. 194, 195).

51.   Peter Bishop has examined a particular tree, the "Karma-Kargyudpa Lineage Tree" in the Tibetan Buddhist tradition, iconographically presented in a temple as the abode of numerous personages—deities, guardians, historical figures. Here, as in many religious depictions, the tree plays a key "role [in] organizing archetypal imagery"; it serves as an introduction to the beginning practitioner of the Kargyudpa tradition, encompassing "in an ordered and systematic unity" the complexities of Buddhist spirituality. But it is double-edged; as Bishop observes, "Especially noticeable . . . is the devaluation of other traditions through the position and use of Hindu deities, trampled underfoot" at the base of the tree—a devaluation that cannot be evaded, whatever "symbolic purpose" is also intended. Political ramifications of such a tree are unavoidable. See Bishop, "Archetypal Topography: The Karma-Kargyudpa Lineage Tree," *Spring 1981: An Annual of Archetypal Psychology and Jungian Thought*: 69–75. The tree is described on p. 67. Quotes are from pp. 69, 70, 72.

52.   Roland Barthes, *Mythologies* (New York: Hill and Wang, 1972), p. 129. See also the discussion of Barthes in Daniels, "Political Iconography," p. 73, n. 2.

53.   Liisa Malkki, "National Geographic: The Rooting of Peoples and the Territorialization of National Identity Among Scholars and Refugees,"

Cultural Anthropology 7, 1 (February 1992): 28, 26, 28. For a psychological discussion of roots, rootedness, and rootlessness, see Peter Bishop, *Greening of Psychology*, pp. 65–67 (on C. G. Jung's images of rootlessness) and 185–90.

54. Pastor Charles V., interviewed for the study of "Nuclear Threat and the American Self."

55. In her argument, Malkki relies heavily on the work of the French authors Gilles Deleuze and Felix Guattari, who mount an attack on the dominance of the tree model in "Western reality and all of Western thought, from botany to biology and anatomy" and in other disciplines including "all of philosophy. . . . The West has a special relation to the forest, and deforestation." They favor a rhizomatic model, not because of its *eternal* quality that Jung emphasizes but because the rhizome is more mobile, antidualistic and antihierarchical. It "connects any point to any other point, and its traits are not necessarily linked to traits of the same nature," and it has no center. The tree model, conversely, is premised on the formula of "one becomes two," so that "binary logic is the spiritual reality of the root-tree." As Deleuze and Guattari themselves acknowledge, their polemic itself sets up a (tree–rhizome) dualism and has its limitations. But it is worth giving them an ear for a moment, because a tree spirit lives in their brief against the dominance of "the spiritual reality of the tree," one that they distinguish from trees "in nature," with their "taproots with a more multiple, lateral, and circular system of ramification, rather than a dichotomous one. Thought lags behind nature." Like all who talk tree spirits, they distinguish between the tree and the spirit; the spirit haunts their work and has political relevance.

The tree spirit they have in mind "fixes an order"; "there is," moreover, "always something genealogical about a tree. It is not a method for the people." Its order, that is, has an authoritarian element. And "the tree and root inspire a sad image of thought that is forever imitating the multiple on the basis of a centered or segmented higher unity." The *sadness* of some thought, then, is *actively* inspired, shaped, by the tree. The vital power of this tree spirit can manifest also in sad images. It is related to "the State's pretension to be a world order, and to root man." This is where deep-rooted nationalisms and prejudices come in, also where the tree's *tendency to ramify into a world* shows itself. It is, argue Deleuze and Guattari, a static world, not like the underground "alliance" that constitutes

a rhizome. Malkki continues: "The territorializing, often arborescent con-
ceptions of nation and culture . . . are associated with a powerful sedentarism in our thinking. . . . This sedentarism is not inert. It actively ter-
ritorializes our identities, whether cultural or national." The sedentarism
Malkki refers to literalizes and *essentializes* roots; that is, it empowers the
formation of images of a pure (or impure) essential identity, and hence
the search for illusory *real* (pure or purified) roots of a national, ethnic,
or religious character. In contrast, one could (say Delueze and Guattari)
"be quick, even when standing still!" For "we're tired of trees. We should
stop believing in trees, roots, and radicles. They've made us suffer too
much." See Gilles Deleuze and Felix Guattari, *A Thousand Plateaus: Capi-
talism and Schizophrenia*, trans. Brian Massumi (Minneapolis: University
of Minnesota Press, 1987), p. 18. The above quotes are from pp. 5, 8, 16,
21, and 24 respectively.

56.   Tolkien, *The Two Towers*, p. 99; subsequent quote from *The Return
of the King* [Part III of *The Lord of the Rings*], p. 319.

57.   Roland Bechmann, *Trees and Man: The Forest in the Middle Ages*,
trans. Katharyn Dunham (New York: Paragon House, 1990 [1984]), p. 276.

58.   "The Crust," in *The Rain and the Trees*, p. 41.

59.   *A Sand Country Almanac*, pp. 9–10.

60.   It would seem that *writing, narrative, and history* are repeatedly
evoked by the power of trees. Trees are in that sense writers' tools. Bechmann
points to the close association between trees, books, and "writing, which
is meant to constitute an objective and perennial memory," in Western European languages (*Trees and Man*, p. 290).

61.   Sherko Bekas, quoted in *The New York Times*, 14 April 1991, Section 4, p. 2.

62.   As related to George Hunt, who collected many tales for the anthropologist Franz Boas; quoted in Boas, *The Religion of the Kwakiutl
Indians*, vol. 2 (New York: Columbia University Press, 1930), p. 163.

63.   Franz Boas, "Ethnology of the Kwakiutl," *35th Annual Report of
the Bureau of American Ethnology* (1913–14), pt. 2 (1921), p. 1290.

64.   Stanley Walens, *Feasting with Cannibals: An Essay on Kwakiutl
Cosmology* (Princeton: Princeton University Press, 1981); following three
quotes from pp. 70, 5, 58. In the following, I rely for the most part on
the English forms of Kwakiutl names given in Walens's account; their spell-
ings vary widely.

65.   Quote from Irving Goldman, *The Mouth of Heaven: An Introduction to Kwakiutl Religion* (New York: John Wiley and Sons, 1975), p. 112.

66.   Walens, *Feasting*, pp. 53–54, 72.

67.   From Franz Boas, "Ethnology of the Kwakiutl," *35th Annual Report of the Bureau of American Ethnology* (1913–14), pt. 1 (1921), pp. 616–17, 619.

68.   This and the following quote from Boas, *Religion of the Kwakiutl Indians*, p. 106.

69.   Boas, "Ethnology of the Kwakiutl," pt. 1, pp. 617–18.

70.   Franz Boas, *Kwakiutl Tales* (New York: Columbia University Press, 1910), pp. 117–19. The spelling of "Dzonoqua" is taken from this volume.

71.   Goldman, *Mouth of Heaven*, pp. 110, 111; following quote from p. 191.

72.   Ibid., p. 97.

73.   Ibid., p. 193.

74.   Franz Boas, "Ethnology of the Kwakiutl," pt. 2, pp. 1181, 1180, 1220.

75.   Ibid., pp. 1337–338.

76.   See Phil Nuytten, *The Totem Carvers: Charlie James, Ellen Neel, and Mungo Martin* (Vancouver: Panorama Publications, Ltd., 1982), pp. 116–26.

77.   Audrey Hawthorn, *Kwakiutl Art* (Seattle / London: University of Washington Press, 1979), p. 70.

78.   Goldman, *Mouth of Heaven*, p. 192.

79.   Franz Boas, *Kwakiutl Ethnography*, ed. Helen Codere (Chicago: University of Chicago Press, 1966), pp. 131–32, 135.

80.   Goldman, *Mouth of Heaven*, p. 177.

81.   *The Living*, p. 237.

82.   Audrey Hawthorn, *Kwakiutl Art*, p. 218.

83.   Boas, *Kwakiutl Culture*, p. 146.

CHAPTER 5

1. Gaston Bachelard, *Air and Dreams: An Essay on the Imagination of Movement*, trans. Edith R. and C. Frederick Farrell (Dallas: The Dallas Institute Publications, 1988), p. 217.

2. Phyllis Windle, "The Ecology of Grief," *BioScience* 42, 5 (May 1992): 363–66.

3. *Observer* staff, "Rare Trees Lost," *The London Observer*, 18 October 1987, p. 1.

4. Mary Oliver, "The Lost Children," *American Primitive* (Boston: Little, Brown and Company, 1984), p. 15.

5. Carson McCullers, *The Ballad of the Sad Café and Other Stories* (New York: Bantam Books, 1990 [1951]), p. 12. Following quotes from pp. 6, 12, 27, 70.

6. Carson McCullers, *The Heart Is a Lonely Hunter* (New York: Bantam Books, 1967 [1940]), p. 244.

7. Toni Morrison, *Beloved* (New York: Alfred A. Knopf, 1987). The following quotes are from pp. 79, 6, 89, 87, 19, 35, 17.

8. Zora Neale Hurston, *Their Eyes Were Watching God* (New York: HarperCollins, 1990 [1937]), p. 18.

9. Annie Dillard, *The Living* (New York: HarperCollins, 1992), p. 50.

10. William Styron, *Darkness Visible: A Memoir of Madness* (New York: Random House, 1990), p. 83.

11. See Hal Hartzell, Jr., *The Yew Tree: A Thousand Whispers: Biography of a Species* (Eugene, OR: Hulogosi Books, 1992).

12. David Rains Wallace, *Bulow Hammock: Mind in a Forest* (San Francisco: Sierra Club Books, 1989), pp. 13, 14.

13. Tim O'Brien, "How to Tell a True War Story," in *The Things They Carried* (New York: Penguin Books, 1990), p. 80.

14. Quoted in Loring M. Danforth, *The Death Rituals of Rural Greece* (Princeton: Princeton University Press, 1982), p. 98.

15. J. R. R. Tolkien, *The Return of the King, Part III of The Lord of the Rings* (New York: Ballantine Books, 1965), p. 374.

16. In the combined edition of *The Charleston News* and *Courier/Evening Post* of 23 September.

17. See Judith Herman, *Trauma and Recovery* (New York: Basic Books, 1992).

18. Elias Canetti, *Crowds and Power*, trans. Carol Stewart (New York: Continuum, 1981 [1960]), pp. 67, 85.

19. Stephen Crane, *The Red Badge of Courage: And Other Writings*, ed. Richard Chase (Cambridge, MA: The Riverside Press, 1960), pp. 165, 192.

20. Jon Winant, personal communication, 5 August 1990.

21. Chuck Sudetic, "West Doubts Yugoslavs Will Send in the Army," *The New York Times*, 29 January 1993, p. A3, col. 1.

22. "Pumping Oil, a Rebounding Iran Strives for Regional Leadership in the Gulf," *The New York Times*, 7 November 1992, p. A6, col. 3.

23. Michael Pollan, *Second Nature: A Gardener's Education* (New York: Laurel, 1991), pp. 55, 58, 59, 63.

24. John Haines, *The Stars, the Snow, the Fire: Twenty-five Years in the Alaskan Wilderness* (New York: Washington Square Press, 1989), pp. 53, 54.

25. O'Brien, *The Things They Carried*, pp. 77–78, 85, 87, 89, 80, 81.

26. Leonard Nathan, "The Election," in *Carrying On: New & Selected Poems* (Pittsburgh: University of Pittsburgh Press, 1985), p. 104.

27. Daniel B. Botkin, *Discordant Harmonies: A New Ecology for the Twenty-First Century* (New York: Oxford University Press, 1990), p. 117.

28. See Charles B. Strozier, Michael Perlman, and Robert Jay Lifton, "Nuclear Threat and the American Self" and Robert Jay Lifton, *The Protean Self* (New York: Basic Books, 1993), ch. 11.

29. Jonathan Schell, *The Fate of the Earth* (New York: Alfred A. Knopf, 1982). The following quotes from pp. 63–64, 65.

CHAPTER 6

1. Georg Kohlmaier and Barna von Sartory, *Houses of Glass*, trans. John C. Harvey (Cambridge & London: MIT Press, 1986), p. 12.

2. Harold F. Searles, *The Nonhuman Environment: In Normal Development and in Schizophrenia* (New York: International Universities Press, Inc., 1960), pp. 294, 295.

3. Roger S. Ulrich, "Aesthetic and Affective Response to Natural Environment," *Human Behavior and the Environment* (New York: Plenum, 1983), p. 116.

4. For a recent article which includes a brief survey of the literature see Virgil L. Sheets and Chris D. Manzer, "Affect, Cognition, and Urban Vegetation: Some Effects of Adding Trees Along City Streets," *Environment and Behavior* 23, 3 (May 1991): 285–304. The authors conduct two experiments indicating that people find the presence of trees helpful in urban areas, resulting in better feelings about treed places and more positive evaluations of them.

5. Roger S. Ulrich, "View through a Window May Influence Recovery from Surgery," *Science* 224, no. 4647 (27 April 1984): 420, 421. Ulrich studied the records of a group of postoperative gall bladder patients at a hospital during the years from 1972 to 1981.

6. Quoted in *Trees: A Celebration*, ed. Jill Fairchild (New York: Weidenfeld & Nicholson, 1989), p. 39.

7. Annie Dillard, *The Living* (New York: HarperCollins, 1992), p. 235.

8. Hale White, '*Mark Rutherford*' *More Pages from a Journal* (London: Oxford University Press, 1910), p. 182. Quoted in Kim Taplin, *Tongues in Trees: Studies in Literature and Ecology* (Ford House: Green Books, 1989), p. 14.

9. Jessica Benjamin, *The Bonds of Love: Psychoanalysis, Feminism, and the Problem of Domination* (New York: Pantheon Books, 1988), p. 29. See chapter 1 above, pp. 3–4.

10. Theodore Roszak, in his recent explorations of "ecopsychology" in *The Voice of the Earth* (New York: Simon & Schuster, 1992), pp. 294–96, critically considers Searles's contribution to a more environmentally aware psychology. Though he overstates his case, Roszak notes "a strenuously defensive stance" in much of Searles; this comes through in Searles's criticism of his appreciation of the tree as "inordinately keen." The defensiveness reflects, I believe, a profound cultural repression of our capacities for "lovingness," in Searles's congenial word, toward the nonhuman world.

11. Fyodor Dostoevsky, *Complete Letters*, vol. 1 (1832–1859), ed. and trans. David Lowe and Ronald Meyer (Ann Arbor: Ardis, 1988), p. 173, letter of 18 July 1849. The following quote is from p. 174, letter to Mikhail of 27 August 1849.

12. John Jones, Introduction to Fedor Dostoevsky, *Crime and Punishment*, trans. Jessie Coulson (New York and Oxford: Oxford University Press, 1981 [1953]), p. x.

13. Dostoevsky, *Letters*, p. 188 (30 January–22 February 1854).

14. Toni Morrison, *Beloved* (New York: Alfred A. Knopf, 1987), pp. 21, 221.

15. Aldo Leopold, "November," in *A Sand Country Almanac: With Essays on Conservation from Round River* (New York: Ballantine Books, 1966), pp. 74, 93.

16. Toni Morrison, *Beloved*, pp. 220, 22.

17. Ibid., pp. 220, 221.

18. Henry David Thoreau, "Walking," in *Thoreau: The Major Essays*, ed. Jeffrey L. Duncan (New York: E. P. Dutton Co., 1972), p. 209.

19. Printed in *Poetry for the Earth*, ed. Sara Dunn with Alan Scholefield (New York: Fawcett Columbine, 1991), p. 5.

20. Quoted in Brian Lanker, *I Dream a World: Portraits of Black Women Who Changed America* (New York: Stewart, Tabori & Chang, 1989), p. 8.

21. Langston Hughes, "Daybreak in Alabama," in *The Panther and the Lash: Poems of Our Times* (New York: Alfred A. Knopf, 1979), p. 101.

22. Gordon Parks, *Voices in the Mirror: An Autobiography* (New York: Doubleday, 1990), p. 327.

23. From panel exhibit, "The Lady and the Tree," Magnolia Tree Earth Center.

24. From A. S. Pushkin, *Sochineniia i pisma* (St. Petersburg, 1903), pp. 206–07; author's translation. I am indebted to Vladimir Maliavin for this reference.

25. See Robert Jay Lifton, *The Broken Connection* (New York: Basic Books, 1983 [1979]), pp. 22–23 and *The Protean Self*, "The Ecology of Proteanism."

26. Jim Peterson, "Stand Still," *Amicus Journal* (Winter 1993): 15.

27. Christopher D. Stone, *Should Trees Have Standing? Toward Legal Rights for Natural Objects* (Los Angeles: William Kaufmann, 1972).

28. Ibid., p. 49.

29. The following quotes from the story are from Carson McCullers, *Collected Stories* (Boston: Houghton Mifflin Co., 1987), pp. 125–33.

30. See Peter Bishop, *The Greening of Psychology: The Vegetable World in Myth, Dream, and Healing* (Dallas: Spring Publications, 1990), pp. 3–18.

31. See discussion of Harold Searles's case above (pp. 155–57).

32. Toni Morrison, *Beloved*, p. 162.

33. J. R. R. Tolkien, *The Two Towers, Part II of The Lord of the Rings* (New York: Ballantine Books, 1965), p. 96.

34. Quoted in Daniel Grotta, *Tolkien: Architect of Middle Earth* (Philadelphia: Running Press, 1992), p. 106.

35. From Zosimos, "The Treatise of Zosimos the Divine Concerning the Art," in C. G. Jung, "The Visions of Zosimos," in *Alchemical Studies, CW* 13, trans. R. F. C. Hull, Bollingen Series XX (Princeton: Princeton University Press, 1967), p. 64. As Jung points out, there are numerous metallic trees in alchemical imaginings (see, for instance, p. 89; also "The Philosophical Tree" in ibid., pp. 310–11). It should be noted that "metal" in alchemical philosophy is not exactly equivalent to our conceptual category of metal, but is understood as a psychic and spiritual component of the cosmos with an origin in one of the seven classical planets. Imagistically, however, alchemical metal embraces what we conceive as metal. Most important, the ecological sense of the alchemists can be considered as a thoroughgoing deconstruction of our usual organic / metallic dualities.

36. Men and women *do* express love—for people, for cars and other things, for ideas and images—by tearing them apart at times in order to hold them together. Sometimes this happens on a concrete level—as my father's surgical practice illustrates. Always, it has metaphoric ramifications. It can be a necessary way of forging a continuity of care, of attention to the things of the world. We sometimes need to get "under the hood" of things in order to get them moving. Though there is plenty of room for disagreement on specific policies, the love of mechanical things and its expression surely has a role to play in our attempts to restore and protect ecological communities.

37. Aldo Leopold, "The Land Ethic," in *A Sand Country Almanac*, pp. 253, 251, 261.

38. Thomas Berry calls forth this sense of solidarity of the natural and technological when he says that "human technologies should function in an *integral relationship with earth technologies*, not in a despotic or disturbing manner or under the metaphor of conquest, but rather in an evocative manner" (*The Dream of the Earth* [San Francisco: Sierra Club Books, 1988], p. 65). The evocativeness of technology, metal, and machine—their metaphors and images—may point the way toward more imaginative and ecologically sustainable technologies. More needs to be said about the relationship between "despotic" and "disturbing" manners, however. Psychologically, despotism can be seen as a defense against disquiet, against metaphoric and actual death, disintegration, fragmentation. Despotism

needs to be disturbed. Considered from an alchemical viewpoint, the disturbing quality of technology is unavoidable, but if we allow disturbance and disquiet their own evocativeness then technology is less prone to despotism—to rule by an old tyrannical king, in an alchemical image. Thus, in speaking of the ways of solidarity of trees, metal, and machines, I don't want to rule out the need for disturbing their images. And, as Berry and others note, given our planetary ecological predicament, we'd do better just now to feel disturbed rather than complacent.

For a thorough discussion of the development of Leopold's ecological philosophy, see Max Oelschlaeger, *The Idea of Wilderness: From Prehistory to the Age of Ecology* (New Haven: Yale University Press, 1991), ch. 7. Oelschlaeger discusses a "creative tension" between Leopold's "arcadian" and "imperial" ecological perspectives (pp. 7–8, 231–32). There is a broader context as well: "If we view Leopold as theoretically and existentially immersed within a cultural matrix that transcended merely disciplinary issues, then the land ethic can be understood as part of an ongoing twentieth-century struggle to link the descriptive world of classical science and the prescriptive world of ethics" (p. 239). One link between these two in Leopold's formulation quoted in the text is the tree. The tree is then part of the nonhuman context of Leopold's typically "twentieth-century" struggle. It becomes part of an image of the *mechanical* that, through its paradoxical partnership with the organic, transcends the merely *mechanistic*.

39. Walt Whitman, *Leaves of Grass* (New York: W. W. Norton, 1973 [1965]), p. 206.

40. See Catherine L. Albanese, *Nature Religion in America: From the Algonkian Indians to the New Age* (Chicago/London: University of Chicago Press, 1990), p. 75.

41. Robert Pogue Harrison, *Forests: The Shadow of Civilization* (Chicago: University of Chicago Press, 1992), pp. 2, 6, 7–8.

42. William Dietrich, *The Final Forest: The Battle for the Last Great Trees of the Pacific Northwest* (New York: Simon & Schuster, 1992), quotes from pp. 43, 42.

43. Whitman, *Leaves of Grass*, pp. 184, 186.

44. John Haines, *The Stars, the Snow, the Fire: Twenty-five Years in the Alaskan Wilderness* (New York: Washington Square Press, 1989), pp. 158–59.

45. Aldo Leopold, "December," in *A Sand Country Almanac*, p. 88.

46. Stephen Young, "Root and Branch in the Groves of Academe," *New Scientist* 23/30 (December 1989): 58, 61.

47. Unattributed, p. 5.

48. Georgia Tasker, "Emerging from Intensive Care," *The Miami Herald*, 27 September 1992.

49. John F. Dwyer, Herbert W. Schroeder, and Paul H. Gobster, "The Significance of Urban Trees and Forests: Toward a Deeper Understanding of Values," *Journal of Arboriculture* 17, 10 (October 1991): 281.

50. See: Anthony Joseph, "Roots," *Mother Jones* (April/May 1990); "Leaves of Gas," *Discover* (February 1989); Gary Moll, "Sex and the Single Tree," *American Forests* (September/October 1989); "A Tree Grows in Manhattan," *Environment* 31 (December 1989); Ari W. Epstein, "Woody Witnesses: Tree Rings Provide Evidence of an 1812 San Andreas Quake," *Scientific American* 259 (September 1988); "How the Wind Rubs Trees Up the Wrong Way," *New Scientist* 144 (2 October 1989); Larry Van Goethem, "Top This!" *National Wildlife* 23 (April–May 1985): 16; Ivars Peterson, "Searching for a Breath of Clean Air," *Science News* 132 (28 November 1987); Peter A. A. Berle, "Turning off the Maples," *Audubon* 86 (September 1987); "Ozone Needles Loblolly Pines . . . and Saps Sequoia Seedlings," *Science News* 136 (16 September 1989); "U.S. Cities Axe Tree Budgets," *Environment* 34 (March 1992); Steve Sandfort and Edwin C. Butcher, "How to Avoid Being Clipped by a Tree Trimmer," *Flower and Garden* 32 (5 April 1988); Jack Schultz, "Tree Tactics," *Natural History* 92 (May 1983); Anastasia Toufexis, "The Trees Are Taking Over," *Time* 125 (17 June 1985); "Happiness Is a Green Tree," *New Scientist* 113 (19 February 1987); "Would You Like to See a Grown Tree Weep?" *Sunset* [Central West Edition] 171 (August 1983); Tom Arrandale, "Go Ahead, Hug a Tree: It's Good for You," *Governing* 5 (September 1992); and Mike Baillie and Jon Pilcher, "Make a Date with a Tree," *New Scientist* 117 (17 March 1988).

The story and methods of TreePeople are explained by its founder, Andy Lipkis, in his book *The Simple Act of Planting a Tree: The TreePeople Guide to Healing Your Neighborhood, Your City, & Your World* (Los Angeles: J. P. Tarcher, 1990).

51. Tolkien, *The Two Towers* [*Part II of The Lord of the Rings*], pp. 82, 83.

CHAPTER 7

1. David Rains Wallace, *Bulow Hammock: Mind in a Forest* (San Francisco: Sierra Club Books, 1989), pp. 2–6.

2. Translation by Robert Pogue Harrison in *Forests: The Shadow of Civilization* (Chicago: University of Chicago Press, 1992), p. 179.

3. Ibid., pp. 181, 182.

4. In *Hesiod, The Homeric Hymns and Homerica*, ed. with facing trans. by H. G. Evelyn-White (Cambridge: Harvard University Press, 1982 [rpt. ed.]), pp. 406–27. I have modified the translation both in accordance with my reading of the Greek text and with stylistic concerns.

5. ". . . pines and high-crowned oaks. . . . Beautiful trees they are": *elátai ee drues hupsikárenoi . . . kalaí*, lit. "pines and high-topped oaks . . . beautiful"; "first the trees, so beautiful, wither upon the ground": *adzánetai mèn prōton epì chthonì déndrea kalá*, lit. "They wither first upon the ground, the beautiful trees."

6. Ted Williams, "Big Timber, the U.S. Forest Service and the Rape of the Northwest," *The Forest Voice* 2 (1 March 1990): 7.

7. Gerry Ellis and Karen Kane, *America's Rainforests* (Minocqua, WI: NorthWord Press, Inc., 1991), p. 31. Following quote from page 39.

8. Jerry F. Franklin, H. H. Shugart, and Mark E. Harmon, "Tree Death as an Ecological Process: The Causes, Consequences, and Variability of Tree Mortality," *BioScience* 37 (September 1987): 550–56.

9. For a good popular account of Franklin, his career, and that of "New Forestry," see William Dietrich's *The Final Forest: The Battle for the Last Great Trees of the Pacific Northwest* (New York: Simon & Schuster, 1992), ch. 6.

10. Quoted in Dietrich, *Final Forest*, p. 101. Following quotes from ibid., pp. 101, 102.

11. Bill McKibben, *The End of Nature* (New York: Random House, 1989), p. 34.

12. Interview transcript, "American Self" study.

13. Wendell Berry, "The Old Elm Tree by the River," in *The Country of Marriage* (San Diego: Harcourt Brace Jovanovich, 1975), p. 3.

14. Robert Jay Lifton, *Death in Life: Survivors of Hiroshima* (Chapel Hill: University of North Carolina Press, 1991 [1969]), p. 95.

15. See Floyd Hiatt Ross, *Shinto: The Way of Japan* (Boston: Beacon Press, 1965), p. 64.

16. Ineko Sata, "The Colorless Paintings," in *The Crazy Iris and Other Stories of the Atomic Aftermath*, ed. Kenzaburo Oe (New York: Grove Press, 1985 [1984]), p. 117. Following quotes are from pp. 115–16, 124, and 120.

17. In the Greek, "shady dwellings" are *skioentas enaulous* ("Hymn to Aphrodite," 74, 124), with *skioentas* the plural accusative form of *skioen*, from *skia* "shadow."

18. Tim O'Brien, "How to Tell a True War Story," in *The Things They Carried* (New York: Penguin Books, 1990), pp. 77–78.

19. "The Homeric Hymn to Pan," 33–34.

20. O'Brien, "Sweetheart of the Song Tra Bong," in *The Things They Carried*, pp. 125, 106, 103–04, 112, 115–16, 124, 125.

21. Wendell Berry, "The Country of Marriage," in *The Country of Marriage*, pp. 6, 7.

22. Rainer Maria Rilke, "Third Elegy," in the *Duino Elegies*. I am indebted to Nancy Billias for her translation of these lines.

23. Virginia Spencer Carr, *The Lonely Hunter: A Biography of Carson McCullers* (Garden City, NY: Doubleday, 1975), pp. 23, 221, 191.

24. Zora Neale Hurston, *Their Eyes Were Watching God* (New York: HarperCollins, 1990 [1937]), pp. 10–11.

25. Michel Tournier, *Friday*, trans. Norman Denny (New York: Pantheon, 1969), pp. 192–94. Excerpts quoted in Al Lingus, "Lust," *Spring 51* (1991): 19–20.

26. Walt Whitman, *Specimen Days, The Portable Walt Whitman*, rev. ed., ed. Mark Van Doren (New York: The Viking Press, 1973 [1945]), pp. 495–96.

27. *Numpholeptos* in Greek; see C. Kerényi, *The Gods of the Greeks*, trans. Norman Cameron (London: Thames & Hudson, 1979 [1951]), p. 179.

28. Ibid., p. 178.

29. Chris Genovali, "Redwood Forests Slated for Slaughter," *Taiga News* 5 (March 1993): 5.

30. Hesiod, *Theogony* 185, and James Hersh, "From *Ethnos* to *Polis*: The Furies and Apollo," *Spring 1985*: 63.

31. See discussion in Bill McKibben, *End of Nature*, pp. 179–82.

32. See Robert Jay Lifton, *The Broken Connection* (New York: Basic Books, 1983 [1979]), pp. 147–51.

33. Nicholas Gage, "My Mother Eleni: The Search for Her Executioners," *New York Times Magazine* (3 April 1983), p. 65; quoted in Hersh, "From *Ethnos* to *Polis*," p. 70.

34. The words of Christopher Columbus as quoted in Howard Mumford Jones, *O Strange New World: American Culture, the Formative Years* (New York: Viking, 1965), pp. 14–15; and in Richard Slotkin, *Regeneration Through Violence: The Mythology of the American Frontier, 1600–1860* (Middletown, CT: Wesleyan University Press, 1973), p. 16.

35. Richard H. Grove, "Origins of Western Environmentalism," *Scientific American* (July 1992): 42.

36. Robin Matthews contrasts paradisal "myths of manageability," which are characterized by "wishful visions of an idealized humanity," from paradisal "myths of religion," which function as "incantations of ultimacy" ("In the Trail of the Serpent: A Theological Inquiry," in *The Meaning of Gardens*, ed. Mark Francis and Randolf T. Hester, Jr. [Cambridge / London: The MIT Press, 1991 (1990)], p. 51). Matthews observes that "there is agreement that the nostalgia for paradise arises from and points back to the present. But unlike religious readings, myths of manageability edit out discontinuity when they envisage their future paradise as humanly brokered and accessible. In a curious form of ingratitude the brokenness that generates their yearnings for wholeness gets deliberately left out in their final vision." Still, I would argue that "myths of paradise," whether of the religious or secular variety, are in part powered by the ideal imagination that is evoked by trees and the forest. Images of "manageability" such as Will's are not only rational-secular readings, but themselves a kind of religious, "final vision," however blinkered. The problem with wholeness of either the religious or rational-secular variety is that it tends to leave out brokenness, which is by contrast never absent from old-growth or Aphrodite's Woods. It's not only that, as Matthews notes, "misadventure and mischance enter into reality on an equal footing with primordial security and salvation" (ibid., p. 52), but that brokenness, rot, decay, and mourning are equally primordial amidst trees.

37. See my "Air Wars, Greenhouses, and Hands of Prey," Occasional Paper Number 7 (New York: Center on Violence and Human Survival, 1990), pp. 7–11.

38. Georg Kohlmaier and Barna von Sartory, *Houses of Glass*, trans. John C. Harvey (Cambridge / London: MIT Press, 1986), pp. 7, 14, 25.

39. "Origins of Western Environmentalism," p. 42.

40.   James Fox Wilson, paper presented to the British Association for the Advancement of Science, 1858; quoted in Grove, "Origins," p. 46.

41.   Darwin, *The Voyage of the Beagle* (New York: Dutton, 1959 [1860, 2d ed.]), pp. 476, 477.

42.   See, for instance, Daniel B. Botkin, *Discordant Harmonies: A New Ecology for the Twenty-First Century* (New York: Oxford University Press, 1990).

43.   McKibben, *End*, p. 47.

44.   In John Haines, *New Poems: 1980–1988* (Brownsville, OR: Story Line Press, 1990), pp. 64–65.

45.   *The Homeric Hymns*, trans. Charles Boer (Chicago: The Swallow Press, 1970), pp. 8, 9.

46.   Toni Morrison, *Beloved* (New York: Alfred A. Knopf, 1987), p. 165.

47.   For a philosophical and historical discussion of archaic ideas of wilderness, see Max Oelschlaeger, *The Idea of Wilderness: From Prehistory to the Age of Ecology* (New Haven: Yale University Press, 1991), ch. 1. Oelschlaeger emphasizes an evolutionary viewpoint that encompasses what I've called the human and nonhuman in nature: "A study of the idea of wilderness . . . assumes the natural history of humankind" (p. 4). For an aesthetic perspective on images of the other world, see Ellen Dissanayake, *Homo Aestheticus: Where Art Comes From and Why* (New York: Free Press, 1992), pp. 49–51. Dissanayake's stress on the evolutionary function of perceiving or creating "other worlds" differs from my sense of such worlds. There could well be evolutionary (motivational and survival) value in the imagination of other worlds, but I would argue that "other-worldliness" or "wilderness" is also a psychological quality given with, inherent in, the realms of physical nature. It has to do with the evolution and form of trees and forests, for instance, as much as with human evolution. Our evolution, that is, assumes the natural history of trees.

48.   Michael Pollan, *Second Nature: A Gardener's Education* (New York: Laurel, 1991), p. 214.

49.   E. O. Wilson, *The Diversity of Life* (Cambridge: The Belknap Press of Harvard University Press, 1992), pp. 350, 351.

Index

Aeschylos (*Oresteia*), 210
African-American experience, trees of: figure pain, 55–56, 105–06, 111, 135–36; have restorative power, 43, 160–61, 162, 163–68; *see also* Peace
Agent Orange (wartime forest defoliant), 141; *see also* Hugo (Hurricane); Vietnam War; War
Alaska, 100, 144, 182; *see also* Wilderness, imagination of
Albanese, Catherine L., 95, 179
Alchemy, of human–tree relationship, 89, 176–78; *see also* Human; Tree('s) spirits
Alciatus, Andreas, 55
Alienation. *See* Estrangement
Amplification, role of in psychological interviewing, 25, 227 n. 3
Anchises, 193, 196, 201
Anderson, William, 228 n. 5
Andrew (Hurricane), 3, 6, 8, 174–75, 182, 185, 214; foreignness of landscape in aftermath of, 4, 5, 23, 24–25, 140, 221; reveals importance of tree(s), 1, 10, 22–27, 88, 115, 139–40, 157, 190; reveals trees of pain, 129, 130, 131, 132–33, 197; stirs anger against trees, 20; "war zone" images and, 141, 148–49
Anger: against trees, 19–21; catalyzed by trees, 64–65, 86–87, 115, 160, 163–64, 188; of humans, on behalf of trees, 175, 208–10; of trees, 36, 37, 101, 118–19, 183, 207–11

Anthropomorphism, 11, 88, 93; concept of critiqued, 90–91
Antietam (Civil War battle), 141; *see also* Hugo (Hurricane); War
Aphrodite, 8, 13, 225 n. 12, 237 n. 20; Artemis and, 216–21; Eden and, 214–16; erotic and sexual power of trees and, 12–13, 190, 203–07; myth of "Aphrodite's Woods" discussed, 192–96, 199, 200–02, 207–08
Apollo, 54, 91–92
Artemis, 12, 200; Daphne and, 91, 92; and imagination of wilderness, 216–20; *see also* Aphrodite; Wilderness, imagination of
Auschwitz, 108
Authoritarianism, figured by trees, 108, 111–12; *see also* Political imaginations, trees and

Bachelard, Gaston, 41, 49, 127
Barthes, Roland, 110
Baudelaire, Charles, 191–92
Beauty of trees, 12–13, 28, 31, 66, 81, 86, 97, 191, 206–07, 215–16; commingles with pain and grief, 128–31, 145; and death (of trees and others), 195-200; in great trees' felling, 180; in "managed" versus old-growth forests, 35, 66, 68–69; vitalizes humane and ecological solidarity, 156–57; vitalizes social inequity and evil, 108–10, 112
Bechmann, Roland, 113, 242 n. 60

Bekas, Sherko, 242 n. 61
Benjamin, Jessica, 53, 88–89, 159;
    see also Feminism
Berry, Thomas, 224 n. 3, 248–49 n.
    38
Berry, Wendell, 41, 86, 114, 170,
    198, 203
Biographical woodscapes: defined,
    9–10; in human life-stories, 55–70,
    72–73, 182–83, 203f.
Biophilia, 221
Bishop, Peter, 92, 94, 173–74,
    222–23 n. 2, 240 n. 51
Bleakley, Alan, 225 n. 12
Boas, Franz, 87, 116, 125, 126
Boer, Charles, 218
Bolander, Karen, 39
Botkin, Daniel B., 150, 254 n. 42
Brooks, Gwendolyn, 86–87, 110
Buber, Martin (I and Thou), 230–31
    n. 17
Buddha, -ism, tree spirits in, 94, 97,
    98, 240 n. 51
Bukwis (of Kwakiutl mythology),
    125–26, 200

Callicott, J. Baird, 234 n. 34
Carr, Virginia Spencer, 204
Casey, Edward S., 46–47
Christianity, tree(s) of, 26, 94, 98,
    113, 136, 146
Climbing trees, tonic power of, 43,
    44–45, 49, 158; see also Peace
Coleridge, Samuel Taylor, 89
Columbus, Christopher, 211–12
Computer, -s (trees inhabit), iii, 15,
    81–82, 150–51
Contradiction, -s, -oriness, in ecolog-
    ical imagination, 4, 33–34, 52–53,
    90, 111, 221
Crane, Stephen, 142
Crest Pole, -s (of Kwakiutl tradition),
    116, 123–24

Dan (South Carolina forester), 57,
    58, 130, 131, 139, 140, 158
Daniels, Stephen, 222 n. 2

Danny (psychotic patient), 154–55,
    158, 183
Dante's Inferno, dark woods of, 136
Daphne, 54, 91–92, 171
Darwin, Charles, 70–73, 213–15
Dave (South Carolina wildlife
    biologist), 32–33, 34, 139, 158,
    195
David (retired Homestead military
    man), 22–27, 49, 90, 94, 98, 102,
    129, 132, 133, 148–49, 153, 161,
    182, 185
Davies, Douglas, 222 n. 2
Dead/dying trees: in Aphrodite's
    Woods, 192–200; and greenhouse
    effect, 196–97, 212–13; power of,
    27, 30–34, 40, 41, 65, 68–70, 71,
    73, 85–86, 102–03, 114, 124, 126,
    212, 213, 216, 221; and war/holo-
    caust-related themes, 128, 140–43,
    146–51, 198–200, 209; see also
    Biographical woodscapes; Bukwis;
    Tree, -s: animal imaginations and;
    War
Death, 10, 11, 20, 21, 22, 39, 53,
    92, 131, 154, 173, 190, 191, 198–
    200, 202, 203, 220, 221; Artemi-
    sian, 216, 218 (see also Artemis);
    estrangement and, 5, 76, 81–82;
    human–tree intimacy or parallels
    and, 26–27, 32–37, 61–73, 76,
    141–51, 169–71; trees draw upon,
    2, 84–87, 98, 121–22, 124–26,
    136–39, 193–96; trees of fear and,
    103–06; see also Aphrodite; Buk-
    wis; Dead/dying trees
Deleuze, Gilles, 241–42 n. 55
Dietrich, William, 180–81, 233 n. 32
Dillard, Annie, 61, 91, 103, 136, 158
Dionysos, 146
Dissanayake, Ellen, 254 n. 47
Dostoevsky, Fyodor, 161–62
Dream, -s (trees in), 10, 64–65, 82,
    90, 105–06, 122, 124–25, 145–46

Earth First!, 28, 129, 210; see also
    Anger: catalyzed by trees
Ecology, -ical concern, 33, 37, 43,

53–54, 56, 58, 82, 84, 115, 141;
and commingling of organic and
machine imaginations, 175–79;
erotic beauty and, 206, 213–16;
and idea of wilderness, 220, 221;
idealization of nature and, 28, 52–
53, 67–68, 100–03, 173, 174, 216,
218; and nuclear threat, 148–51,
198–200; trees shape psychological
aspects of, 1–10, 12–15, 46, 59,
65, 74, 89–90, 94, 113, 126, 129–
32, 159–60, 165, 167, 170–74,
187–89, 190, 193–95, 196–97,
198, 200, 210–11, 213–15; *see also*
Aphrodite; Artemis; Machine, -s;
Wilderness, imagination of

Ecstasy, -ic experiences amidst trees,
45–46, 91, 92, 95, 121–23, 124–
25, 126, 136, 144–46, 157, 159,
162–63, 164, 171–72, 175–76,
188, 190, 205–07, 218

Ed (South Carolina public agency of-
ficial), 19–20, 21, 24, 25, 146,
147, 157

Eden (imagination of trees in), 64,
153, 211–16; *see also* Idealization,
-izing, of nature

Elias, Canetti, 107, 142

Ellen (New York shopkeeper), 60,
84, 85, 90, 100, 103

Emerson, Ralph Waldo, 25–26

Ent, -s (of J.R.R. Tolkien's *Lord of
the Rings*), 21, 82–84, 111–12, 175,
208; *see also* Treebeard

Erotic, power of trees as, 3–4, 12,
41, 42, 53–54, 72, 159, 160, 189,
190–92, 200–01, 203–07, 214–16

Estrangement, 11, 55–56, 82, 93,
121; from trees, as psychologically
generative, 2–5, 12, 19, 24, 34–37,
60–61, 73–77, 81, 132, 143–44,
172, 179–83, 220–21; and trees of
fear, 103–06, 202–03; and trees of
pain, 127, 218–19

Evans, Mari, 12, 53, 164, 172

Evolution. *See* Human

Fairchild Tropical Garden, 8, 9, 26,

130, 131, 141, 149, 168, 187, 197,
214

Fear, of / among trees, 99–106, 127,
136–37, 143–46, 177, 178, 221;
and tree humor, 186, 202–03; *see
also* Pan

Feminism, 51–53, 95, 232 n. 20, 238
n. 21; and tree "genders," 50–54

Forest, -s, 7, 27, 38, 41, 72–73, 77,
78, 81, 82, 92, 96, 97, 112, 172,
174, 186, 190–92, 200, 201; destruction of, 5, 26–27, 92, 127–
29, 130–31, 137–38, 139, 140–43,
146–50, 196–98, 208–11; distinct
from biographical woodscapes, 10;
Francis Marion National, 7, 8, 57,
58–59, 66, 68, 69, 86, 115, 127–
29, 139, 140; managed, 68–70,
95; military images and, 108–09,
160–61; old-growth (primary), 11,
68–70, 86, 92, 116–26, 180–81,
190–91, 193– 95, 196, 208, 210;
as place of foreignness / estrangement, 4–5, 34– 37, 56, 62–63,
75–76, 77, 99– 106, 117–21, 143–
44, 202–03, 217–20, 221; as place
of solidarity / communion with
trees, 42–43, 45, 48–49, 58–59,
65–67, 75–76, 121–23, 152, 153–
54, 155, 157– 61, 165, 169–70,
175–76, 177–80, 187–89, 203–07,
217–20, 221; pre-anthropoid, 13–
15, 77–78; "timeless" (primordial),
12–13, 21, 27, 190, 211–17; *see
also* Aphrodite; Eden; Garden, -s;
Shadow, -s; Tropical rainforest, -s;
Wilderness, imagination of

Fowles, John, 56–57, 58

Francis Marion (South Carolina national forest). *See* Forest, -s

Franklin, Jerry Forest, 194–95

Gadon, Elinor, 238 n. 21

Garden, -s, 10, 32, 213; botanical, 8,
131, 149; of Eden, 213, 215–16
(*see also* Eden); of Gethsemane,
112–13; give-and-take relation of
trees and humans in, 2, 45–46,

49–50, 59–60, 63–65, 88–90, 93, 176 (*see also* Alchemy, of human–tree relationship); tension between forest images and, 56–57, 111–12, 143; trees of, during Dostoevsky's imprisonment, 161–62 (*see also* Peace); Zen, 198; *see also* Fairchild Tropical Garden; Treebeard

Genocide, trees figure themes of, 108, 111, 142, 146–51

Gilgamesh, 237–38 n. 20

Goldman, Irving, 243 n. 65

Green, -ed: eyes, of the ecological imagination, 173–74, 202, 221; *see also* Idealization, -izing, of nature

Greene, Mott T., 226 n. 14

Greenhouse, -s, 152–53, 213; *see also* Eden; Greenhouse effect

Greenhouse effect, 212–14, 216

Grove, Richard H., 212, 214

Gruber, Howard E., 70, 72

Guattari, Felix, 241–42 n. 55

Hades, 126, 201

Haines, John, 144, 217–18

Hammer, E. F., 39

Harrison, Robert Pogue, 5, 15, 74, 179–80, 192, 225 n. 13

Heather (painter), 75

Hektor, 142

Henry, O., 84–85, 90

Hermes, in Aphrodite's Woods, 193, 200–03; *see also* Bukwis; Death; Hades

Hersh, James, 210, 211; *see also* Anger: catalyzed by trees

Hillman, James, 3, 11, 87, 97, 222 n. 2, n. 3

Hiroshima, 128, 148–49, 198–99, 200

History, -ical, witness and memory of trees, 1, 6, 24, 46–49, 83, 84, 104, 112–15, 152, 179–80, 201; cultural images and, 29, 48, 107–09, 110–11, 114–15, 122, 123–24, 163–68, 198–200; evokes religious images, 6, 26, 112–13; pre-historic power of trees and, 12–15,

73, 76–78, 133–36; scientific images and, 94, 184; war images and, 140–46, 148–49, 198–200

Holocaust, planetary and human, figured by trees, 108, 142, 148–51, 197

Homestead (Florida), 1, 2, 4, 9, 10, 22, 88, 132–33, 139–40, 190, 221

Hughes, Langston, 12, 87, 163–64

Hugo (Hurricane), 2, 6, 8, 19, 20, 26, 31–32, 49, 52, 57, 65, 66–67, 68, 69, 76, 84, 86, 88, 115, 127–29, 130–31, 139–41, 146–47, 154, 157, 158, 165, 177–78, 187–88, 196, 197, 209; *see also* Andrew (Hurricane); War

Human: evolution and trees, 13–15, 41–42, 73–78, 220, 254 n. 47; life configured partly by trees, 9–12, 15, 31–34, 46–50, 55–70, 83–84, 106–12, 131–36, 138–39, 154–57, 165, 186–87, 195–96, 198, 218–19; life in continual "conversation" with nonhuman world, 6–7, 116–20, 121–23, 124–25, 176, 190–91, 207–11; relationship with trees combines intimacy and estrangement, 19–20, 21, 34–37, 38ff., 81, 88–93, 103–05, 113, 116–26, 168–74, 179–83, 217–21; relationship with trees as kinaesthetic, 23–24, 41–43, 128–29; sexuality shaped by trees, 51–54, 203–06, 207

Humor, figured by trees, 82, 83, 95, 99, 145, 154–55, 183–87

Hurston, Zora Neale, iii, 38, 53, 99, 135, 204, 205

Hussein, Saddam, 114, 142

"I-You" relationship, of human and tree, 230–31 n. 8; *see also* Buber, Martin

Idealization, -izing, of nature, 4, 28, 173–74, 216; image of Eden and, 211–13, 253 n. 36; power of trees distinguished from, 19–22, 27–34, 88ff., 102–03, 159, 218; sexual images and, 51–53; *see also* Eden; Forest, -s; Garden, -s

Image, -s, -ination, -ining, ecological, 13–15, 87–91, 100–03, 172–74, 178–79, 193–95, 196–97, 205–07, 220–21; Edenic, 211–16, 253 n. 36 (*see also* Eden); evolutionary, 13–15, 73–78, 221; historical, 112–16, 160–61, 179–80; involved in relationship(s) with trees, 1–3, 21–22, 22–27, 36–37, 38–221; spirit–soul differentiations and, 93–99, 100ff., 122, 186–87 (*see also* Spiritualizing, of trees; Tree[s'] spirits); of trees, quickened by pain, 127–36, 152–54, 157, 163–65, 169, 196–98, 218–20; of trees, unconsciously embedded / literalized in social forms, 110; "true" and "false" in relation to trees, 89–90, 99; violent, 209–11 (*see also* Violence; Violent feelings; War); in visual media, related to tree spirits, 10, 11, 137–38, 141–42, 150, 166–67

Intimacy, of trees and humans. *See* Alchemy, of human–tree relationship; Ent, -s; Human; Treebeard

Ire, Trees of, 87, 118, 119, 125, 208ff.; *see also* Anger

Ishtar, 237–38 n. 20; *see also* Aphrodite; Gilgamesh

Ivan (homeless man), 56–58, 152–55, 158, 188, 197

Jaime (Filipino rainforest activist), 42–45, 53, 54, 76, 89, 100–03, 112, 116, 157–58, 169, 175–76, 179, 187–89, 204

Jane (New York artist), 30–31, 33–34, 35–37, 40–41, 49, 51–52, 53–54, 55, 60, 75, 76, 78, 89, 91, 95–96, 98, 99, 102, 103, 109, 112, 114, 116, 118, 127, 131–32, 135, 141, 148, 159, 178, 179, 186, 195, 199, 203, 204, 211

Japan, religious imagination of trees in, 96–97, 98, 198–200

Jenkins, F. A., Jr., 13–14

Jim (energy-conservation consultant), 213

Johnson, Sophie, 167–68

Judaism, tree(s) of, 94, 95–96

Jung, Carl Gustav, 3, 6, 25, 39, 54, 55, 98, 124, 144, 195, 236 n. 13

Kerényi, Carl, 54

Kevin (South Carolina urban forester), 20, 60, 139, 146–47, 177

Kinaesthetic, relation of trees to human body, 24, 41–42, 46ff., 55, 75, 93–94, 128–29, 133

Klein, William, 168, 197

Kluger, Rikvah Schärf, 237 n. 20

Kohlmaier, Georg, 152

Kwakiutl Indians, tree images of, 8, 11, 82, 87, 90, 116–26, 136, 137, 169, 179, 181, 188, 194, 220

Lacan, Jacques, 229–30 n. 8

Lapham, Lewis, 109

Leaf, -ves, iii, 1, 30, 38, 46, 49, 55, 72–73, 83, 91, 166; embody tree power or spirit(s), 44, 84–85, 97–98, 130, 132, 133ff., 161, 165, 173–74, 207, 221 (*see also* Tree[s'] spirits); erotic nature of, 42, 72, 191–92, 204–07, 214; importance of loss or lack of, 33, 72–73, 197–98, 217; loss of, in hurricane winds, 1, 4–5, 23, 25, 132, 149, 175; regrowth of, after hurricane, 24–25, 130, 209; spooky shadows of, 144–45, 200–02

Leopold, Aldo, 12, 84, 114, 162–63, 165, 178–79, 184

Lewis (South Florida farmer), 4, 25, 88, 132–33, 135, 140, 174–75

Lifton, Robert Jay, 3, 7, 108, 171, 198–99, 210, 223 n. 3, 236 n. 16, 245 n. 28

Lingus, Al, 206

Lipkis, Andy, 250 n. 50

Logging, -ers, 210; connection to intimacy with trees, 28, 34, 35, 37, 48, 67, 179, 180–81, 188, 212

Loss: ecological, 1–2, 13, 20, 49, 73, 82, 115, 129–31, 139–41, 173–74, 189, 215; of erotic dimension of ecological thinking, 12; lives in trees, 136, 161, 204; of trees, as mode of arboreal presence, 1–2, 10, 26–27, 84–87, 128–33, 139–51, 161–62, 182, 190, 196–98, 221

Love, 45, 138, 192–93; Artemisian, of wilderness, 218ff.; erotic and sexual, linked with ecological awareness, 3–4, 12, 51ff., 95, 97, 157–60, 172–74, 188–89, 190, 203–07, 211; of trees, 5, 21, 28, 59, 61–62, 77, 82–84, 97, 111, 129–31, 168–72, 175, 186, 195, 203–07, 208, 210–11, 221; trees of pain and, 134–36

Macbeth, trees of, 107, 108, 141

Machine, -s, role of in ecological and arboreal imaginations, 11, 15, 24, 81, 174–79, 181, 194

Macy, Joanna Rogers, 224 n. 3

Magnolia Tree Earth Center, 9, 165–68

Malkki, Liisa, 110–11, 241–42 n. 55

Man Eater (forest spirit of Kwakiutl mythology), 120–21, 136

Manatee, -s, relation of to forested imagination, 187–89; *see also* Tree, -s: animal imaginations and

Mark (South Carolina businessman), 58–59, 209–10

Markusen, Eric, 108

Martin, R. D., 227 n. 15

Matthews, Robin, 253 n. 36

McCullers, Carson, 12, 133–34, 172–74, 202, 203–04

McKibben, Bill, 196, 216–17

Merwin, W. S., 5, 48–49, 60–61, 88, 114

Midwestern flood (of 1993), iii, 81

Mischa (Russian writer), 26–27, 43, 52, 75–76, 113, 160–61, 170, 187, 210, 215

Morrison, Toni, 8, 53, 108, 135–36, 161, 162, 163, 174, 218–19

Mount St. Helens, devastated forests of, 150

Mountain–tree images, 13, 35, 66, 68, 84, 113, 120–21, 137, 146, 192–93, 200, 201–02, 211, 216–17

Nakashima, George, 46

Nathan, Leonard, 149–50

Nature, 2, 46, 56–57, 107–13, 116, 130, 145, 156, 172, 183, 191–92, 197; Artemisian, 216ff. (*see also* Artemis; Wilderness, imagination of); communion with, through conquest, 179; Darwin's Tree of, 70–73; defined as nonessential: as Ecological Pandaemonium, 90, 221, 236 n. 14; "end" of, 216; as form of imaginal conversation, 6–7; idealized, 28; is psychological, 3, 136, 222–24 n. 2, 3; lack of primary unity with, 3–4, 74ff.; no dichotomy between "artificial" realm and, 9, 168 (*see also* Machine, -s; Organic imagination); nonhuman, *see* Nonhuman nature; personified, 25–27, 90–91, 94–99, 102; "return" to, 4–5, 22, 81, 219; sexual, 204; of soul, as ecological, 6, 10, 40, 53

Nawalak (tree power of Kwakiutl mythology), 117ff., 188, 221

Nazism, 108

Nick (social activist), 112–13, 115

Noel, Dan, 6, 224–25 n. 8

Nonhuman nature: adorns itself, 192; continual commingling with human nature, 2, 3–4, 5, 7, 10–11, 14, 35, 38, 43, 46, 50, 63, 74, 81, 88–91, 113, 118, 122–23, 129–33, 159–60, 165, 179, 206, 211, 216, 219–20; distinction from human mediated by trees, 74–76; friendship of trees expresses, 168–72; grief over loss of important, 129–31, 133; inspires human harm, 108–12; is foreign, 4–5, 74, 156, 216ff.; personified in trees, 86, 87–88, 97, 100–03 (*see also* Nature); relationship with human figured in Kwakiutl mythology, 116–17, 118, 120–26

Nonviolence, fostered by trees, 74, 160, 183, 210–11; *see also* Ecstasy, -ic experiences amidst trees; Peace

Nuclear threat, 7; prompts restorative imagining of trees, 153–54, 165; trees figure, 108, 148–51, 197, 198–200, 213; *see also* War

O'Brien, Tim, 8, 144–46

Oddness, of arboreal imaginations, 10, 31ff., 63ff., 97, 112, 230 n. 8; and tree humor, 186–87

Odin, 146

Odysseus, 59, 60

Oelschlaeger, Max, 224 n. 3, 228 n. 5, 235 n. 48, 249 n. 38, 254 n. 47; *see also* Wilderness, imagination of

Old trees: command particular respect, 27, 29–34, 42–43, 52, 82–83, 115, 131–32, 162, 165–68, 169; inspire fear, 100–02; political / social authoritarianism and, 111–12; power of, 19, 38, 55, 63–70, 85–86, 107–11, 136, 155, 176, 186–87, 196, 198, 200, 221

Organic imagination, as intimate with the mechanical, 11, 15, 24, 88, 108, 174–79, 181, 194, 248–49 n. 38; *see also* Machine, -s

Pacific Northwest (forest ecosystems of), 116, 125, 126, 168, 210; debate over logging in, 48, 67, 86, 92; felling of trees in, 62, 180–81; portrayed in literature (fictional and scientific), 61–63, 103–05, 193–94; shape Kwakiutl mythology, 8, 11, 76–77, 116–26; *see also* Aphrodite; Bukwis; Kwakiutl Indians, tree images of

Pain, trees of / and, 11, 31, 59, 86, 127–41, 144ff., 161, 173–74, 179; distinct from spiritualizing tenden-

cies, 92, 93, 99; uprootedness and, 57–58

Pamela (South Carolina car rental agent), 2, 43, 53, 88, 130–31, 135, 139, 141, 158, 160–61, 164–65, 215–16, 219–20, 221

Pan, 201–02

Paradox, -es: in human–tree parallels, 3–5, 15, 56–58, 60–61, 69–70, 73–78, 88–93, 179–83; in images associated with greenhouse effect, 212–13; wilderness as, 221

Paris, Ginette, 225 n. 13

Parks, Gordon, 55–56, 57, 58, 105–06, 110, 111, 165

Paul (South Carolina geographer), 140–41

Peace, 3, 14, 153; felt in connection with felling trees, 182–83; inspired by trees, 152ff.; of trees, energizes psychological and physical healing, 154–57, 160–65; of trees, and religious experience(s), 157–59, 171–72

Peattie, Donald Culross, 50

Pentheus, 146

Perlin, John, 225 n. 14, 237 n. 20

Perry, Donald R., 235 n. 51

Persephone, 126, 201

Peterson, Jim, 171–72

Political imaginations, trees and, 55, 96, 97, 108–12, 116, 146, 149, 212; *see also* Authoritarianism; Ecology, -ical concern; Nonviolence; Nuclear threat; Peace; War

Pollan, Michael, 88, 89, 143, 144, 220, 240 n. 50

Pownall, Thomas, 38

Pruning, of trees, deepens tree–human relationship, 88; *see also* Trees, felling of

Psyche, 91; ecological, 222–23 n. 3 (*see also* Soul, -s); human biographical, 40; tendency to personify, 87; tendency to seek restoration amidst trees, 153; *see also* Reforesting, of soul

psyché, 195

Pushkin, Alexandr, 170–71

Rainforest, -s. *See* Temperate rainforest, -s; Tropical rainforest, -s
Ramos, Maximo D., 101
Reforesting, of soul, 1–3, 78, 90–93, 153ff.; in Kwakiutl traditions, 116–26; and particulars of tree spirits, 93–99; *see also* Dream, -s (trees in)
Rilke, Rainer Maria, 49, 203
Rolston, H., 235 n. 51
Rooted Woman (of Kwakiutl mythology), 121, 136
Roots, -edness, 3, 28, 33, 39, 42, 46, 48, 74, 83, 88, 92, 99, 104, 105, 106, 124, 128, 139, 142, 159, 170, 175, 182, 183, 184, 185, 191, 208; connected with memory, 47–48, 114–15, 127; of ecological concern, 214; erotic, 54, 203, 205; figure images of evil, 106, 108, 110–11; human evolutionary, in forest, 4, 13–15, 41–42, 76–78; prebiblical, of hostility toward trees, 237–38 n. 20; shared by humans and trees, 30, 45–46, 54, 58, 75, 87, 121, 131, 136, 152, 163, 210–11; trees present in generic image(s) of, 85, 92, 106ff.; of uprootedness, 55–56, 57, 58, 61; *see also* Biographical woodscapes
Roszak, Theodore, 223 n. 3, 225 n. 12, 246 n. 10
Ruether, Rosemary Radford, 228 n. 5

Sacred Earth Network, 227 n. 16
Sacrifice: of trees, 148–51, 179; on tree(s), 146
Sally (English-born shopkeeper), 32, 34, 45–46, 47, 48, 49–50, 53, 54, 58, 63–65, 90, 112, 114, 116, 136–38, 159, 169, 176, 179, 186–87, 196, 204
Salmon (of Kwakiutl mythology), 124–26, 194, 200
Samuels, Andrew, 223 n. 3, 234 n. 45
Sata, Ineko, 199–200

Scarry, Elaine, 21
Schell, Jonathan, 150–51, 213
Schroeder, Herbert W., 3
Searles, Harold, 155–57, 158, 223 n. 3, 246 n. 10
Seed, John, 224 n. 3
Sex, -ual desire: energized or figured by trees, 39, 50–54, 95, 178, 190, 203–07 (*see also* Aphrodite; Artemis; Feminism); retreat or distancing from, into trees, 91, 163; role of in ecological awareness, 3–4, 12, 173–74, 206–07
Shadow, -s: of deep forest evoke unease, 35, 77, 78; of Edenic image, 211–13; as metaphoric power, 3, 201–02; of trees evocative of fear, 100, 144–46, 190, 200–03; of trees in political and social dilemmas, 106–08, 111, 134, 202–03 (*see also* Political imaginations, trees and); variegated nature of tree spirits and, 11, 97–98, 170, 207, 218
Shakespeare, William, 85 (*Sonnet 73*), 107 (*Macbeth*); *see also Macbeth*
Shaman, -s, -ism, 121–22, 124–25; *see also* Ecstasy, -ic experiences amidst trees
Shintoism. *See* Japan
Slotkin, Richard, 212
Smith, Jonathan Z., 234–35 n. 46
Solitude, among trees, importance of, 42–45, 122–23, 190, 203–07, 216–17, 219–21; *see also* Peace
Soul, -s, 24, 38, 39, 47, 59, 60, 153, 156, 172, 174, 178, 179, 194, 217 (*see also* Psyche); beauty as fundamental requirement of, 206; conversation of, with earth, 6; ecological nature of, 10, 46, 49–50; in manufactured as well as organic beings, 11, 88 (*see also* Machine, -s; Organic imagination); as quality of tree spirits, 85–86, 87–98, 116, 118, 119, 121, 122ff., 149, 170, 176, 181, 193–94, 200 (*see also* Spiritualizing, of trees; Tree[s'] spirits); world, 222 n. 2

Soutar, George, 226 n. 14

Spiritualizing, of trees, 52, 100–03, 110–12, 122, 184; contrasted to soulful tree spirits, 93–99

Steve (worker at Fairchild Tropical Garden), 26, 131, 149, 214

Stone, Christopher D., 172–73, 228 n. 5

Styron, William, 136

Susan (South Carolina secretary), 128–29, 131, 132, 135, 140

Swamp–tree images, 27; as place of fear or dying, 35, 66, 68–69, 78, 99–100, 103, 104, 169, 199–200

Taiga (Russian forest), 92, 196, 227 n. 16

Taiga Rescue Network, 227 n. 16

Ted (South Carolina biology teacher), 20, 25, 26, 52–53, 92–93, 98, 99, 115, 135, 139, 197

Temperate rainforest, -s, 194; *see also* Forest, -s; Pacific Northwest; Tropical rainforest, -s

Tenacity, of arboreal images, 58, 179–80; affirms life and ethical witnessing, 115, 153–54, 162; figures human inequities and evils, 106–12; shapes human–plant distinction, 74ff.; of Treebeard, 83, 111–12 (*see also* Ent, -s; Treebeard); *see also* Roots, -edness

Thomas, Keith, 109

Thoreau, Henry David, iii, 12, 163, 203

Tolkien, J. R. R., 21, 82–84, 175

Tolkien, Michael, 175

Tournier, Michel, 205–06

Tree, -s: animal imaginations and, 42, 68, 69, 81, 116, 143, 144, 195, 197, 213, 218; distinct from human world(s), 217, 221; express tree sensuality, 14, 42, 77, 97, 187–89, 191; in Kwakiutl mythology, 117, 120, 122–26; personified (*see* Tree[s'] spirits); shape human relations with trees, 13–15, 77, 111, 178, 187–89

Trees, felling of: evokes tree spirits, 34–37, 78, 98, 101, 118–19, 137–38, 175, 179, 181; expresses tree–human solidarity, 179–83; figure of human death, 63, 108, 137–38; figures human birth, 62; psychological ramifications of, 34–37, 163, 179–83; *see also* Logging, -ers

Trees of Fear. *See* Fear, of / among trees

Tree(s) of Life, 19, 184; complex nature of Darwin's evolutionary, 71–73, 106–07, 214; juxtaposed with mushroom cloud, 150

Tree(s') spirits, 3, 81–126, 188, 192, 195, 208, 209; animal imaginations and, *see* Tree, -s: animal imaginations and; as bisexual, 54; defined, 10–11, 81–82; embody power of wilderness, 126, 221 (*see also Nawalak*; Wilderness, imagination of); ensouled, distinct from spiritualized, 93–99, 102–03, 122; evolve through combinations of intimacy with and estrangement from trees, 36–37, 45–46, 78, 81–82, 84–87, 117–19, 127, 128–29, 137–38, 179, 181 (*see* Human); figure social and political power, 97–98, 106–12, 116–17, 140ff., 149–51, 198–200 (*see also* Political imaginations, trees and); humor of, 82, 95–96, 99, 184–85, 186–87 (*see also* Oddness, of arboreal imaginations); kinaesthetically embodied, 93–94, 128–29, 133, 198–99, 203; present in machines, 11, 15, 81–82, 141, 150, 176–79, 183 (*see also* Machine, -s; Organic imagination); sentient presences of, 5, 25–27, 32, 49–50, 63–64, 78, 89ff., 112–15, 118–19, 122–23, 124–26, 127, 137–38, 144–45, 154–55, 157, 164, 165–68, 169–70, 192, 193, 201–03, 207

"Tree Lady of Brooklyn / Bedford-Stuyvesant" (Hattie Carthan), 8–9, 12, 165–68, 209, 211

Tree shrew, Mesozoic, 13–15, 77, 90; see also Tree, -s: animal imaginations and

Treebeard (of J.R.R. Tolkien's Lord of the Rings), 21, 37, 82–84, 111–12, 139, 175, 183, 186, 208

Tropical rainforest, -s, 10, 92, 157; activity and imagining on behalf of, 45, 100–03, 187, 188, 213–14, 221; human origins and, 11, 13–15, 76–78; relationship to Darwin's evolutionary Tree of Life, 70–73; relationship with image of Eden, 211–13; sensual nature of, 42–43, 45, 72, 73, 100, 102–03, 175–76, 204–06, 214–15; threatened, images of, 7; uncanniness in, 137, 144–46, 202–03 (see also Fear, of/among trees; Vietnam War)

Turner, Victor, 36

Ulrich, Roger S., 157

Vietnam War, 22, 210; related to imagination of trees, 8, 128, 141, 142, 144–46, 201–02, 212, 218

Violence: figured by trees, 146ff.; relationships with trees can help lessen, 74ff., 122, 152–54, 160, 183; vitalized by tree images, 108, 122, 143; witnessing of trees and, 114–15; see also War

Violent feelings, on behalf of trees, 209–11; figured by trees but distinct from actual violence, 210–11; place of, in ecological protest, 209, 210–11

von Sartory, Barna, 152

Walens, Stanley, 117

Wallace, David Rains, 137, 190–91, 192, 221

War, 22, 96, 115, 122, 167, 208; against trees, 76, 143–44, 212; concern about as ecological, 3, 14, 160, 211; tree spirits in images of,

11, 22, 107–08, 128, 140–46, 148–50, 201, 218

Water, -s, and trees as mutually evocative, 48, 99, 153, 187–89

Welch, Joan M., 109

White, Lynn, 228 n. 5

Whitman, Walt, 179, 180, 206–07

Wilderness, imagination of, 144, 165, 213, 216; as erotic, 12, 190, 220–21; figures social fears, 106, 202

Will (South Carolina sawmill operator), 8, 27–30, 31, 32, 34–37, 39, 41, 48, 49, 51, 65–70, 76, 78, 85–86, 89, 90, 94–95, 98, 102, 109, 112, 116, 118, 119, 129, 136, 137, 153–54, 158, 169, 177–79, 187–89, 195, 196, 200, 210, 216, 219–20

Williamson, John, 228 n. 5

Wilson, E.O., 221

Windle, Phyllis, 129

Yellowstone National Park (1988 fires in), 68–69, 86

Yggdrasil, 146

Young, Stephen, 184

Zeus, 142, 192, 195, 201

Zosimos, 248 n. 35; see also Alchemy, of human–tree relationship; Machine, -s

Credits

Grateful acknowledgment is made to the following for permission to use the material listed:

Excerpt from *Beowulf* by Burton Raffel, translator. Copyright © 1963 by Burton Raffel, Afterword copyright © 1963 by New American Library. Used by permission of Dutton Signet, a division of Penguin Books USA Inc.

Excerpt from "The Election" reprinted from *Carrying On: New & Selected Poems*, by Leonard Nathan, by permission of the University of Pittsburgh Press, copyright © 1985 by Leonard Nathan.

Excerpts from "The Old Elm Tree by the River" and "The Country of Marriage" in *The Country of Marriage*, copyright © 1971 by Wendell Berry, reprinted by permission of Harcourt Brace & Company.

Excerpts from *Forests: The Shadow of Civilization*, by Robert Pogue Harrison, reprinted by permission of University of Chicago Press, copyright © 1992 by the University of Chicago.

Excerpts from *The Living* by Annie Dillard. Copyright © 1992 by Annie Dillard. Reprinted by permission of HarperCollins Publishers, Inc.

Excerpt from "Tornado at Talladega" reprinted from *The Near-Johannesburg Boy: And Other Poems*, by Gwendolyn Brooks, by permission of Gwendolyn Brooks, copyright © 1986 by Gwendolyn Brooks Blakely.

Excerpts from "Ancestor of the Hunting Heart," reprinted from *New Poems: 1980–1988*, by John Haines, by permission of Story Line Press, copyright © 1990 by Story Line Press.

An earlier version of Chapter 5 was published in *Spring 55: A Journal of Archetype and Culture* (1994).

THE WORLD SOUL

The Ecology of Imagination in Childhood
EDITH COBB

Cobb's collection of autobiographies and biographies of creative people, as well as her direct observations of children's play, persuaded her that genius is shaped by the imagination of the early years. Childhood imagination, participating in the world's "outerness," inspires us to abandon our reliance on "inner" powers alone for mutually fecund relations with people and things. Introduced by Margaret Mead and Shaun McNiff. (vii, 139 pp.)

The Thought of the Heart and the Soul of the World
JAMES HILLMAN

Two pivotal essays move archetypal psychology toward the world. Once the heart is no longer seen as only a pump or only the seat of personal feelings, it reclaims its place as organ of aesthetic perception responding directly to the world's beauty. Social and environmental catastrophes evidence the world's suffering and appeal to us to attend to its soul. (130 pp.)

The Greening of Psychology
PETER BISHOP

Revives the fertile but deeply downward and uncanny roots of our vegetable soul, thereby radically dislocating our usual assumptions about consciousness. Explores the vegetative nervous system and its symptoms (reading anew Freud, Jung, Reich), addictions to plant concoctions (cocaine, coffee, sugar, etc.), social rootlessness, the worship of growth, and the fear of rot. Illustrations, index. (237 pp.)

The Book of Life
MARSILIO FICINO—CHARLES BOER, TR.

In this fluent translation—the first in English—this underground classic of the Italian Renaissance is a guide to food, drink, sleep, mood, sexuality, song, and countless herbal and vegetable concoctions for maintaining the right balance of soul, body, and spirit. Translator's introduction (with bibliography), index. (xx, 217 pp.)

FOR A CATALOG, WRITE:
Spring Publications, P.O. Box 222069, Dallas TX 75222
TO ORDER BOOKS, PHONE:
Publisher Resources, 1–800–937–5557